NATURE,
HUMAN NATURE,
AND SOCIETY

Recent titles in
Contributions in Philosophy

The New Image of the Person: The Theory and Practice of Clinical Philosophy
Peter Koestenbaum

Panorama of Evil: Insights from the Behavioral Sciences
Leonard W. Doob

Alienation: From the Past to the Future
Ignace Feuerlicht

The Philosopher's World Model
Archie J. Bahm

Persons: A Comparative Account of the Six Possible Theories
F. F. Centore

Science, Animals, and Evolution: Reflections on Some Unrealized Potentials of Biology and Medicine
Catherine Roberts

The Philosophy of Human Rights: International Perspectives
Alan S. Rosenbaum, editor

Estrangement: Marx's Conception of Human Nature and the Division of Labor
Isidor Walliman

The Concept of Ideology and Political Analysis: A Critical Examination of Its Usage by Marx, Lenin, and Mannheim
Walter Carlsnaes

Soviet Marxism and Nuclear War: An International Debate
John Somerville, editor

Understanding: A Phenomenological-Pragmatic Analysis
G. B. Madison

Guilt and Gratitude: A Study of the Origins of Contemporary Conscience
Joseph Anthony Amato II

NATURE, HUMAN NATURE, AND SOCIETY

MARX, DARWIN, BIOLOGY, AND THE HUMAN SCIENCES

Paul Heyer

CONTRIBUTIONS IN PHILOSOPHY, NUMBER 21

Greenwood Press
Westport, Connecticut • London, England

Library of Congress Cataloging in Publication Data

Heyer, Paul, 1946-
  Nature, human nature, and society.

  (Contributions in philosophy, ISSN 0084-926X ;
no. 21)
  Bibliography: p.
  Includes index.
  1. Anthropology—Philosophy.   2. Social evolution.
3. Man—Animal nature.   4. Marx, Karl, 1818-1882.
5. Darwin, Charles, 1809-1882.   I. Title.   II. Series.
GN365.9.H49   306'.01   82-937
ISBN 0-313-23161-3 (lib. bdg.)   AACR2

Library of Congress Catalog Card Number: 82-937
ISBN: 0-313-23161-3
ISSN: 0084-926X

First published in 1982

Greenwood Press
A division of Congressional Information Service, Inc.
88 Post Road West
Westport, Connecticut 06881

Printed in the United States of America

10 9 8 7 6 5 4 3 2 1

To Heather Trexler-Remoff

It is a real piece of good fortune that nature has intervened, drawn the essence of the humanities to itself, and opened to us the way to a true humanism from its own side.

—Goethe

Contents

Preface

In nineteenth-century England a revolution in human thought, with repercussions still being felt, was effected by Marx and Darwin. Although they worked in and influenced different traditions, this book examines some important and unsuspected parallels in their thinking. It also highlights a historical situation where significant connections between the natural sciences and human understanding were explored.

The project was born in response to difficulties I encountered when, as a student of anthropology and sociology, I sought to understand humanity and society by drawing from the natural sciences, especially biology. On one hand, I wanted to learn about the antibiological bias of twentieth-century social science. Why, for example, has sociobiology, despite numerous inadequacies, been confronted with hostile attitudes as entrenched and unbending as those that nineteenth-century theology leveled at Darwin's work? My primary concern, however, and the main focus of this book, was to seek a historical foundation for a unified human-natural science perspective, especially one unconstrained by the conservative ideological shackles that several contemporary critics claim must invariably accompany any attempt to deal with human behavior using biological approaches. My search led to a comparative study of two of the most definitive and influential thinkers of the modern age: Marx and Darwin.

This book is a strange species. It is primarily an essay in comparative social thought, but of necessity it contains elements of intellectual history and biography. The study attempts to highlight possible sources for a biosocial perspective in the contemporary human sciences. Of necessity this endeavor is accompanied by a critical, but I trust not ungrateful, account of relevant developments in several of the human sciences over the past 100 years, particularly anthropology and sociology. In addition, connections are drawn between various points raised by Marx and Darwin and recent thinking on related issues. The overall strategy should clarify the original context of their analysis and highlight its continuing relevance.

In part I, I provide a rationale for the study. I also endeavor to enlarge the way in which Marx and Darwin, and the Marx-Darwin relationship, have been perceived traditionally. Here groundwork is laid for the comparative assessment that follows by emphasizing Marx's little-known concern with the natural sciences and Darwin's often-overlooked preoccupation with philosophical and humanistic issues. Finally, using a brief biographical focus, I compare the generally acknowledged major contributions of Marx—the materialist conception of history—and Darwin—the theory of evolution by natural selection. My emphasis is on the complementary rather than parallel nature of these formulations.

Part II is the centerpiece and, for me, the key segment of the book. It is an interpretation of the human theory of Marx and Darwin—in other words, their ideas on human nature and society. This necessitates a rather unusual comparison. I contrast the anthropological and biological cast of the early Marx with the anthropological and philosophical interests of the later Darwin. In addition, I examine several other nineteenth-century writers also having a biosocial perspective, and I give several reasons for the failure of the twentieth-century social sciences to develop this possibility.

In part III, I extend several aspects of the human theoretical framework of part II by dealing comparatively with the ideas of Marx and Darwin on primitive society, race, and slavery. The role these concerns played in their understanding of the human condition is important. This section closes with a reassessment of Engels's contribution to the Marxian legacy, in particular his formulations on biology and human evolution.

In part IV, the conclusion, I briefly assess the contemporary significance of the Marx-Darwin contribution and argue for the importance of biology to the human sciences by critiquing some recent misconceptions regarding the relationship. Finally, I high-light some important recent contributions in the biosocial field and suggest further paths of inquiry.

It should be noted that a chronological bibliography of the major works of Marx, Engels, and Darwin appears at the beginning of the bibliography. This will provide the reader with a full citation for the captions used for the sources in the main body of the text. In addition, consulting the chronological bibliography at the outset, as well as periodically, will provide the reader with a sense of the closeness in time of major research stages in the careers of Marx and Darwin, and the circumstances surrounding the publication of several key texts.

There are several idiosyncratic usages in this book. For example, the terms *Marxian* and *Marxist* are a source of ongoing confusion and misunderstanding; consequently, I have stabilized my usage by employing *Marxian* when referring directly to the texts and views of Marx and *Marxist* to the traditions following from Marx openly proclaiming affiliation to his world view. Perhaps I take Marx's famous declaration, "I am no Marxist," too seriously. Nevertheless, delineating a Marxian-Marxist separation has greatly aided my understanding of a rather controversial legacy to the human sciences. Another problem area that surfaces in doing a study such as this is the use of the masculine *mankind* or *man* to signify the human species. This is a wide-spread bias not only in the nineteenth century but in our own as well; it is both discriminatory and bad biology. When dealing with the nineteenth-century context, or interpretation pertaining to it, it would be somewhat misleading not to follow such usage; however, when speaking in the present sense, I use *humankind, humanity, the human species,* or an equally nonsexist term.

Ten years of research and thinking underwrite this book. It began when I was a graduate student. I learned that Marx wished to dedicate an edition of his major work, *Das Kapital,* to Darwin, or so many commentaries stated. Over the past several years, however, research has shown this event probably did not occur; there is a continually growing literature on the incident, and some of it is assessed in chapter 1. Although beginning from what now appears to be a false assumption, I stumbled across many other points for effecting a comparative assessment. I thought they were rather obvious and would have explored the matter no further than a programmatic outline were it not for the suggestions and inspiration provided by Lionel Tiger and Robin Fox. They stressed the importance of the problem and encouraged me to pursue it.

The preliminary results, primarily dealing with Marx's interest in the natural sciences, became my Ph.D. dissertation in anthropology at Rutgers University completed in 1975. This was followed by a postdoctoral research internship from the Harry Frank Guggenheim Foundation, which enabled me to look more closely at the problem of human nature in the social sciences and the contribution in the area to be made by both Darwin's work and contemporary biological theory. More recently, as a faculty member in the Department of Communication at Simon Fraser University, I aired the results of these studies to a receptive and critical audience of students and faculty. This prompted important revisions, and in due course I finished the manuscript for this book.

Much of what follows will undoubtedly be controversial. Writing about Marx invites unparalleled scrutiny, and when one is not a member of the prevailing interpretive camps attacks can be merciless—one of my students has aptly noted that there might be more "fundamentalist archbishops" in the Marx arena than in any religious sect. Nevertheless, I have tried to make the book operate on two levels. There is, of course, the comparative assessment and the perspective it represents, which can be agreed or disagreed with. However, in articulating this problem, I was forced into a scrutiny of some of the basic concepts of Marx and Darwin and to a degree have attempted to convey them to readers in a basic jargon-free language. In no way do I intend this book to be a definitive interpretation or to supplant other efforts. Instead it represents a fruitful reexamination from an as-yet-untried context. In this spirit, I have surveyed and assessed an area that I hope will be of interest to readers of diverse backgrounds who are united by a curiosity regarding the human species and the ways we have, and might develop, to comprehend it.

The road leading to this work has been paved with encouragement and inspiration. To thank everyone involved would be an awesome task. Yet certain individuals must be mentioned, despite the fact that support did not in every case imply agreement. For first enlightening me in critical social science while I was at the New School for Social Research, I shall be forever in debt to Stanley Diamond, Mike Harner, and Sol Miller. The understanding faculty at Rutgers University immeasurably aided me. I wish to thank Warren Shapiro for showing me that important concepts need not defy clarity in communication; Dieter Steklis for his encouraging interest in the importance of the history of the natural sciences for the social sciences; and Tim Perper, who as a biologist shed invaluable light on the relevance of several aspects of the work I had taken for granted.

During the period when I first struggled with the idea presented here, many friends were unyielding in their support, especially Barbara Blei, Vicki Burbank, Jim Chisholm, Carol Jennings, Tony Pfeiffer, and most of all, Heather Trexler-Remoff. Heather's warm, unyielding personal support, as well as her quest into biosocial understanding, inspire the dedication of this book.

I must also bequeath a special debt of gratitude to those oft-misunderstood scholars, Lionel Tiger and Robin Fox. The inspiring exchange between us, although often punctuated by disagreement, was united by a concern for the relevance of biology to the social sciences. Without their encouragement and support, this venture would have never been possible.

For immeasurably encouraging me during the final reworking of the manuscript and allowing me to pursue some of my unorthodox teaching and research interests, I give wholehearted thanks to students and faculty in the Department of Communication at Simon Fraser University, in particular those who persuaded me to stay when other possibilities loomed.

Financial aid for portions of this work was generously provided by the Harry Frank Guggenheim Foundation and the Canada Council. For typing the manuscript during its many stages, I thank Carole Akazawa, Rosemarie Bakker, Shelly Strudwick, Cynthia Lee, and Velma Watters.

Finally, I am indebted to those involved in the production of this book: Bill Gum, who when he was at Elsevier did the preliminary editing, constantly encouraging me with his overt enthusiasm and off-beat humor; and James T. Sabin, Susan Baker, and the others at Greenwood Press, who allayed my impatience and made working so far from one's publisher easier than I thought.

Part I
OVERVIEW

Establishing Connections — 1

On Tralfamadore, says Billy Pilgrim, there isn't much interest in Jesus Christ. The Earthling figure who is most engaging to the Tralfamordian mind, he says, is Charles Darwin.
—Kurt Vonnegut, Jr.

The doctor stared thoughtfully at Charles. He had just set a little test to prove his guest's mihd. And it had revealed what he had expected. He turned and went to the bookshelves by his desk and then came back with the same volume he had shown Charles before: Darwin's great work. He sat before him across the fire; then with a small smile and a look at Charles over his glasses, he laid his hand, as if swearing on a bible, on *The Origin of Species.*
—John Fowles

Almost any discussion of great thinkers who have significantly influenced the course of history will yield the names of Marx and Darwin. Frequently they are mentioned in the same context. One reason is that they were contemporaries. Less well known is the striking overlap in their respective life histories. They were born, underwent a developmental period, wrote major works, and died at about the same time. These parallels generally can be accepted without contention. It is when we go beyond the facts of their historical existence, to a comparison and interpretation of ideas, that controversy surfaces.

As a recent encyclopedia of Marxism has pointed out, nearly every mayor study of Marx or Darwin has commented briefly on a possible relationship between the two.[1] Current opinion on the problem is divided, with several points of view. Two lend themselves to an obvious comparison. On one hand there is the Marxist-Leninist or Soviet-Marxist stance that dogmatically regards the legacies of the two thinkers as integrally related. This perspective sees Marx and Darwin as partners in revealing the inexorable laws of history and nature, respectively, laws often assumed to be the same, and as brothers in championing the matter-before-mind materialist world view that served to upend the explanations of man and the universe proffered by traditional theology. This is the prevailing view in the Soviet Union, in some Eastern European nations, and in orthodox Marxist-Leninist circles in the West. Contrasting with this position is a heterogeneous group composed of philosophers and social scientists of the critical theory school, existenialists and phenomenologists of Marxist persuasion, and several contemporary historians of Marx. They contend that the root of much that is valid in Marx's writings is not to be found in the influence of the natural sciences and hence Darwinism but in their humanist cast and indebtedness to the method of Marx's great philosophical precursor, Hegel.

Despite the potential insights to be derived from a Marx-Darwin comparison, the Anglo-American social science tradition has refrained from an assessment of the possibility. It has located Darwin almost exclusively in the natural sciences or believed that any social application of his ideas would lead to something resembling social Darwinism, and although Marx had been an influential figure, what has been appropriated are those aspects of his thought that serve to mesh with and extend already acceptable models of analysis. Overall assessments of Marx's work, which might consider his assumptions regarding human nature and the nature of society, have been conspicuously absent.

The biographical and critical literature on both Marx and Darwin is enormous. Marx without doubt is one of the most written about historical personages of all time, and recently Darwin's contribution has been the subject of an evergrowing number of books and articles. The present work will be biographical and historical, but only as a means. Although Marx and Darwin have been associated in the historical literature numerous times, there has been no sustained comparative examination of the scope, convergence, and divergence of their ideas. Thus my primary purpose is to elaborate a comparative theoretical analysis, one that also assesses a historical precedent for linking critical human inquiry to the insights of the natural sciences.

Any case to be made for the relatedness (or even the separateness) of the thought of Darwin and Marx that discusses only points of comparison between their most well-known contributions—the theory of evolution by natural selection with its notion of the struggle for existence and the materialist conception of history and class struggle—will be incomplete. Nevertheless this has been the track taken in most previous evaluations. It is, of course, a crucial issue and will receive appropriate consideration here. However, the major emphasis of this study is on assessing what I call the human-theoretical framework. Broadly conceived this refers to the interest Darwin and Marx shared in the subject of human nature, the nature of society, and the significance of primitive people in understanding the human possibility. Also important to my argument is a concern with the involvement each had in areas usually deemed to be the other's field of expertise. For example, Darwin was not averse to straying into philosophy, particularly the sector that we might today call philosophical anthropology, and Marx's interests frequently included extensive surveys of the natural sciences.

Both Marx, coming out of the German philosophical tradition, and Darwin, emerging from roots in a number of the natural sciences, sought a unified science of humankind. Marx was the bolder and more widely ranging of the two. This caused him to seize immediately upon the significance of Darwin's work, somewhat to the latter's puzzlement. Darwin, as his unpublished notebooks reveal, thought deeply and critically about more than he released in his published works. These notebooks are now accessible, and necessary, if we are to understand the significance of his thought in its entirety. The common ground the two men independently sought would, if it were realized today, be a meeting place for the humanities and the social and natural sciences. This is not to suggest that their approaches, even when applied to similar topics, are ever congruent. Often the respective points of focus vary considerably and I indicate where and why this is the case. Although Marx and Darwin had independent visions, the case to be made for juxtaposing their legacies rests with the complementary rather than parallel nature of these visions.

REASSESSING DARWIN

Unlike Darwin Marx has a reputation as a multifaceted intellectual figure. From a schooling in classical philosophy during the 1830s, he established himself as the most important political economist of the capitalist regime with the publication of *Das Kapital* in 1867. It has been contended that although Marx was not a sociologist, there is sociology contained in his writings.[2] A similar case can be made regarding Marx and a number of other disciplines. For example, Marx is also relevant to economics, political science, philosophy, history, and anthropology.

Darwin's range of acceptance is considerably narrower, serving to belie the magnitude of his contribution. Over the past century Darwin has been acknowledged primarily for his role in establishing the theory of evolution by natural selection, though at times even his priority in this area has been called into question.[3] His reputation derives mainly from *The Origin of Species*, which in 1859 put before public and scientific scrutiny the theory of evolution along with massive supporting evidence. Yet he published several lesser-known works having critical importance to a whole range of disciplines. The first work in this direction was *The Voyage of the Beagle* (1845), a journal of his travels in popular form containing numerous anthropological as well as naturalistic observations and perceptive comments on the politics of slavery and race. In overall conceptual dimension the book is not unreminiscent of anthropologist Claude Lévi-Strauss's recent narrative *Tristes tropiques*.[4] After Darwin's reputation was secured and the controversy surrounding *The Origin of Species* had abated, he dealt with the nature and origins of mankind and society in *The Descent of Man* (1871) and *The Expression of the Emotions in Man and Animals* (1872). These texts provide considerable insight into what the fields of psychology, sociology, anthropology, and philosophy purport to represent. In his later work, Darwin, coming from a biological direction, gave much attention to the nature of the human species, a topic to which the early Marx devoted extensive philosophical speculation. Evaluating this as a combined legacy is long overdue, and it will be a major point of focus here.

The scientific credentials of Marx's work have often been questioned because of the philosophical and political overtones in it. Karl Popper's critique in this direction is probably the most formidable.[5] Ironically Darwin has suffered what amounts to a reverse fate. Because of an alleged lack of sophistication in theoretical and philosophical issues, he has at times been portrayed as a master fact gatherer rather than as a truly creative thinker. For example, the historian Jacques Barzun has deemphasized Darwin's genius by trying to cast him in the role of a Hegelian world historical character (one who is in the right place doing the right thing at the right time, and whose efforts, not extraordinary in themselves, suddenly take on crucial historical significance).[6] Darwin probably would have been in partial accord with this view. In a letter to Herbert Spencer, he remarked, "I never believed in the reigning influence of great men on the World's progress" (*Life*, 3:165). That genius is the product of circumstances was not an uncommon notion during the century. The idea was shared in almost equal measure by Marx, Darwin, Herbert Spencer, and John Stuart Mill.

While Darwin may not have regarded himself as a genius, he firmly believed that he was an innovator. His letters to a number of people illustrate that he did not deem evolution to have been "in the air." He saw himself as making a crucial breakthrough in his effort to convince, by tremendous weight of evidence, an otherwise skeptical scientific and lay public in the plausibility of evolution by natural selection.

In placing its arguments outside the framework of classical philosophical concepts and terminology, Darwin's *The Origin of Species* appeared to signal the emancipation of science from philosophy.[7] This may have been partly responsible for Marx's fascination with Darwin's work, for Marx was frequently outspoken in his belief that science, not philosophy, is the repository of truth. Here, as elsewhere, he remained a true child of the nineteenth century. Although Darwin lacked philosophical pretensions, he did not lack refined philosophical and scientific understanding. Two recent works have done much to unveil his abilities in these areas. Michael Ghiselin has written a definitive study of Darwin's theory and method, demonstrating that Darwin's conception of science and philosophy was extremely sophisticated, that his extraordinary scientific achievements cannot be attributed to the collection of facts as previously believed but to the development of theory, and that his "philosophical prowess was in no small measure responsible for his scientific triumphs."[8] Darwin's genius has been further studied by Howard Gruber and Paul Barrett.[9] They have highlighted the creative process and imaginative flourishing that were so much a part of his work and made us aware of the extent and depth of his ideas on human nature and philosophy. With respect to the continuing validity of Darwin's major contribution, the theory of evolution by natural selection, biologist Ernst Mayr has noted that it tends to come as a surprise to all—but biologists—to learn that contemporary evolutionary theory is closer to Darwin's original formulations than at any other time in the past 100 years.[10]

MARX AND THE SCIENCES

Few would deny the judgment that Marx and Darwin were highly influential thinkers whose theoretical contributions have revolutionized the modern age.[11] Frequently their major texts, *Das Kapital* (1867) and *The Origin of Species* (1859), have been referred to as being among the handful of books significantly influencing historical direction. And in a number of ways they are similarly structured. Although Darwin was addressing himself to a biological argument and Marx to the domain of political economy, both works exude the same wide observation of phenomena, meticulous assembly of data, and conclusions that appear to express a fundamental determinism.[12] Of the two books, *Das Kapital* is the more flamboyant, though both epitomize the nineteenth century style. However, because Marx was a political philosopher and revolutionary, the scientific credibility of his work has suffered.[13]

Popper has argued that Marx's view represents historicism, an approach to the social sciences that takes historical prediction to be their primary aim.[14] He rejects what he terms theoretical history or historical social science on the grounds that historical prediction cannot have any scientific foundation. Popper's argument is doubtlessly consistent within the canons of science he espouses. However, the plausibility of Marx's approach does not necessarily hinge on its ability to predict the future. It is more valid to see it as being concerned with an explanation or retrodiction of past historical occurrences using the strictures of nineteenth century science, strictures similar to those utilized by Darwin. It is also worth noting that one can adhere to a science of history having a materialist or economic viewpoint without accepting the Marxian perspective. The vision of Marx contains more than a way of incorporating economic theory into social-scientific methodology. It implies a certain understanding of human nature and the nature of society, a fact more readily acknowledged by philosophers than by social scientists.[15]

Popper's critique of Marx and historicism is particularly interesting because he levels a similar argument against Darwin and evolutionism by contending that any search for the laws of evolution cannot fall within the scope of the scientific method.[16] Popper's position is that the evolution of life on earth is a unique one-time process. He holds that while evolution may be the most successful explanation of the various facts of biology and paleontology, it is not a universal law but only a particular statement about the specific ancestry of the various life forms.[17] Though Popper does not specifically state that the doctrine of historicism might be similarly useful for explanatory purposes, he refers to it as being pro-naturalistic and holds that by dealing with natural laws of succession, it can be seen as being supported by Darwinism.

One of Popper's main criteria for the establishment of any notion as scientific is that it must be capable of being refuted. That their theories defy refutation is a criticism often leveled at Marx and Darwin. While not addressing himself directly to Popper, Ghiselin delves into the scientific status of Darwin's formulations:

the hypothesis of natural selection is predictive, testable, and capable of refutation. But in its implications it has no need to predict, with great accuracy, the long-term course of historical events, any more than the law of gravity should be expected to predict the path of every drop of rain.... The difference with respect to historical sciences lies in the degree of complexity of the generalizations and in the conditional reasoning which is rather unfamiliar to most experimentalists. Natural selection does not prophesy—it only implies that matter will tend to assume certain configurations more often than others, and that such regularity is intelligible in terms of theory. . . . Any objection to the theory of evolution as an explanatory hypothesis on the grounds that it does not predict some particular event may be reduced to an absurdity.[18]

These observations could, with slight modification, be used to describe Marx's attempt to apply scientific insight to historical processes. That he tried to predict the course of history and was occasionally wrong cannot be denied; Marx, like Darwin, overreached his methodology on a number of occasions. Yet, the materialist conception of history, like the theory of evolution by natural selection, has enduring validity. If, as Maurice Cornforth suggests, Marx's historical insights are to be rejected as pseudoscience on the basis of Popper's criteria, then the theory of evolution by natural selection must also be disregarded.[19]

Establishing whether Marx's research has scientific validity when considered from the vantage point of contemporary philosophy of science would be a useful project, but it is beyond the scope of this work. My primary task is to reveal Marx's involvement with, and the degree to which his views reflected, a scientific approach considering the science of his day; also, I am concerned with the actual efforts that he and Engels devoted to studying the theoretical sciences, and the influence these studies had on their views of human nature and history. Each time Marx is dealt with, one or more of these questions will at least be partially answered.

It is significant that Marx thought highly enough of Darwin that he sent him a copy of *Das Kapital*, and for nearly a century, it was believed that Marx intended to dedicate an edition of the work to Darwin. This respect and concern for Darwin's opinion cannot be viewed as an isolated occurrence. It must be seen as one outcome of an intense preoccupation with the natural and physical sciences that Marx and Engels shared throughout their intellectual lives. Not only in their economic perspective on history but regarding the nature of humankind and society, their approach shared a kinship with natural scientific understanding. This was inextricably linked to a critical social theory that had, and has, continuing human relevance. Today such a juxta-position seems unusual. Yet Marx, on numerous occasions, in both his early and later writings, spoke of the necessity for a constant dialogue between critical human theory and the revela-tions of theoretical science. This vision has been abandoned in the West largely in reaction to the blatant steering of theoretical research toward political ends that accompanied the rise of So-viet Marxism; the frustration felt in the face of the appropriation of science by an imperialist technology bent on domination; and the "specialized" blinders imposed upon research in the quest for academic security and acceptability.

An evaluation of the relationship Darwin had with Marx can be understood properly only when it is placed within the con-text of Marx's ongoing interest in nineteenth century scientific discovery. As Engels remarked on several occasions, Marx was heir to three great intellectual traditions: classical German phi-losophy, British political economy, and French socialism. Nota-bly absent from this list is a reference to the natural and physical sciences, probably because they constituted an immediate rather than a purely historical influence. Their relevance takes on obvi-ous significance when Engels remarked at the graveside of Marx, "Just as Darwin discovered the law of development of organic nature, so Marx discovered the law of development of human history."[20] It is indeed puzzling that a number of the foremost Marx scholars have taken pains to deny the validity of the com-parison.[21] Regardless of whether it is legitimate, to downplay Marx's quest for what he thought were scientific laws of devel-opment, as many recent writers have done, is to miss a crucial aspect in the intellectual drama of his life.[22] We can only assume that if Engels at such a sensitive moment elected to draw the parallel, it must have held meaning for Marx. During the course of this brief eulogy, Engels also deemed it relevant to mention the breadth of Marx's interests, in particular the constant enthu-siasm he showed for new developments in the field of theoreti-cal science.

Marx's belief in the importance of theoretical science is also evident from an incident that took place shortly before his death in 1883. At an informal family gathering he was asked by one of his daughters to play a popular Victorian parlor game in which one is asked to give a favorite color, motto, writer, and so on. When he was asked to name his favorite hero, he gave two names: Spartacus and Kepler. This juxtaposition of the man of action with the thinker, the political revolutionary with the genius of pure science, is indicative of the way Marx perceived himself. That his thinker was Kepler, not Hegel or even Aristotle, demonstrates Marx's high regard for theoretical science.

The fascination that science held for Marx did not come about as a result of the Darwinian revolution; it was present earlier and underwent continuous development. As a schoolboy, he was deeply interested in the natural sciences. Before Hegel's philosophy captured his imagination, he was enthralled by Goethe's naturalism. While studying at Trier (to about 1830), he did work under the renowned geologist Steininger, and shortly thereafter when in Berlin he attended lectures by Heinrich Steffens, a natural philosopher who was also a noted geologist.[23] Subsequently and largely on his own, he studied Kirkwood, Laplace, Kepler, and Newton in astronomy, Schleiden and Schwann, Kölliker, Trémaux, Huxley, and Helmholtz in chemistry and biology, and a number of lesser-known figures in these and other fields. He also had an interest in agronomic chemistry, and his collected writings demonstrate a wide knowledge of this history of science, particularly its applied effects on the history of technology. While in London, from 1849 to his death, he often attended lectures by Moleschott, Liebig, Huxley, and others. Thomas Huxley's lectures are especially noteworthy. Given in the fall of 1862, they were titled "On Our Knowledge of the Causes of the Phenomena of Organic Nature" and were an attempt to communicate Darwin's ideas to a wide audience, many of them English workers.

During the 1830s while Darwin was sailing around the world on the *Beagle* making observations and gathering the information he utilized in the later development of his evolutionary theory, Marx was a student of philosophy engaged in a similar venture in the classroom and library. His dissertation, although in philosophy, showed a concern for scientific theory. He contrasted the strict physical determinism of Democritus with the more open-ended approach of Epicurus that allowed freedom as well as determinism. In his subsequent historical writings, Marx did not hold freedom and determinism in opposition. This is not necessarily a contradiction, for it is not freedom and determinism that are in eternal opposition but freedom and predeterminism. Thus one aspect of Darwin's theory of evolution by natural selection that must have pleased Marx's philosophical sensibility was its stress on the interplay of random chance, opportunism, and environmental determinism. While many of Darwin's critics wrongly referred to his approach as being mechanistic—what philosophers sometimes label mechanical materialism—Marx believed that Darwin provided a materialist perspective compatible with his own, although it was being applied to a different set of phenomena.

From about 1840 to 1845 while Darwin was secretively outlining preliminary sketches of this theory of evolution, Marx was defining a philosophical and scientific portrait of human nature, which can be referred to as a philosophical anthropology. A number of his writings from this period only recently have been discovered and/or translated into other languages. Much of the work remained unpublished during his lifetime, but its significance in understanding his thought as a whole is unquestionable. The early texts are unsystematic and impressionistic. Hegel and Feuerbach are the major influences. At times these writings have been labeled humanist and existentialist.[24] Those who find the later Marx distasteful as a result of his rigorous attempt to render history and economics scientific can find solace in the early philosophical texts. Here is a Marx that even poets can come to know and love. Marx deals here with generic man, alienation, and the nature of society. Although the early work cannot be labeled scientific in the formal sense, the influence of science can be continually felt; there is a strong belief in the necessity of a synthesis between the humanities and the natural sciences. In 1844 he stressed that

the *natural sciences* have developed an enormous activity and have accumulated an ever-growing mass of material. Philosophy, however, has remained just as alien to them as they remain to philosophy. . . . *One* basis for life and another basis for *science* is *a priori* a lie. . . . History itself is a *real* part of *natural history*—of nature developing into man. Natural science will in time incorporate into itself the science of man, just as the science of man will incorporate into itself natural science: there will be *one* science. [*Paris Manuscripts*; 142-43]

The vision of the *Paris Manuscripts* is nothing less than a cumulative interdisciplinary science of humankind, a vision still awaiting realization. In many ways it is a philosophical precursor of the more empirical map of modern anthropology drafted by Sir Edward Burnett Tylor in 1881, one of the major founders of that discipline.[25] Both Marx and Tylor began their researches independently of Darwin, and in due course both recognized the significance of the great English naturalist's work and the necessity for its inclusion into their perspectives.

It is hard to conceive of two persons, not scientists in the strict sense, who were more well read in the physical and natural sciences than were Marx and Engels. Both at times wrote down a number of their ideas on science. Engels' exploits in this direction are well known. Unfortunately a number of writers have argued, inaccurately, that the scientific bent belonged to Engels alone.[26] This has probably resulted from the fact that Marx's efforts, significant as they are, remain largely unknown. During the latter part of his life he drafted about nine hundred pages of mathematical manuscript accessible today only in Russian. They include abstracts of textbooks, along with notes, comprehensive accounts of special subjects, and independent investigations ranging from preliminary sketches to finished manuscripts. A summary of their contents is now available in English.[27] Although the mathematical manuscripts were geared toward self-clarification rather than publication, Engels had planned to publish several excerpts along with some of his own essays. Marx's death hastened other matters, such as the preparation for publication of the second and third volumes of *Das Kapital*. Eventually Engels's essays were published posthumously as *Dialectics of Nature* without the inclusion of any of Marx's studies.

Marx began to study algebra, analytical geometry, and calculus seriously in 1858. The drafting of the manuscripts proper did not take place until 1870 when geology and physiology were added to his realm of systematic inquiry. Perhaps Marx saw in Darwin's theory of natural selection the potential for mathematical precision that contemporary evolutionists have since developed. However, Darwin did not have an proclivity for, or interest in, mathematics. It was one of his worst subjects, along with languages—the latter a field in which Marx and Engels both excelled.

THE MARX-DARWIN CORRESPONDENCE

On the Origin of Species was published on November 14, 1859. The second edition, which differed little from the first, appeared on January 7, 1860. By December 19, 1860, Marx indicated in a letter to Engels that he had finally read the work.

During my time of trial, these last four weeks I have read all sorts of things. Among others Darwin's book on Natural Selection. Although it is developed in the crude English style, this is the book which contains the basis in natural history for our view. [*Torr.*, 126]

Engles had earlier, December 12, 1859, to be exact, indicated to Marx that he was reading the work, which he found "splendid." Marx's initial reaction to *The Origin* lingered, and on January 16, 1860, he wrote to his inconstant socialist ally, Lassalle:

Darwin's book is very important and serves me as a basis in natural science for the class struggle in history. One has to put up with the crude English method of development of course. Despite all deficiences not only is the death blow dealt here for the first time to "teleology" in the natural sciences but their rational meaning is empirically explained. [Ibid., 125]

Marx read the work several times making notable comments on it in *Das Kapital*. According to one biographer, when Marx first read *The Origin*, he could talk of nothing else for months other than the tremendous importance of Darwin and his discoveries.[28] "Crude English style" and "crude method of development" could refer to Darwin's ponderous, drawn-out technique of marshaling fact upon fact to support his theory. As a result, the evidence often gets in the way or causes one to lose track of the theoretical argument. Gruber gives a somewhat different interpretation. He believes the crudity alluded to by Marx refers to Darwin's avoidance of any discussion of the philosophical issues underlying his scientific thought.[29]

In the spring of 1873 Marx sent Darwin a copy of the second German edition of *Das Kapital* (1872), with the following passage inscribed:

Mr. Charles Darwin
On the part of his sincere admirer
[signed] Karl Marx
London 16 June 1873
[illegible number] Modena Villas
Maitland Park [30]

This was accompanied by a letter that has not survived. Darwin wrote back on October 1, 1873:

Dear Sir—I thank you for the honour which you have done me by sending me your great work on *Capital*; and I heartily wish that I were more worthy to receive it, by understanding more of the deep and important subject of political economy. Though our studies have been so different, I believe that we both earnestly desire the extension of knowledge; and this in the long run, is sure to add to the happiness of mankind. I remain, dear Sir/yours faithfully/Charles Darwin.[31]

The book, which still survives, is cut only as far as page 105. Darwin therefore did not see the references to him that come later in the text. Difficulty in reading German and the fact that the subject held no particular interest for him were probably responsible for the cursory examination. Also, at this stage in his life he was mentally and physically exhausted, having in the two previous years finished *The Descent of Man, Expression of the Emotions in Man and Animals*, and the sixth and last edition of *The Origin of Species*.

Seven years later it appears as if Marx again wrote to Darwin, in a letter that has not survived. In a letter dated October 13, 1880, Darwin replied:

Dear Sir:

I am much obliged by your kind letter & the Enclosure.—the publication in any form of your remarks on my writings really requires no consent on my part, and it would be ridiculous in me to give consent to what requires none.—I Sh. prefer the Part of Volume not be dedicated to me (though I thank you for the intended honour) as this implies to a certain extent my approval of the general publication, about which I know nothing.—Moreover though I am a strong advocate for free thought on all subjects, yet it appears to me (whether rightly or wrongly) that direct arguments against christianity and theism produce hardly any effect on the public; & freedom of thought is best promoted by the gradual illumination of men's minds' which follow from the advance of science. It has, therefore, been always my object to avoid writing on religion, I have confined myself to science. I may however, have been unduly biased by the pain which it would give some members of my family, if I aided in any way direct attacks on religion.—I am sorry to refuse you any request, but I am old & have very little strength, & looking over proof-sheets (as I know by present experience) fatigues me much—I remain Dear Sir/ yours faithfully/ Ch. Darwin.[32]

Until recently this letter was assumed to be a response to Marx regarding an edition of *Das Kapital* allegedly dedicated to Darwin. In a number of recent and fruitful exchanges, considerable new light has been shed on the incident.[33] It now appears the letter was intended for Edward Aveling, a biologist and common-law husband of Marx's youngest daughter, Eleanor. Aveling wrote a series of articles on Darwin and eventually a book, the *Student's Darwin*, for which he sought Darwin's approval. A letter indicating this situation has recently come to light.[34] Darwin's response can now be regarded as a reaction to Aveling's book. Aveling was a member of the Free Thought movement and an avowed atheist. He continually tried to show how Darwin's ideas serve to discredit traditional religious beliefs, although Darwin always refrained from publicly discussing his views on religion. Since Darwin shunned controversy, particularly in his later years, the thought of being affiliated with Aveling's position dissuaded him from accepting the dedication, as the text of his letter reveals.

Although Aveling was a pioneer in the popularization of science, he had a reputation as a scoundrel, a thief, and a forger.[35] Since he was the one who first made public the 1873 letter from Darwin to Marx in an 1897 article titled "Charles Darwin and Karl Marx," there has been some speculation that it may have been a forgery.[36] Further appraisal, including an analysis by a handwriting expert, new evidence regarding knowledge of the

letter on the part of Engels, and a more extensive examination of Darwin's character, lend strong support for the letter's
authenticity.[37]

LATER PERSPECTIVES ON THE RELATIONSHIP

After Darwin died in 1882 and Marx in 1883, various socialist
thinkers, aware of Marx's fascination with Darwin and natural
science, felt the need to establish a theoretical compatibility between the Marxian and Darwinian perspectives. This was partly
in reaction to the misappropriation of Darwin's views by the
so-called social Darwinists, who were for the most part a group
of laissez-faire capitalists—neither very social nor Darwinian.[38]
The social Darwinists took their inspiration primarily from terms
employed in *The Origin*, such as the *struggle for existence* and the
survival of the fittest (the latter admittedly borrowed by Darwin
from his philosophical contemporary Herbert Spencer), ignoring the broad and often metaphoric way these concepts were
applied. As Hofstadter accurately notes, in *The Descent of Man*
(1871) Darwin expounded social and moral conclusions completely antithetical to the postulates of social Darwinism.[39] Not
only were Darwin's ideas incompatible with the social Darwinist position, had he lived long enough to see what would be
done in his name, he might have come up with an aphorism
similar to Marx's notorius, "Je ne suis pas Marxiste."[40] Even
Darwin's defender and friend, the always outspoken Thomas
Huxley, a staunch advocate of free enterprise, at one time considered the possibility that socialism rather than the individualism of the social Darwinists might be the end product of natural
selection.[41]

The socialist defense of Darwinism actually began during Marx's
lifetime, with studies by Friedrich Lange and Ludwig Buchner.
Their conceptions were as simplistic as those of the social Darwinists. Marx was scornful of their work, dismissing it as a
travesty, unrigorous, and inaccurate in the understanding of
both history and Darwin.[42] Later, in 1897, Edward Aveling wrote
comparatively about Darwin and Marx.[43] Aveling must have been
one of the few people to have known both men personally, and
although he wrote fair and competent introductory texts on each,

his attempt to link up their respective positions in the 1897 article remained superficial.

Socialism and evolutionary theory also came under discussion during the 1887 congress of naturalists in Munich, and the consequences were bizarre. The spectre of a possible relationship between the theory of evolution and socialism became a pressing topic at that time. The noted German scientist Rudolf Virchow attacked Darwinism as leading directly to what he called "collectivism." He thought he saw a connection between the two currents in political upheavels—like the Paris Commune of 1871—and feared that a similar occurrence might take place in Germany. In part he was addressing himself to a speech given earlier by his contemporary, Ernst Haeckel, defending Darwin. A rumor was spread that Haeckel was sympathetic to the Communards. Virchow's battle cry was "Darwinism leads directly to socialism."[44] In retrospect the attack seemed to accuse Darwinism of being in error because it was dangerous.[45] Unfortunately for Haeckel this controversy came at a time when Bismarck was conducting a witch hunt for suspected socialists. In defending himself Haeckel proclaimed that Darwinism was not a collectivist ideology at all and that its social theory is more favorable to the ruling classes than to the oppressed, an equal distortion. In 1892 Haeckel again addressed himself to the controversy by stating that Darwinism was an aristocratic doctrine emphasizing the survival of the best.[46] What Darwin actually said was "survival of the fittest," a phrase he used to indicate reproductive success. It was Spencer, from whom he borrowed the term, who confused *fittest* with *best* or *strongest*.

Shortly after the turn of the century, several works tried to connect the ideas of Marx and Darwin. Because they expounded on overt socialist position, they were largely ignored by the Western social science tradition despite some intriguing observations. Enrico Ferri produced a critique of social Darwinism that attempted to combine the views of Marx, Darwin, and Spencer.[47] His effort to examine the biological foundations of collectivist social notions was praised in a review by the great maverick American economist Thorstein Veblen.[48] In another work dating from the same period, Anton Panneköek compared Marx on the social nature of man with observations on the behavior of the social animals, using Darwin's chapter on sociability in *The Descent* as a reference point.[49] A similar approach was taken by Karl Kautsky.[50] In endeavoring to find the ethical foundations of socialism never rendered explicit in Marx, he looked to Darwin's later writings on the connection, through the social instinct, between human and animal societies.

These writers all tried to consider human society from a biological point of view; however, the tide at this time was moving strongly in the opposite direction largely under the influence of Emile Durkheim, a founding father of modern sociology. Durkheim preached the separation of sociology and what he called social facts from the realm of biology and psychology. Since he was such a powerful and influential force, history has tended not to do justice to contemporaries who professed an alternative perspective. Durkheim himself was not without socialist leanings, but he avoided any discussion of Marx in his work, and although Darwin played a part in his earlier writings, the influence did not persist.

The bleakest chapter in the history of the relations between Marx and Darwin occurred in the Soviet Union. Early in the twentieth century Lenin began the trend by putting forth a materialist philosophy, showing an incomplete understanding of Marx's principal tenets.[51] The stage was set for subsequent misinterpretations. Under Stalin a crass misappropriation of science was effected by T. D. Lysenko. The modern science of genetics was abolished, books on the subject burned, and academies purged of scholars who criticized the position advanced by Lysenko affirming the inheritance of acquired characteristics. This episode is now well documented and would not merit restating here were it not for the fact that the approach of Lysenko has often been called Soviet Darwinism.[52] Ironically, after once claiming that his work was based on Darwinian principles, Lysenko then confessed that he had not studied Darwin properly—a profound understatement.[53] His tirade against classical genetics and heredity did not, according to one commentator, contain one theoretical argument based on fact.[54]

In an unfair historical assessment, Conway Zirkle has elected to call Lysenko's approach Marxian biology rather than Soviet Darwinism.[55] To indict Marx and Engels for sins committed in their name, as Zirkle does, unjustly obscures the open spirit of scientific inquiry they adhered to throughout their lives. Historian Loren Graham, in criticizing a number of authorities, including Zirkle, has pointed out that there did not exist a peculiarly Marxist form of biology from Marx and Engels onward.[56] He notes that nothing in Marx's philosophical system of materialism lends obvious support to Lysenko's views and that the inheritance of acquired characteristics is an aspect of nineteenth century biology as a whole not necessarily the product of Marxism. The interpretation of Lysenko arose among neither Marxist biologists nor established Marxist philosophers. It constitutes a chapter in the history of pseudo-science, not science.[57] Lysenko alone cannot be seen as representative of Soviet science during the period of his reign, which coincided closely with the span of Stalin's regime. During this period, a number of Soviet scientists and philosophers criticized Lysenko and similar careerists and ideological zealots whenever conditions permitted.[58]

THE CONTEMPORARY VIEW

The mesh of politics, philosophy, and science in the Soviet Union has weighed heavily on the minds of contemporary Western interpreters of Marx. In reaction to the scientific mishandling of Marx by Soviet Marxists, there has been a tendency to put the blame on science instead of on the system of political monopoly endeavoring to control it.[59] As a result, Western philosophers, sociologists, and historians of Marx have tended to downplay or disavow the link between his approach and scientific understanding, focusing on the German intellectual tradition as the source of all that is valid in Marx. The 1960s have been referred to as the period when the relationship of Marxism to its Hegelian origins was discussed at an intellectual level proper to the subject.[60] Without doubt this is a worthy enterprise. Marx is a figure of such breadth that it can be highly revealing to scrutinize his work from a number of different angles, but they need not be exclusive. Nevertheless, several recent Marx interpreters, although of diverse intellectual persuasion, seem to be in accord in denying the possibility of a synthesis between critical human theory and a natural science perspective. This is totally alien to Marx's spirit of inquiry. In *The Holy Family* (1845), he attacked the "critical critics" of his day for making the same separation.[61]

Among those writers seeking to redirect interest in Marx from scientific to philosophical issues, two, Jean-Paul Sartre and Herbert Marcuse, have extensive international reputations. Their ideas have been a powerful influence on radical thought since the 1960s. Sartre has attempted to marry certain tenets of existentialism to his own vision of Marxism, a vision owing a considerable debt to Hegel's *Phenomenology of Mind*.[62] In so doing, he has disavowed all affiliations between human, or cultural, understanding and the natural sciences, thereby taking a track diametric to the one pursued by Marx. Marcuse's well-known attempt to apply a critical philosophy deriving from Marx and Hegel (the influence of the latter cannot be underestimated)[63] to the contemporary Western situation continually evades confrontation with the scientific understanding that Marx would have held to be crucial to such an enterprise. Marcuse has also played an important part in synthesizing the contributions of Marx and Freud. However, this daring and worthy enterprise has suffered from a failure to consider either the scientific framework of Marx or Freud's theory in light of modern biological concepts.

Most writers who emphasize the philosophical and humanistic side of Marx also contend that there is a crucial hiatus between the thought of Marx and Engels. One is Alfred Schmidt, who has written a book on the concept of nature in Marx, a topic relating closely to the subject of this book.[64] Schmidt comes out of the same tradition of German critical theorists as Marcuse and like them places the philosophical and humanistic concerns of Marx on a separate plane from the scientific. He insists that Marx's approach, or dialectic as he prefers to call it, is applicable only to human, not natural, history. Although the book is purportedly about Marx and nature, it refrains from discussing Darwin. The concept of nature that Schmidt endeavors to affiliate with Marx derives from the metaphysics of Hegel rather than from the materialist world view shared by Marx and Darwin. He and other critical theorists rightly stress the importance of the recently discovered early humanistic Marx. These writings must now be acknowledged and made an integral part of future Marx assessments. Yet, although the early writings are couched in philosophical language, to say that here Marx is interested only in human nature and not in physical nature, as Schmidt does, belies the scope of Marx's intellect. Going against this increasingly fashionable intellectual trend, Graham is forced to remind us that

Marx's doctoral dissertation written in 1839-40, several years before the now noted *Economic and Philosophical Manuscripts*, was suffused with the realization that an understanding of man must begin with an understanding of nature. . . . Those recent writers who have tried to divert Marxism of all remnants of inquiry into physical nature have not only misrepresented Marx but have also deprived Marxism of one of its intellectual strengths. . . . The same man who wrote the *Economic and Philosophical Manuscripts* also inquired into the concept of mathematical differentiation, criticized Newton's method of quadratures, and discussed the mathematics of Lagrange, Maclaurin, and Taylor. Science was not only an area of knowledge that Marx attempted to bring within his purview, but also a model to him of a methodology of investigation.[65]

Although there are striking similarities in the writings of Marx and Darwin—for example in their biologically grounded views of human nature and society—the differences between them are no less real and at times more obvious. Marx was heir to a humanistic tradition of social involvement that he forged into a revolutionary politics. Darwin cast himself into the role of the pure scientist, though on a few issues, such as in his criticism of slavery, he became politically outspoken. Marx realized that Darwin would always remain outside the political arena. Marx believed in pure science, a science for science's sake.[66] He was sure in the long run it would lead to truths ultimately serving the interest of the masses, a view promulgated prior to the massive constraints put on scientific research by the giant military-industrial complexes of this century.

Marx's politics were predicated on the belief that in order to change the world, one must first understand it, chiefly through science, and it is those aspects of his work devoted to this understanding that invite comparison to Darwin. Connecting Marx to science does not invariably lead to Leninism, Stalinism, or Lysenkoism. Similarly, looking at the human and social implications of Darwin's research is not tantamount to doing that great misnomer, social Darwinism.

Evolution and History

> In general there is no force whatever that is not a principle of change.
>
> —Denis Diderot

In the middle of his critical analysis of capitalist production, the subject of volume 1 of *Das Kapital*, Marx made the following comment in a brief footnote:

Darwin has interested us in the history of Nature's technology, i.e., the formation of the organs of plants and animals, which organs serve as instruments of production for sustaining life. Does not the history of the productive organs of man, of organs that are the material basis of all social organization deserve equal attention....[*Capital*, 1:372]

He was alluding to *The Origin of Species*. Earlier in the text he referred to it as an epoch-making work (ibid., 1:341).

In addition to the speech made by Engels at Marx's graveside, the Marx-Darwin connection surfaces again in the 1888 edition of *The Communist Manifesto* when Engels remarked that Marx's perspective would do for history what Darwin's had done for biology (*Manifesto*, 6). Although not drawing the Marx-Darwin parallel, the contemporary French theorist Althusser has accurately pointed out that Marx's intent was to open up for scientific understanding the "continent" of history.[1] The fact that Marx sought such an understanding is also mentioned by a number of his biographers, plus several who deal with Darwin, and brief comparisons of the similar way the two men independently sought laws of development in their respective spheres have been convincingly elaborated by several.[2] Marx himself was forthright and unambiguous in stating that his purpose was to discover the natural "laws of movement" in modern society and to view "the evolution of the economic formation of society...as a process of natural history" (*Capital*, 1:10), a proclamation that is almost surprising considering the endeavor of recent Marx scholarship in the West to steer clear of any scientific affiliation.[3]

Although Marx enthusiastically accepted Darwin's contribution to his inclusive science of history, he was never directly influenced by the great naturalist's method. True, he received the publication of *The Origin of Species* with an unbridled excitement, vividly expressed in his correspondences and writings after 1859, but it was the excitement of one who discovers an intellectual cousin having a complementary perspective in another discipline. Marx saw in Darwin a materialism similar to his own: a matter-before-mind scientific perspective capable of explaining the transformation of lifeforms by the observable struggle of those lifeforms through time. This perspective dispensed with teleology, religious or otherwise, and avoided the ahistorical and mechanical view common to the natural sciences of the eighteenth century, a view that derived from Descartes's physics and Newton's world machine. In a somewhat ebullient manner Himmelfarb has expressed the Marx-Darwin connection in the following way:

What they both celebrated was the eternal rhythm and course of life, the one the life of nature, the other of society, that proceeded by fixed laws undistracted by the will of God or men. There were no catastrophes in history as there were none in nature. There were no inexplicable acts, no violations of the natural order. God was as powerless as individual men to interfere with the internal, self-adjusting dialectic of change and development.[4]

This statement would coincide more completely with some of the tenets of Marx if the phrase *variable laws* is substituted for *fixed laws*, an important point.

Darwin's major contribution remains the theory of evolution by natural selection and Marx's the materialist conception of history as employed in his economic analysis of nineteenth-century capitalist society. This must not be forgotten even though much of this study focuses on their other and more frequently over-looked contributions.

A major task for both men was to explain change in their respective domains of evolution and history. In Darwin's case the labor was twofold: he had to establish that change had actu-ally taken place in the biological realm and to provide an ade-quate mechanism, natural selection, to explain how such change had occurred. The two tasks were so intertwined that the solu-tion to the second provided him with an affirmation of the first. Marx's task was more singular. Prior to the formulation of his materialist perspective, history had been regarded as a devel-opmental process, but it often was perceived in terms of a divine plan or held to be the inevitable unfolding of a destiny predi-cated on reason. Marx sought to show that historical change begins at the level of survival, with active men engaged in pro-curing their means of subsistence in real life processes working under definite material limitations (*German Ideology*, 36-37). The ramifications of this earthly struggle are what lead ultimately to changes in social, political, and ideological relations. In nature, as Marx was aware, sustenance is primarily gathered rather than produced through cooperative social labor. Therefore evolution and history are not synonymous. But because nature is the foun-dation of history, the two are continuous. Marx often referred to history as "an evolution," both before and after 1859. History, as the development of human technology, was held by Marx to be an extension of the development of nature's organic technology.

The two realms, Darwinian evolution and Marxian history, deal systematically with the process of change, development, and adaptation. In both cases a theory is given and a method formulated. Neither approach is, or pretends to be, all inclusive. For Darwin, the source of the variations that occur in organisms, the foundation of the evolutionary possibility, remained a mys-tery. He was forced to accept variation in nature as given, and from there to go on to demonstrate evolution through elaborat-ing how these variations were selected for and preserved. Simi-larly, Marx's perspective has come under criticism for its failure to reckon with the role of the individual subject in history. Marx avowedly steered clear of explaining historical change in terms of the motivations and innovations of particular individuals, whose behavior is usually seen as a result of economic categories and class relations (*Capital*, 1:10). Marx did not deny that certain individuals could subjectively raise themselves above these categories and relations; however, even when this happened, it could affect the movement of history only insofar as the totality of economic and social relations, always the final arbiter, would permit.

Despite a number of revealing points of convergence between the theory of evolution by natural selection and the materialist conception of history, the two were independently conceived and will be separately assessed. Rather than make a case for specific parallels between the two, I prefer to state the relationship in the following way: there is nothing in Darwin's theory of evolution antithetical to Marx's concept of history, and there is much that is complementary, as Marx himself recognized. Of course, many aspects of Darwin's work are irrelevant to an understanding of historical processes, an inevitable consequence of the fact that the two men worked in different areas. It might be pertinent to note that while one can be a Darwinian in biology and reject Marx on the grounds that history is not subject to scientific understanding, a respectable if somewhat limited intellectual position, one cannot proclaim fidelity to the Marxian world view and reject Darwin. The reason is basic. Central to Marx's vision is the assumption that nature and history fit together to comprise a totality. Since man emerged from and continues to depend on and transform nature, history as a science will remain incomplete until this foundation is fully comprehended. And no one has contributed more toward this comprehension than Darwin.

DARWIN'S EARLY DEVELOPMENT

Darwin's scientific and personal life is exceptionally well documented. Most of his biographers portray a curious, diligent, modest man caught in the historical vortex that resulted from his scientific insights. There is near consensus regarding his personality and the growth of his ideas. The major difference of biographical opinion seems to center around whether his contributions were extraordinary because they were timely or timely because they exhibited a creative prowess that approached genius.

Unlike Marx, whose reputation derived from several areas, among them radical journalism, theoretical economic essays, and the practical politics that infused his destiny, Darwin's fame came primarily from a single source, *The Origin of Species*. This work has made 1859 probably the most memorable date in the history of science. While it cannot be denied that *The Origin* represents Darwin's foremost gift to subsequent generations, it is only one of several remarkable studies. And indeed the climate of opinion seems to be changing; Darwin is slowly being recognized not only as the author of *The Origin* and founder of the modern theory of evolution but as one who also extended evolution's explanatory powers into areas we are only now coming to recognize as significant. A prime example is his formulations on human nature and society.

It is not my intent to present a full biographical sketch of Darwin or to elaborate the details of his theory; these undertakings have been blessed with able interpreters from whom I draw. Rather I wish to point out facets in the development of his theory that invite comparison and contrast to the process of history as conceived by Marx. Nevertheless, it is impossible to effect this undertaking without mentioning some key points and influences in the development of Darwin's life and thought.

Darwin commentators frequently point out that the idea of evolution was a family heirloom, being a major preoccupation of Charles's grandfather, Erasmus Darwin (1731-1802), as evidenced in his epic and poetic work, *Zoonomia*. However, not only did this work not influence Charles directly, he seems to have been critical of the imaginative license that so richly imbued Erasmus's thinking. In the century preceding the publication of *The Origin of Species*, a number of speculative attempts to affirm evolution had been drafted to explain various aspects of natural phenomena unconvincingly dealt with by traditional interpretation, but these attempts were unsupported by any critical tests.[5] Natural selection, Darwin's major contribution to knowledge, was rarely even hinted at by earlier writers.[6] The evolutionary formulations of Erasmus Darwin, rather than forming the basis of a scientific hypothesis, were a response to what the great historian of ideas, Lovejoy, has called the temporalization of the "great chain of being" that took place during the Enlightenment.[7]

The great chain of being was the concept whereby all manner of natural, human, and heavenly phenomena were ranged in an ideal scheme that allegedly reflected their hierarchy of importance and order of creation. Each species was held to be separately created and occupied its own sacred link on the great chain. Similarities among species were explained on the basis of proximity in time of creation, not through any kind of relationship of descent.

During the eighteenth-century Enlightenment new developments in science and technology were eroding the earlier world view based on the conception of a static but harmonic relationship between categories.[8] History became viewed in terms of cumulative change and through concepts of progress and perfectibility (the capacity for improvement). At that time the belief that economic, social, and intellectual phenomena were in a state of flux and open to continuous transformation was widespread in the literature, vividly expressed in the writings of Turgot, Condorcet, de Brosses, Ferguson, Kames, Millar, and a host of others. The Enlightenment represented not only a temporalization of the great chain of being but also a secularization in thought. The ubiquitous and observable process of social change, largely brought about through technoeconomic innovations, rendered theological explanations of world order less authoritative. Reality could now be measured and related to a newly emergent theoretical imagination owing no debt to religious orthodoxy, as the rise of classical political economy vividly demonstrated.

But what of species during the Enlightenment? Were they considered to be immutable or to be capable of modification? To elaborate on the mutability of species in the next century, as Lamarck (1744-1829), Robert Chambers (1802-1871), and Darwin did, was to invite unbridled criticism and ridicule. Yet for a number of intriguing reasons the spirit of inquiry was more open in the eighteenth century. Buffon (1707-1788), de Maupertuis (1698-1759), and Erasmus Darwin all intimated the evolutionary possibility to varying degrees, and escaped unscathed. Even historical writers as secular and daring as Jean Jacques Rousseau

(1712-1788) in his *Discourse on the Origin of Inequality* and James Burnet (1714-1799) in his *Origin and Progress of Language* came close to a biological evolutionary perspective, ultimately rejecting the position for want of evidence, not because of constraints exerted on their thought by previous or contemporary orthodoxy.

Rousseau, Burnet, and other Enlightenment sages were primarily concerned with evolution and development in a historical frame. However, the period also saw important theories of change elaborated in two other areas: Kant's nebular hypothesis on the cosmic plane and Hutton's uniformitarian perspective in geology. By the onset of the nineteenth century, although change and theories purporting to explain it were transpiring in the study of history, astronomy, and geology, species were held to be as self-contained as they were on the day of creation.

In 1809 two important events occurred: Lamarck first published his evolutionary ideas in *Zoological Philosphy*, a work that may or may not have been influenced by Erasmus Darwin; and Charles Darwin was born. Despite the presence of Erasmus on the family tree and the fact that Lamarck's work was fairly well known to the generation in which Charles Darwin grew up, he regarded both these precursors as highly speculative thinkers. He appeared totally unswayed by their arguments for the mutability of species. Even after becoming convinced, probably around 1837, of the transformation of species, he was reticent to admit that his newly found evolutionary vision had been influenced by previous writers, although he did give Malthus credit for helping him discern natural selection. It was not until the third edition of *The Origin of Species* that Darwin added a brief historical sketch, largely under the insistance of several close friends. Even so, the sketch, right through to the sixth and last edition of the work, remains a half-hearted effort. It was, I believe, a subtle attempt on the part of Darwin, a perennially unassertive personality, to emphasize his originality by downplaying earlier contributors.

Although notions regarding evolution did not preoccupy the young Darwin, he was unabashed in his interest in things natural. For the most part this interest was extracurricular. School was more of an obligation than a source of inspiration. Under the insistence of his father, Dr. Robert Darwin, a tyrannical figure about whom much psychohistorical speculation has been written with respect to his influence on Charles's personality, Charles went to Edinburgh in 1825 to study medicine. He was bored by the lectures, depressed by what he saw practiced in the name of medicine, and sickened by dissections. He wanted out. This was facilitated by a small legacy bequeathed to him by his father that enabled him to live comfortably.[9] Despite abandoning his plans for a medical career, however, Darwin remained at Edinburgh for another year reading widely in the natural sciences, the works of Lamarck and Erasmus among others, and meeting and conversing with several faculty interested in geology, zoology, and botany.

In 1828, still feeling obliged to embark on a respectable career, Darwin went to Cambridge to study for the ministry. During his sojourn there, Darwin managed to pursue his interest in the natural sciences, despite the fact that at that time they were still peripheral to the mainstream of academic life. Beetle-collecting became a passion, the resurfacing of a boyhood interest. While at Cambridge he came under the tutelage of three inspiring teachers: John Henslow, a botanist, Adam Sedgwick, a geologist, and William Whewhell, whose interest was mineralogy. Like Darwin they were newly emergent amateurs. They had a commitment to their subjects and an enthusiasm in communicating it. Although lacking a highly specialized systematic understanding, this was not necessarily a drawback. Not having a backlog of obsolete information, they perceived afresh the significance of new discoveries. In this community of enthusiastic amateurs turned professional, Darwin fitted well.[10] He pursued no degree program in science while at Cambridge but learned an enormous amount from a rich exchange and several field trips that took place outside the bounds of required learning. In 1831, he graduated as a cleric, but as one more interested in observing earthly phenomena than in preaching divine revelation.

Hesitant to take on the responsibilities of a country parson, Darwin led the life of a gentleman of leisure while pursuing his wide naturalistic interests, much to the dismay of his father. In the summer of 1831 an opportunity arose that he freely and frequently admitted changed the course of his life. Henslow recommended him for the position of naturalist (unpaid) on board H.M.S. *Beagle*, which was due to sail around the world on a voyage of exploration. As in the case of most of his other endeavors, Darwin was both enthusiastic and reluctant, the latter a result of his father's less than supportive reaction to the possibility. However, thanks to the persuasion of Charles's maternal uncle, Josiah Wedgwood, Robert Darwin gave his son aquiescence. From December 1831 to October 1836, the *Beagle* sailed the globe on its epoch-making voyage of discovery.

THE THEORY AND ITS SOURCES

While on the *Beagle* voyage, Darwin observed, collected, and pondered. Although he did not theorize about the mutability of species, he saw nature in ways that the explanations given by previous scientific orthodoxy had failed to satisfy. If he had doubts about the mutability of species during the voyage, they were subliminal. His return to England was characterized by a brief period of illness, some hectic traveling, and an enduring marriage with cousin Emma Wedgwood. His immediate task was to work on the journal of the voyage, the first edition being published in 1839. In March 1837 he began compiling his first notebook on the possibility (he was still unconvinced) that species were mutable.[11] Gradually his doubts and uncertainty regarding the transformation of species became displaced by insight into the processes by which such an incredible happening might have transpired.

A real contributor to Darwin's doubts regarding orthodox explanations of the species question was the work of Charles Lyell (1797-1875) whose heretical book, *Principles of Geology*, was regular reading for Darwin while he was on the *Beagle*. It is not an exaggeration to state that Lyell was the greatest influence on Darwin's thinking.[12] Darwin himself was no stranger to geology. His contributions in this area would have been sufficient to ensure him a niche in the history of science even if he had not authored *The Origin of Species*.[13] During the eighteenth and nineteenth centuries, geology and biology were more closely allied spheres of inquiry than they were destined to be in the century following Darwin's death. Therefore a work rethinking the question of transformation in the earth's history, such as Lyell's *Principles of Geology*, was bound to have repercussions in, and be influenced by, biology. However, it must be pointed out that although Lyell's evolutionary perspective on the history of the earth was a radical view that deeply influenced Darwin, and although the two men became fast friends, it was only some time after the publication of *The Origin of Species* that Lyell came reluctantly around to accepting Darwin's theory.[14]

Lyell championed an approach known as uniformitarianism. He was not the first to elaborate this view. James Hutton (1726-1797), John Playfair (1778-1819), and William "Strata" Smith (1769-1839) all contributed to the formulation of uniformitarianism as a definitive scientific perspective. In the period from 1790 to 1830, since known as the Heroic Age of Geology, they struggled valiantly to establish an evolutionary perspective on the history of the earth, thereby paving the way for both the reception of Lyell's views and later Darwinian thinking in biology. It was Lyell's work in geology, by captivating both scientific and lay public, that finally marshalled substantial support for uniformitarianism. Even Marx, who was a student in philosophy at that time, indicated in the *Paris Manuscripts* a familiarity with and an enthusiastic acceptance of Lyell's views.

Uniformitarianism bequeathed to the world the conception of a gradual history through processes observable every day in nature such as erosion, sedimentary deposition, and volcanic activity. It opposed two earlier modes of interpretation: the "Neptunist" and the "Catastrophist." The Neptunist adherents postulated that the earth's landscape had been laid down by a universal sea—the biblical deluge. As the sea receded, it sequentially deposited landforms in the manner in which we apprehend them today. Like the Neptunist view, the Catastrophist interpretation could also preserve the notion of special creation; however, instead of postulating one biblical event it argued for a series of creations transpiring sequentially in the various geological epochs.[15] Uniformitarianism, by contrast, saw an eternal earth perpetually recreating itself. In Hutton's words, echoed by Lyell, "We find no vestige of a beginning, no prospect of an end."[16] The processes seen to be operative during the eighteenth and nineteenth centuries were held to be identical to those operative since the dawn of time; this is one sense in which uniformitarianism differs from modern historical geology, which recognizes that the ratio between, and preeminence of, certain processes varies in different geological epochs.

Despite the controversy surrounding several details in the uniformitarian perspective, it dealt a fatal blow to the notion that creation took place in 4004 B.C., a viewpoint worked out by Archbishop James Ussher in 1650 by means of calculations of the post-Adamite generations, an accepted view prior to 1800. For the idealism of special creation, uniformitarianism substituted the conception of gradual processes operating according to natural law and capable of being revealed through reason. It occupied a segment in the great scientific trajectory, along with the discoveries of Copernicus, Kepler, Galileo, Newton, and eventually Darwin. By stressing that the explanation of earthly phenomena must be sought in the everyday workings of nature, not through spiritual intervention, uniformitarianism helped displace both theological and philosophical idealism with a newly emergent naturalism and realism. In history this trend received expression in Marx's attempt to shift emphasis from heaven to earth—to deal with active human beings engaged in real life processes. This concern with the reality of everyday life activities also became a preoccupation of the nineteenth-century arts. Millet and Courbet dramatized it in their painting, and Balzac (about whom Marx at one time wanted to write a book), Flaubert, and Zola etched it into the literature of the period.

From the moment he read Lyell, Darwin looked at geological phenomena from a historical perspective. He noticed, as many before him had, that in certain geological deposits, sequences of fossils could be found; and as one moved from lower to higher in the geological beds, one moved from an earlier to a later time. Very often these fossils would resemble one another and yet exhibit certain key differences. The closer the fossils were situated in the stratigraphical hierarchy, the more they resembled one another; the more they were separate, the more they diverged. The catastrophists explained the situation in terms of separate creations. Darwin doubted the plausibility of this view, and, speculating about the subject after his return from the *Beagle* voyage, began seriously to consider that, like the substance of the earth itself, biological species might be modifiable: that present varieties could be the result of a transformation of earlier forms. This notion was fueled by his extensive observations on the variations that occur in domestic plants and animals. Far from being immutable, domestic species illustrate incredible diversity, a subject that would take up a number of pages in *The Origin of Species*. Cutting across these observations was the memory of situations encountered during the voyage. For example, in the Galapagos Islands, various islands in the chain that differed geographically and climatologically had life forms, such as the famous Darwin's finches, that resembled related species on other islands and on the South American mainland (their probable place of origin) yet also exhibited crucial differences, deriving he believed, from their changed circumstances. But how could these changes, which must surely demonstrate the mutability of species, have come about?

In pondering the experiences of the voyage, as well as his earlier efforts as an observer of nature, Darwin became privately convinced that biological evolution had occurred. He had indirect evidence in abundance. What he lacked was a plausible theory to explain this evidence. In October 1838, while systematically going over his earlier observations, he read the well-known *Essay on Population* by the clergyman Thomas Malthus (1766-1834). It appears that this was the moment of birth of the theory of natural selection:

> I happened to read for amusement Malthus on population and being well prepared to appreciate the struggle for existence which everywhere goes on from long continued observation of the habits of animals and plants, it, at once, struck me that under circumstances favourable variations would be preserved, and unfavourble ones to be destroyed. The result would be the formation of new species. Here then I had at last got a theory by which to work. [*Life*, 1:87]

The relationship of Malthus to Darwin has been much discussed over the last several decades. Harris has contended that Darwin received inspiration for his greatest idea, natural selection, from Malthus and that since Malthus was a social scientist of sorts rather than a natural scientist, Darwin's notions are therefore an application of social science concepts to biology.[17] Freeman has countered by arguing for the priority of Darwin's own observations.[18] According to Eiseley, Darwin may have been groping his way toward the principle of natural selection before he read Malthus.[19] In Vorzimmer's opinion, the perspective of Malthus acted as a catalyst, awakening Darwin's memory to past observations.[20]

Despite his reputation as a political economist, Malthus had a diligent interest in the natural sciences and in fact was an active member of several scientific societies. In an interesting reinterpretation, Himmelfarb cites the following passage from *An Essay on Population* as evidence that Malthus may have derived his ideas on political economy from natural processes:

Through the animal and vegetable kingdoms nature has scattered the seeds of life abroad with the most profuse and liberal hand; but has been comparatively sparing in the room and nourishment necessary to rear them. . . . The germs of existence contained in this earth, if they could freely develop themselves, would fill millions of worlds in the course of a few thousand years. Necessity, that imperious all pervading law of nature, restrains them within prescribed bounds. The race of plants and animals shrink under this great restrictive law; and man cannot by any efforts of reason escape it.[21]

In *An Essay on Population*, Malthus tried to refute the progressive view of history as a process of inevitable improvement, the view put forth by Godwin and Condorcet. In the age of the Enlightenment, characterized by such rampant optimism, Malthus, along with Rousseau (for quite different reasons), stand out because of their negative assessments of the trends they perceived. Yet despite Malthus's supposed or apparent intent, Himmelfarb has claimed that what Darwin did was to use Malthus to prove the case of Condorcet: "As surely as Marx stood Hegel on his head, so Darwin did to Malthus.[22] In other words, Darwin, inspired by the model of Malthus, saw in both the animal and human realm a constant pressure of population against the means of subsistence leading to a struggle for life. In human populations this was said to result in infant mortality, epidemics, emigration, war, infanticide, and any of a number of population checks. From this situation Malthus conceived a self-regulating model, conservatively mitigating against any long-term change or improvement. Darwin discerned another possibility. Although he conceded the acuity of Malthus in observing how the struggle for existence could limit population numbers, innumerable observations of nature led him to conclude that under such circumstances favorable variations would be preserved and unfavorable ones destroyed; the character of the population could, through time, alter in response to its circumstances. In other words, Darwin used elements in the Malthusian theory to refute the inevitable consequences predicted by it.

While Darwin drew inspiration for the theory of evolution by natural selection from Malthus, Marx and Engels drew inspiration of a different sort. They regarded the approach of Malthus as a singular and antihistorical way of viewing the human condition. A brief assessment of the Marx-Engels position on Malthus can serve as a contrast to Darwin's reception of his ideas and also illustrate some fundamental tenets underlying the materialist conception of history and their relationship to evolutionary thinking.

When Marx read Darwin's description of the struggle for existence as "the doctrine of Malthus applied with manifold force to the whole animal and vegetable kingdom" (*Origin*, 78), he expressed amusement. In a letter to Engels dated June 18, 1862, he noted how remarkable it was that Darwin recognized among plants and animals the struggles of modern English society (*Moscow*, 57). Several years later when Friedrich Lange attempted to apply a similar model to all of history, Marx became critical. On June 27, 1870, he wrote to Kugelmann, a long-time friend and confidant:

Herr Lange you see had made a great discovery. The whole of history can be brought under a single great natural law. This application is the *phrase* (in this application Darwin's expression becomes nothing but a phrase) "the struggle for life," and the content of his phrase is the Malthusian law of population. So instead of analyzing the struggle for life as represented historically in varying and definite forms of society, all that has to be done is to translate every concrete struggle into the phrase "struggle for life." [*Kugelmann*, 111]

Lange had written a book that, in conceiving historical struggles in Darwinian terms, also acknowledged a debt to Marx's perspective. Marx, however, had forewarned Lange in a letter, dated March 29, 1865, that "to us so-called economic laws, are not eternal laws of nature but historic laws which arise and disappear" (*Torr*, 198).

Marx adhered to the belief that although history is underwritten by economic laws and that they are subject to scientific scrutiny in a manner comparable to the history of species, the laws themselves evolved; those governing the asiatic, ancient, feudal, and modern bourgeois modes of production are quite different. It is unfortunate that Marx's view of history has often been dismissed as a single-factor explanation when he sought so assiduously to show the many ways in which this factor is operative. Frequently those who profess a many-sided historical perspective seem narrow in comparison. It is also unfortunate that in lauding Darwin's view of nature, Marx nevertheless saw it in a singular way. He, along with most of his contemporaries, overlooked Darwin's broad usage of the concept of the "struggle for existence," a term Darwin avowedly applied in "a large and metaphorical sense including dependence of one being on another" (*Origin*, 77; *Origin 1st*, 62). To say that a given structural or behavioral complex arose through the "struggle for existence" and natural selection is not to imply casually that some naturalistic factor must be responsible; it is to make reference to the profound guiding principle by which particular manifestations of nature can be related to the general scheme of evolution. When John Herschel, an esteemed colleague of Darwin, called natural selection the law of "higgilidy piggilidy," he was not alone in demeaning its significance. Now over 100 years later modern biological science has established his principle as a guiding concept. In the opinion of the eminent contemporary biologist, George Gaylord Simpson, the hand of time rests more lightly on *The Origin of Species* than it does on any other scientific classic.[23]

While Darwin was gaining inspiration from the *Essay on Population*, Marx and Engels bludgeoned Malthus at every turn. Their wrath was directed more toward the political implications of his theory than to its scientific plausibility. In the *Grundrisse*, Marx attacked Malthus with a fervor, indicting the theory of population as the model of capitalist society given universal application. He claimed that when it does function, it is not the expression of some immutable law of nature but of human society at a given level of productivity. Laws of population he argued, are "natural laws," but they are the natural laws of humanity at different historical epochs. Therefore they are variable. To say, for example, that a primitive or modern society is overpopulated explains nothing. If, as he observed, overpopulation resulting in warfare exists among a hunting people, it does not prove that the land could not support their number, only that their productive circumstances require a great amount of territory for a few people.

In an earlier work Engels had compared the population question between Australian hunters and English society (*Outline*, 216). He concluded that to be consistent, the Malthusian doctrine would have to contend that the world was overpopulated when only one man existed—an obviously overdrawn example. Since Malthus could not explain actual historical change, which seemed to occur in spite of his theories, he was mockingly chastised. Marx and Engels believed that man has and will continue to produce the changing conditions of his own historical evolution and that although laws underlie the procedure, they are continually subject to change through the social recognition of new necessities.

Part of the difference between the way Darwin and Marx received the ideas of Malthus is based on the fact that for population biology, Malthus hit on a first approximation of truth, whereas in human history, human food production, and the sources of misery, he was merely an idealogue.[24] Darwin perceived the first and built on and extended it; Marx perceived the second and rejected it. In other words, it is possible for a materialist perspective to accept Malthus with reference to certain natural regularities in biology (Marx failed to note this) and to reject him regarding the laws of political economy.[25] Although the debate regarding the influence of Malthus on Darwin continues, it is clear that Darwin saw fit to cite his influence on a number of occasions, a notable situation since Darwin was so often lax in citing the influence of other predecessors on the development of his theory.

On the Origin of Species exhaustively argues for the transmutation of species (the term *evolution* did not appear until the third edition) from geological, paleontological, and geographical observations. It meticulously documents the variations that occur in domestic plants and animals, comparing this to the situation regarding variation in nature, and makes conjectures about the necessary consequences. The work then links this evidence together using the principle, or agent as Darwin often referred to it, of natural selection. Ghiselin succinctly summarizes the main tenets of Darwin's great principle:

Organisms differ from one another. They produce more young than the available resources can sustain. Those best suited to survive pass on the expedient properties to their offspring, while inferior forms are eliminated. Subsequent generations therefore are more like the better adapted ancestors and the result is a gradual modification or evolution. Thus the cause of evolutionary adaptation is differential reproductive success.[26]

Like many other great discoveries, this is a simple idea, and one not only intimated by Malthus but by a number of other writers as well.[27] Nevertheless it was Darwin who meticulously, and at times brilliantly, wove the principle through the fabric of nineteenth century biological knowledge, changing an entire world view in the process.

On the Origin of Species was first published in 1859. Indeed 1859 can be referred to as the year of evolution for the suddenness in which the presentation of the theory and its arguments burst upon the scene. Even careful followers of science, such as Marx and Engels, gave no evidence of grappling seriously with the species question until after the publication of *The Origin*. True there were writers who, earlier than Darwin, believed and wrote about species transformation, and every once in a while in a book or article someone will rescue and resuscitate one of these figures and bequeath to them priority at Darwin's expense.[28] Nevertheless, it is Darwin who marshalled the greatest amount of evidence, came up with the most insightful explanatory principle, and succeeded in communicating his findings to a degree unmatched by earlier writers. As Darwin himself interestingly noted with respect to the fact that Fritz Muller and Ernst Haeckel were given greater acknowledgment than he for certain embryological researches, although he had written on the subject earlier and compiled considerable information on it, "It is clear that I failed to impress my readers; and he who succeeds in doing so [referring to Muller and Haeckel] deserves, in my opinion, all the credit" (*Life*, 1:46).

The suddenness with which Darwin's theory appeared stands in sharp contrast to the gradual and protracted way he developed and elaborated the argument. Perhaps it is fitting that a theory of gradual change through inumerable small variations should have unfolded through the accumulation and variation of inumerable supporting details over a 20-year period. Marx by contrast was ready to publish the materialist conception of history within a year after having outlined its major premises.

Having been opened up to the possibility of evolution while on board the *Beagle*, Darwin began elaborating, in 1837-1838, a number of ideas relating to the problem; 1838 was also the year that he felt the influence of Malthus. In 1842 Darwin produced a brief 35-page sketch outlining his evolutionary ideas. He did this in great secrecy; the sketch remained unknown until his son Francis unearthed it in 1896. In 1844 he drafted a 230-page essay, with instructions to his wife that it should be published only in the case of his death.[29] In many ways this essay is a much better introduction to Darwin's theory than the more ponderous text of *The Origin of Species*. It contains the theory lucidly outlined and supported with enough facts to render it convincing, while in *The Origin* there is a tendency for the facts to bury the theory.

During the period from 1839 to 1859 Darwin wrote about barnacles, coral reefs, and various problems in geology, constantly prolonging and delaying the release of his great work. From September 1854, largely under the continued encouragement of Lyell, Darwin worked on what would become *The Origin of Species*. In 1858 he received a letter from Alfred Russel Wallace (1823-1913) who appeared also to have conceived evolution in terms of natural selection. This resulted in their joint paper on natural selection presented to the Linnaean Society and the publication of *The Origin* the following year. When Darwin wrote *The Origin*, he thought it would be only the abstract of a proposed longer work. However, the text was awesomely detailed, and it, rather than another book, became one of the most important treatises in the history of science.

MARX'S EMERGENCE

Unlike Darwin, Marx wrote no autobiography, nor was his immediate family, and in this I include his spiritual brother, Engels, as concerned about the events of his life as was the circle that surrounded Darwin. Marx's coterie was, however, very much interested in his writings, their impact and implications. As a result, a remarkably complete corpus of published and unpublished work has survived to the present. These texts and the historical events surrounding them, coupled with a voluminous correspondence, have provided ample material for biographers, and there is no dearth of attempts in this direction.[30] Most are in accord regarding the major points in his life and thought, though there is considerable divergence from writer to writer regarding the significance of his contribution and its theoretical validity.

Marx's domestic situation can be viewed in terms of three broad phases: an early comfortable period lasting to about 1840, the results of a middle-class upbringing and privileged student experience; a period of unintended but self-imposed poverty lasting until nearly 1870 in which he made the transition from political journalist to historical theoretician; and the period lasting until his death in 1883, one of relative comfort in which he traveled and corresponded but produced little formal writing.

With respect to what we would today call social science, Marx did not have an extensive reputation in his own lifetime. It is only in the twentieth century that Marx's perspective has been appropriated by a number of academic disciplines. It is intriguing to speculate on how Marx might have felt had he known that his major works would be appropriated by and become required reading in the social science curriculum of many bourgeois universities. In any case, it is important to note that although his writings were certainly not unknown in his lifetime, the audience was not an academic one. Today we can look at Marx's work in the context of nineteenth-century social evolutionary thought and see the relationship of his ideas to those of his contemporaries; however, in his own time, he was not assimilated into debates within that context.

Like Darwin, Marx had a middle-class background. Interestingly enough neither man practiced a formal profession, though both received professional training. Darwin studied medicine, a program he never completed, but he did graduate from a university, albeit with a degree in divinity. However, the *Beagle* voyage beckoned more strongly that the possibility of being a country pastor, and when he returned, a family legacy enabled him to embark on a lifelong career of research and writing. Marx began in law, switched to philosophy, and eventually obtained his doctorate in that discipline in 1841. Attempts at a professional academic career were thwarted by the political climate of the day. Discounting intermittent early stints as a journalist, Marx did not undertake formal work. As a result, he assumed a life-style of poverty. Numerous biographers have painted a vivid portrait of the abject circumstances of his middle years—hunger, sickness, and the death of several of his children. More than one biographer has admonished him for not seeking gainful employment. Small sums from his journalism, family, and the redoubtable Engels kept him afloat, but barely. Yet these were the most theoretically productive years of his life. Although Darwin experienced no such dire circumstances, it must be remembered that the *Beagle* voyage was arduous, and Darwin was frequently ill, mostly by being seasick, but he did acquire an illness that would plague him throughout his life.[31]

Marx was born in 1818 in Trier in the Rhineland region of Prussia, the second of eight children. He was the son of a lawyer and was encouraged to pursue his father's path. But father and son had sharp differences in their personalities, and Marx made the break with tradition much more easily than did Darwin. His father came out of an extensive rabbinical tradition; however, he was forced to convert to Protestantism in order not to jeopardize his career. Following his high school experience, Marx went to the University of Bonn in 1835 and enrolled in the law program. Here he confronted his romantic spirit—writing bad poetry, carousing, and joining a dueling club.

During his romantic phase, Marx fell in love with and became engaged to Jenny von Westphallen, whom he married in 1843. During the courtship, Marx had an amiable relationship with Jenny's father, Baron von Westphallen. The baron took Marx under his intellectual wing. He encouraged young Karl to read a number of classic works in both literature and social thought, and the two would then engage in extended discussions of the particular texts. Marx had no such relationship with his father, who for the most part was a stern authoritarian. The relationship between young Karl and the baron recalls the relationship between a male and his mother's brother as it is so often described in anthropological literature. For example, while a father is usually a disciplinarian, it is often the mother's brother who befriends the young male, teaches him hunting, the lore of the tribe, and on occasion provides him with his daughter as a wife—although in this case the baron was not related by blood to Marx. The pattern also appears in Darwin's life. It was his mother's brother, Josiah Wedgwood, with whom Charles was extremely friendly, who persuaded Dr. Robert Darwin to allow his son to go on the *Beagle* voyage. The situation is classic because it was Josiah's daughter, Emma, whom Charles married, an instance of what anthropologists refer to as a matrilateral cross-cousin marriage.

In 1836 Marx transferred to the University of Berlin where he developed his latent philosophical interests. Here he came under the influence of the awesome system of Hegel. Hegel's perspective was a powerful one, and countless writers have properly stressed, but at times overstressed, its influence on Marx.[32] During this period, Marx began to elaborate a critique of religion and to manifest a concern with human destiny and the economic and political factors constraining it. His doctoral dissertation, completed in 1841, contrasted the atomic theories of Democritus and Epicurus. It demonstrated an interest in an area that today might be referred to as the history and philosophy of science, not a surprising concern considering Marx's preoccupation with science.

Like a number of other great thinkers Marx continued his education beyond the formal confines of the university. Although he became a journalist with the *Rheinische Zeitung*, a politically inspired paper, he avidly read philosophy and struggled to forge a link between deep theoretical explanation and the practical politics of the cultural present in which he lived. He eventually became editor of the *Rheinische Zeitung*, struggling at times to couch his searing critiques in a way that would slip past Prussian censorship. The effort failed, and in 1843 he fled to Paris.

During this time he had matured to the point where he began a series of related writings confronting Hegel's theories of society, law, and the state.

While in Paris, Marx sporadically continued his journalism and exchanged points of view with a circle of notables that included Heine, Proudhon, and Bakunin. He continued wrestling with Hegel's philosophy, pinning, he believed, that worthy opponent on a number of occasions. In critiquing Hegel, Marx found a powerful ally in the philosophical theory of Ludwig Feuerbach whose writings were much discussed at the time. Feuerbach's influence became crucial to Marx's attempt to understand human nature and society. Into the theoretical cauldron of Hegel and Feuerbach, Marx added a new-found interest in political economy. The result was *The Economic and Philosophical Manuscripts of 1844*, known also as the *Paris Manuscripts*, a perplexing and at times brilliant dialogue with himself, crucial to a complete understanding of Marx's later historical writings. The year of 1844 was also the one in which Marx met Engels, who inspired Marx into further exploring political economy and adding to it the historical dimension that so many previous writers had neglected.

Together Marx and Engels wrote *The Holy Family* in 1845, a critique of the so-called critical critics, a circle of German intellectuals proclaiming a radical philosophy based on an interpretation of Hegel. This group has sometimes been referred to as the left Hegelians or young Hegelians to differentiate them from the old Hegelians whose conservative and orthodox stance they were rebelling against.[33] In attacking the idealist biases of the critical critics, Marx at the same time sharpened his sense of history. The collaboration with Engels continued in another work, *The German Ideology*, written in 1845-1846 in Brussels, where Marx then lived. This is the text in which the materialist conception of history, the overall plan to which Marx's later studies of nineteenth century capitalism would relate, was first elaborated. From this point on, history and political economy became his dominating interests.

Prior to publishing his major work, *Das Kapital* in 1867, Marx produced several writings that served to clarify his historical understanding. In 1847, still in Brussels, he attacked Proudhon's idealist utopian socialism and naive sense of history in *The Poverty of Philosophy*, a reply to the latter's *Philosophy of Poverty*. A year later, *The Communist Manifesto* was drafted in response to a request from the Communist League in London. The work endeavored to wed the materialist conception of history to the practical strategy of an immediate revolution. Fleeing to London in 1849, where he would remain for the rest of his life, Marx maintained a low political profile for the next ten years, burying himself in the study of history and political economy. In 1857 and 1858, amid dire poverty, he produced a series of notebooks that in effect contained a rough draft for *Das Kapital*. The *Grundrisse*, as they have become known, can be seen as the second stage in a grand historical vision that began in 1845 with the writing of *The German Ideology*. Recently published in English with an excellent introduction, the *Grundrisse* represents the confluence of many themes in Marx.[34] It vividly illustrates continuity in his thought: what he gleaned from the early studies and the direction his future research must take.

During the 1860s Marx returned to active politics, becoming a central figure in the International Association of Workers, an involvement that delayed the eventual publication of *Das Kapital* and thwarted him from completing its remaining volumes. The 1870s were a time of relative security, although factionalism in the International and recurring illness frustrated any concerted attempt at writing. Marx died in 1883, known and revered in socialist circles throughout the world and yet virtually unacknowledged for his theoretical contributions by the British intellectual milieu that surrounded him for thirty-four years.

UNDERSTANDING HISTORY

Marx did not call his method of historical inquiry *dialectical materialism* or *historical materialism*; these are labels affixed to his perspective by later Marxist traditions.[35] He called his approach the *materialist conception of history* or the *materialist perspective*, always being careful to differentiate his open-ended evolutionary view from the closed-system analysis of eighteenth-century mechanical materialism. For Marx the study of history was based upon comprehending productive activity through time and the various forces and circumstances constraining it. In his writings, "materialist" signifies the physical-environmental-economic circumstances to which a particular society is bound, but it also indicates the organic biological and psychological make-up of humankind itself—the same sense in which Darwin used the concept in his unpublished notebooks.

While Marx adhered to the belief that history was constrained by economic laws subject to scientific scrutiny, the laws themselves evolved: those governing the Asiatic, ancient, feudal, and modern bourgeois modes of production were quite different. It is unfortunate that Marx's view of history has often been dismissed as a single-factor explanation when he so consistently sought to show the multitude of ways in which this factor is operative. Nor can it be said that Marx viewed history as a drama in which the participants, according to Popper, are "mere puppets irresistibly pulled by economic wires."[36] It is also obvious from even a superficial reading of Marx that his materialist interpretation of history has no connection to an alleged economic striving as the fundamental drive in man.[37]

When Marx embraced *The Origin of Species*, he believed that Darwin had done for nature what he had done for history. He was strongly motivated by the nonmechanistic and nonteleological character of Darwinian theory. Although several of his conservative contemporaries accused Darwin of reducing life's creative expression to mechanical laws, Marx knew otherwise. To him, natural selection had the scientific legitimacy of Newtonian theory coupled to an open-endedness capable of framing the reality of continual change, an element absent from Newton's perspective.

Marx was concerned with the relationship between nature and history and with rendering historical analysis scientific. Considerable inspiration for this task was provided him by the universal historians of the eighteenth century. Since most writers have, and I am no exception, stressed the influence on Marx exerted by Hegel, Feuerbach, and classical political economy, the impact of the eighteenth-century historians is often overlooked. During that century, particularly in what has become known as the Scottish Enlightenment, writers such as Adam Ferguson and John Millar did not deal with the subject of history in terms of kings and wars—what Marx would refer to as the "high sounding dramas of princes and states" (*German Ideology*, 48)—or as a succession of ideas. Instead they stressed the importance of economic stages, such as hunting, pastoralism, agriculture, and commercialism.[38] Similarly, several writers from the French Enlightenment couched history in terms of a perspective that Marx found informative. Turgot and Condorcet emphasized key developments in the arts and sciences, and Rousseau outlined a critical historical perspective, the stamp of which became indelibly etched in Marx's writings.

In his *Discourse on the Origin of Inequality* (1755), Jean Jacques Rousseau conceived history in terms of epochs based on the development of social organization and technology. His main argument was that these humanly created phenomena have become tyrannical and suppressive of creativity, spontaneity, and freedom, an anticipation of Marx's view of the alienation of labor that occurs with the rise of the state. It is not surprising, then, that Engels eventually claimed that the sequence of ideas Rousseau elaborated in *Discourse* correspond exactly to those used by Marx right down to "a whole series of the same dialectical developments" (*Anti-Dühring*, 153). In dealing with the entire breadth of human social evolution, Rousseau also considered the importance of what we now term the passage from nature to culture, the human transition. In explaining the emergence of human society out of an earlier prehuman and individualistic state of nature, Rousseau even speculated on the possibility of biological evolution but wisely noted that at the time of his writing, insufficient evidence mitigated against the acceptance of such a perspective. One of the few recent writers to perceive the crucial link between Rousseau and Marx is the sociologist Robert Nisbet:

If Darwin had his Lyell, Marx had his Rousseau (*vide* the *Discourse on the Origin of Inequality*). That Darwin's statement of continuous and cumulative variation in genetic change has had a degree of acceptance that Marx's statement of dialectical change in society has not had in sociology is not the point. The point is simply that the prestige of one in the study of biological evolution has been precisely paralleled in the prestige of the other in the study of social stratification, and that in each we are dealing with ideas that have deep eighteenth century roots.[39]

Fundamental to Marx's perspective is both the historical character of nature and the natural character of history. Although the latter concept emerged as a recurring theme in *The German Ideology*, it was not until 1859 that Marx emphatically accepted the former concept as part of his world view. Nevertheless, even in his earlier writings he was critical of the idealist's attempt to separate nature from history.

In attacking the grandiose vision of the idealist tradition, Marx claimed that history is not an autonomous or abstract force; it is always rooted in a naturalistic or materialistic base. The following passage is one of his most succinct:

History is nothing but the succession of the separate generations, each of which exploits the materials, the capital funds, the productive forces handed down to it by all preceding generations, and thus on the one hand continues the traditional activity in completely changed circumstances and, on the other, modifies the old circumstances with a completely changed activity. [*German Ideology*, 59]

The materialist conception of history was in part a reaction to the earlier idealist view that history was some kind of divine unfolding, "a metaphysical subject of which real human individuals are but the bearers" (*Holy Family*, 107). Phrases such as "history does this" or "history does that" were held to be meaningless abstractions. Marx identified perspectives that regarded history as an autonomous, almost personal force with the old teleology, which proffered the notion that plants exist to be eaten by animals and animals by people (ibid.). One of his targets in this critique was Hegel, who conceived history in terms of the gradual emergence or unfolding of what he called the "idea" or "spirit" or the "notion" (tantamount to what we might today refer to as consciousness) at successively higher levels of organizational complexity. All earthly events were seen as acting in a manner geared to the more efficacious actualization of "spirit." For Hegel, as spirit rose historically, it evidenced greater freedom. However, he always held that the mass of humanity, whom Marx saw as the builders of history, were only the agents in which spirit was realized, not its creators.

The criticism of history as the abstract logical formula of movement leveled at Hegel and other idealist visionaries, resurfaces in Marx's polemic against the views of the French utopian socialist Proudhon. In his flamboyant work, *The Philosophy of Poverty*, Proudhon took relations of economic production outside the context of human activity and placed them in the realm of the autonomous and abstract. Marx accused him of making a metaphysics out of political economy.

If we abstract thus from every subject all the alleged accidents, animate or inanimate, men or things, we are right in saying that in the final abstraction, the only substance left is logical categories. Thus the metaphysicians who in making these abstractions, think they are making analyses, and who the more they detach themselves from things, imagine themselves to be getting all the nearer to the point of penetrating to their core. [*Poverty Philosophy*, 106]

This incisive critique is equally apropos of the great French sociologist Emile Durkheim who at the turn of the century proposed a theory of society based on the belief that social phenomena are autonomous, self-contained entities, not understandable in terms of biology, psychology, or techno-economic organization. It also forewarned against the danger inherent in the superorganic approach to culture that has been integral to American anthropology in the twentieth century. It is ironic that one of the most outspoken of the superorganicists, Leslie White, has been affiliated with Marx's theoretical position. White's constant elaboration of the premise "culture does this" and "culture does that" recalls the idealist assumption that "history does this" and "history does that" to which Marx was so antagonistic.

Although in his materialist conception of history, Marx reacted to idealist and purely conceptual approaches, such as Hegel's, this is not to say that his perspective was dominated by an empiricism that endeavored to explain the totality of external circumstances on every occasion. As he noted, "Science would be superfluous if the outward appearance and the essence of things directly coincided" (*Capital*, 3:817).

The materialist perspective is in effect a dialogue between scientifically inspired conceptual formulations and an observable world continually in a state of flux. The latter constrains, the former explains that constraint, but always after the fact, as in the case of open-systems approaches such as the theory of evolution by natural selection. The contemporary French theorist Maurice Godelier comes close to this position when he claims that Marx's dialectic is more than merely the inversion of Hegel's; it is an attempt to reveal the hidden internal structure beneath visible empirical operations and is therefore quite consonant with a modern scientific approach.[40] But it must be kept in mind, as Wilden has recently pointed out in his communicational interpretation of Marx, that this internal structure itself is open to change in response to the various levels of environment that constrain it.[41] Assuming this to be the case, and there is good evidence upon which to ground such an assumption, then the materialist conception of history has legitimate claim to a scientific affiliation—one that is Darwinian rather than Baconian.

As historian of science Loren Graham has noted, if Marx's perspective "either as an explanation of nature or of social history, is to be discussed in terms of science, the comparison must be with nondeterministic theories of low predictive power, such as the theory of evolution or probability theories."[42] Just as by using natural selection Darwin could not predict exactly when a new species would arise or what it would be like, Marx was in the same situation regarding a new form of society. That he did attempt such prediction, and was sometimes wrong, does not diminish the explanatory power of his perspective. To say that history is determined is not to say that it is predetermined.

The disjunction between the theoretical explanation of physical events, whether in history or in evolution, and the events themselves as recurring processes, was a situation Marx grasped intuitively rather than explicitly; this is one reason why his work has spawned so much interpretation. It remained for Engels, only a few months from death, to attempt a discussion of the problem of the relation between reality and theory with respect to the concept of history that he and Marx had striven for so long to develop. It is no accident that evolutionary theory provided him with a model. In a letter to Schmidt, dated March 12, 1895, he wrote:

Are the concepts which prevail in the natural sciences fictions because they by no means always coincide with reality? From the moment we accept the theory of evolution all our concepts of organic life correspond only approximately to reality. Otherwise there would be no change. On the day when concepts and reality completely coincide in the organic world development comes to an end.... The concept of fish includes a life in water and breathing through gills: how are you going to get from fish to amphibian without breaking through this concept? And it has been broken through and we know a whole series of fish which have developed their air bladders further into lungs and can breathe air. How, without bringing one or both concepts into conflict with reality are you going to get from the egg-laying reptile to the mammal which gives birth to live young? And in reality we have the monotremata a whole sub-class of egg-laying mammals—in 1843, I saw the eggs of the duck-bill in Manchester and with arrogant narrow mindedness mocked at such stupidity—as if a mammal could lay eggs and now it has been proved. [*Torr*, 530]

The fact that Marx called his approach the materialist conception of history has led numerous later writers to assume that he was talking only about the economic determinants of social formation. Marx's model, however, was not so one-sided. It also accommodated the organic. History, like evolution, according to Marx, was predicated on the activity of organisms engaged in the life process. Therefore the bedrock of history consists of human beings' manifesting their given capacities and capabilities. Human nature underscores historical development. To grapple fully with this, the naturalistic basis of human action must be understood: "The first fact to be established is the physical organization of these [historically producing] individuals and their consequent relation to the rest of nature" (*German Ideology*, 31).

Human beings make history because of the way their species characteristics are expressed through labor at a particular period of social development. This part of historical interpretation consists in having an understanding of what Thomas Huxley referred to, in the book of the same name, as "man's place in nature." It is little wonder that Marx was enthralled when he attended Huxley's lectures, although he would hardly have been in accord with the latter's politics. It was Marx's belief that a knowledge of something akin to a combination of what we would today call physiology and biopsychology is an essential prerequisite for the comprehensive historian. In the *Paris Manuscripts* he attempted to improvise such a perspective by defining human species characteristics in terms of a model provided by Feuerbach's philosophical naturalism. He abandoned the quest a year later in *The German Ideology*, not because he lost interest in its importance but because he realized it was beyond his scope at that time and his newly emergent interest in economics was fast becoming a total preoccupation. The plea for and attempt at investigating human nature in the *Paris Manuscripts* gave way, in the *German Ideology*, to only a plea for that investigation. Nevertheless, Marx avidly kept up with the relevant literature in the field, even though he was never able to integrate it fully into his later historical writings.

In historically setting into motion various activities relating to their species requirements, human beings are inextricably linked to a social context. Marx took as an inherent characteristic of our species a predisposition toward the social, a perspective grounded into the biologic of evolution by Darwin in his 1871 work, *The Descent of Man*. For social beings at the base of history, the tasks, according to Marx, are twofold: production of the means of subsistence and the reproduction of the species itself. The urge to propagate leads the species into various biosocial relationships, such as the link between the sexes, the parent-child bond, and the various forms of the family (*German Ideology*, 40). Later in the *Grundrisse* and *Das Kapital*, he would come to regard the various types of blood organization, based on the tribal clan, as a similar fundamental expression. The production of the means of subsistence, particularly through cooperative social labor, is what differentiates historical beings from the rest of nature. In *Das Kapital*, he would refer to hunting societies, which do not produce in the true sense, as the starting point for history. At that time, aware that pack-hunting carnivores also evidence cooperative social labor, Marx began increasingly to stress the role of tool manufacture in human emergence.

Since human history at its most basic level is predicated on the production of life through labor and procreation, it is therefore both a social and a natural phenomenon. Through labor, man participates in nature by starting regulating and controlling reactions essential to his survival (*Capital*, 1:77). Each generation in so doing exploits, in accordance with its species wants, the productive and reproductive capacities handed down to it by the preceding generations. Marx referred to this process as an "evolution" that takes place naturally, not as a result of a plan of freely combined individuals (*German Ideology*, 88). The evolutionary character of history is nowhere more clearly expressed than in the following passage:

Men make their own history, but they do not make it just as they please; they do not make it under circumstances chosen by themselves, but under circumstances directly encountered, given and transmitted from the past. The tradition of all the dead generations weighs like a nightmare on the brain of the living. [*18th Brumaire*, 15]

Although Marx held that men are free individually, he did not believe that they were free absolutely in relation to history. The productive forces that are the basis of their identity are an acquired force, always the product of former activity (*Poverty Philosophy*, 181). In generating these productve forces, men enter "into definite relations which are independent of their will...and these relations result in the specific mode of production of material life which...conditions the general process of social, political, and intellectual life" (*Critique*, 20). Inextricably bound up with the development of production in any historical epoch is the existence of classes and their ensuing struggle (*18th Brumaire*, 139).

For Marx, the class struggle began with the dissolution of primitive tribal society and the common ownership of the means of production that typified it (*Manifesto*, 6). As society differentiated into ruling classes and exploited oppressed classes with the rise of the state, those in power generated ideologies designed to rationalize and legitimize their interests. These ideologies have taken the form of religion, law and, of course, science, frequently being proffered to the masses as universal truths. At times the class struggle has been seen as the historical analogy to Darwin's struggle for existence in nature; indeed, Marx and Engels drew the parallel on several occasions. It is important to note, however, that just as Darwin's concept of the struggle for existence in nature did not usually refer to an interspecies or intraspecies warfare but rather to a struggle on the part of species and individuals to appropriate their wants from nature, so in Marx's view the class struggle did not necessarily imply actual warfare (although it could) but the struggle to appropriate the results of productivity.

Each historical epoch is underwritten by a repertoire of productive forces. They can be analyzed and the economic character of the epoch discerned through a study of the instruments of labor and their manufacture and functioning. In approaching this task Marx again evidenced Darwin's influence by using a biological metaphor: he likened the procedure to the search for fossil bones in determining extinct species of animals (*Capital*, 1:180). In both examples, the concrete remains are viewed not as final entities but as examples of process: the instruments of labor are evidence of history and the fossil bones evidence of evolution. Engels later elaborated on this notion when he wrote that it was the old natural science, predominantly a collecting science, that investigated living things as finished objects, while the natural science of Marx's era, largely under the influence of Darwin, dealt with process and interconnection: "What is true of nature, which is hereby recognized also as a historical process of development, is also true of the history of society in all its branches" (*Feuerbach*, 47).

Engels went on to explain the proximity of evolution and history in Marx's work. He noted that in nature various agencies act on one another, and what he called general laws arise from this interplay. In history men are endowed with conscious purposeness; they act with deliberation toward definite goals. While recognizing the importance of these motivations in the investigation of particular events, he pointed out that their power diminishes over the course of total history where the operation of more general laws comes into effect. Therefore the conflict in history of many individual wills and actions partly "produces a state of affairs analogous to the realm of unconscious nature" (ibid., 48), adding that to be complete, the study of history must take into account forces, conscious and unconscious, that lie behind the motives of men. It therefore appears that Engels opened up the materialist conception of history to the possibility of psychoanalytical or psychohistorical interpretation not as the explanatory vehicle for historical processes but rather to give us a fuller understanding of these processes.

Just as organic life must meet the exigencies of an environment that is often changing or else become extinct, man's historical mode of productive relations is continually adapting to physical conditions. But unlike the animal that only slightly modifies its environment, man, through social labor and manufacture of tools, is capable of rendering wide changes to the world he inhabits. Nevertheless he must reckon first with physical conditions. Marx responded to this situation by postulating two classes of external environmental factors: natural wealth in terms of direct subsistence, which includes rich soil, bountiful wildlife, and so on, and natural wealth that can be an instrument of the labor process at a given period in history, including waterfalls, navigable rivers, fuel supply, metals, and the like (*Capital*, 1:512). In man's historical evolution, the first factor was the important one during the early phases of development, whereas the second became significant with the advent of civilization. This approach, while conceding primacy to physical factors, avoids a simplistic or reflexive environmental determinism. For example, Marx noted that although a natural force such as a river exists apart from human intervention, it has no intrinsic economic value until it is acted upon, or we can say "mediated," by a particular form of social labor—the social relations of production—in a given historical period.[43]

In an anticipation of the gradualist perspective of cumulative change intrinsic to Darwin's theory, Marx noted that during the course of historical evolution, no social order is ever displaced before all its productive forces have been developed; new forms never replace the older until the conditions for their existence have evolved within the framework of the old society (*Critique*, 21). Elsewhere, using yet another biological metaphor in a similar context, he stated that "human anatomy contains a key to the anatomy of the ape" (*Grundrisse*, 105).[44] The biological credo, *Natura non facit saltum*, thus applies equally to history.[45] There were no miracles or chasmic leaps, only a gradual evolution brought about by productive social labor and the ensuing class struggle for its appropriation.

In Marx's nineteenth-century cultural present, the class struggle was expressed in terms of the relations of production of bourgeois capitalist society. For him, this was a transitory historical period—not the universal human condition rationalized by the political economists. According to Marx, earlier economic writers had defined two kinds of institution: the artificial and the natural. They had deemed the productive relations of feudalism artificial and those of the bourgeois epoch natural, an expression of the relations "in which wealth is created and productive forces developed in conformity with the laws of nature" (*Poverty Philosophy*, 121). This ahistorical way of viewing political economy was severely criticized by Marx, who likened it to a theology that claimed one true religion. He saw each epoch as expressing some aspect of human self-realization. Capitalism, with its exploitation of the worker through wage labor, reducing mind and body to an appendage of the machine, restricted this self-realization more than did any prior epoch.

The materialist conception of history reached its zenith with the case study of nineteenth-century capitalism contained in *Das Kapital*. In it Marx showed how forces of production constrain the mode of social organization and the mode of social organization the ideology. It is a systemic analysis, a cross-section of the internal relations of a particular historical period, yet it illuminates historical movement as a whole. Similarly Darwin, in *The Origin of Species*, highlighted the temporal dimension of evolution through a systemic analysis of the interactions of living communities of plants and animals. In his historical quest, Marx. early on abandoned the idealist search for absolute truth in favor of relative truths pursued along the paths of the theoretical sciences, with their results mediated by human necessity.

Hegel's Vision of Nature

> Fire and water married, and from them sprung the earth, rocks, trees and everything. The cuttlefish fought with the fire and was beaten. The fire fought the rocks and the rocks conquered. The large stones fought with the small ones; the small ones conquered. The trees fought with the creepers; the trees were beaten and the creepers conquered. The creepers rotted, swarmed with maggots, and from maggots they grew to be men.
>
> —Polynesian myth

Few studies of Marx fail to discuss the influence exerted on his thought by the great German philosopher Georg Wilhelm Friedrich Hegel (1770-1831).[1] Most of these studies deal with Marx's appropriation of Hegel's method[2] or the continuities that exist in their respective historical approaches.[3] Darwin, too, has been compared to Hegel, and although it is unlikely that Darwin ever seriously read Hegel, the fact that the idea of evolution is a prominent theme in both their writings has been used as the basis for comparison.[4]

Hegel's vision of nature and its transformation is a philosophical melange of pre-Darwinian concepts, and there is little evidence to indicate that Marx ever seriously subscribed to it. While Marx took and extended certain aspects of Hegel's philosophy and rejected and criticized others, he was largely silent in assessing Hegel's natural and scientific writings. Although Marx was impressed by the encyclopedic range of Hegel's thought, he was also sensitive to the developments taking place in nineteenth-century science that at every turn were rendering eighteenth-century formulations like Hegel's obsolete.

During the 1840s Marx was deeply concerned with nature and its relationship to human nature. What he took from Hegel, and later from Feuerbach, during this period was a phenomenology of the natural. Although in his early work Marx tried to develop a consistent natural science perspective, he does not appear to have achieved this objective until Darwin's evolutionary research was published in 1859. *Das Kapital* contains the first complete scientific assessment of nature to appear in Marx's writing. While a thorough understanding of this text requires a knowledge of Hegel's *Phenomenology of Mind* and *Logic*, as many commentators have noted, the scientific credentials of the analysis spring directly from the nineteenth-century context. As one critic, Jean Hyppolite, has aptly noted, in *Das Kapital* Marx thinks like a Hegelian but adopts a stance on nature that reflects Darwin, not Hegel.[5]

Although Hegel's vision of nature influenced Marx less than did the great philosopher's historical and logical mode of interpretation, this vision is of some importance if we are to understand the intellectual shift brought about by the Darwinian revolution, a revolution that powerfully caught Marx in its swirl. It was not simply a matter of Darwinian evolution's displacing biblical creation. There were a number of scientific views prior to Darwin that tried to deal with the continuity of life forms. Many, including Hegel's, were what I call cataclysmic-creationist; although they recognized continuity in form, they disavowed direct, continuous descent. The new forms were held to have arisen through a sudden upheaval. Since each new form invariably contained vestiges of what preceded it in time, any resemblance, such as between ape and humankind, need not imply lineal descent, only close proximity in time of creation on the great chain of being. The cataclysmic-creationist model is obviously consonant with biblical ideology; however, it could also be formulated on the basis of speculative inference without recourse to postulates emanating directly from the Scriptures, and this is the way the doctrine was expressed in Hegel's philosophy. It is a useful vantage point from which to look back at biblical notions and ahead to the gradualism of Darwinian theory.

SUCCESSION IN NATURE

Although Hegel's philosophical interpretation of nature was not published in its entirety until 1842, summaries and outlines of the material contained in it began appearing in 1817 in his *Encyclopedia*. Marx and Engels, in their personal correspondence, give evidence of having read Hegel's ideas on nature and science as late as 1858. It appears that they were fascinated by his method of argumentation rather than with his specific conclusions. Both in his natural scientific and other writings, Hegel attempted to present a synoptic view of all knowledge. In an effort herculean in scope and evolutionary in design, he strove to comprehend qualities inhering in all phenomena in the cosmos. It is not difficult to imagine Marx as a student of philosophy reading Hegel's entire available corpus a number of times. The breadth of concern in Hegel recalls Aristotle, another of Marx's philosophical influences. The evolutionary cast of the argument foreshadowed, in a more spiritual and less materialist manner, the philosophical system of Herbert Spencer, a contemporary of Darwin, Marx, and Engels, about whom they said surprisingly little.

Almost all of Hegel's writings are permeated with concepts of evolution and development. This is most apparent in his *Philosophy of Nature* and *Philosophy of History*; even in *The Phenomenology of Mind*, probably his most important work, which focuses on the abstract realm of knowing, evolution is used to characterize thought moving upward from sensations, to consciousness, to self-consciousness. Hegel has few peers as a philosopher of evolution, a tradition that includes the less profound but nonetheless interesting figures of Auguste Comte and Herbert Spencer in the nineteenth century and Teilhard de Chardin in the twentieth. Although the Hegel-Marx connection is by now a well-interpreted historical fact, at least one notable attempt has been made to tie Hegel's idealism to Darwin, and it was done in the 1870s by the British philosopher F. H. Bradley.

Marx, in dealing with history, and Darwin, with evolutionary biology, endeavored to link their perspectives to a scientific approach, in that they weighed evidence and sought to establish relationships of constraint that were at least in part empirically testable. Hegel's approach to nature was more conceptual and intuitive. Nevertheless, by affirming development and change in nature and, more significantly, history, even if he lacked the wherewithal to give convincing scientific demonstration, he became one of a number of late eighteenth- and early nineteenth century thinkers, among them Goethe, Buffon, Geoffroy Saint-Hilaire, Lamarck, and Erasmus Darwin, whose efforts prepared the intellectual climate of the second half of the nineteenth century for the reception of Darwinian theory.

In Hegel's vision of nature, movement and change can be evidenced everywhere: in day-to-day activity as well as through eons of time. This may sound like a typically Darwinian viewpoint, but Hegel's manner of explaining how the process operated differed significantly from Darwin's. In Darwinian theory, evolution is held to be a long, slow, protracted continuum of events characterized by the "preservation of favourable individual differences and variations, and the destruction of those which are injurious" (*Origin*, 91). The gradual nature of the process was suggested by uniformitarian geology, one of Darwin's early influences. Although the latter years of Hegel's life, spanning as they did the late eighteenth and early nineteenth centuries, coincided with the rise of uniformitarianism in geology, Hutton, Playfair, Smith, and Lyell being its major disseminators, Hegel's *Philosophy of Nature* failed to absorb this influence.

For Hegel, transformation in nature did not take place through the gradual processes suggested by uniformitarianism but by a series of cataclysmic successions. These successive creations moved nature from the simple to the complex through a series of hierarchical stages. The scheme he elaborated was designed to meet the criticism that the great chain of being provided no reliable method by which the gradations linking its extremities might be enumerated and ranged in a rational sequence.[6] Hegel held that succession from one stage to another always takes place through a sudden and dramatic leap. In this sense he shares kinship with the opponents of uniformitarianism, the catastrophists in geology and biology, the most notable being the French naturalist Georges Cuvier (1769-1832), one of Hegel's contemporaries.

The mode of reasoning whereby nature moves in leaps or sudden spurts has, despite the Darwinian revolution, never entirely disappeared from the Western intellectual tradition, nor is it exclusively the preserve of the biblical special creationists. Early in the 1900s, the discovery of mutation theory in biology led to the belief in some circles that these sudden transformations of nature might be the primary agent of evolution. For a brief period of time, Darwin's gradualism was severely questioned. However, rather than refuting the Darwinian perspective, mutation theory was ultimately absorbed by it, the result being the modern synthetic or neo-Darwinian theory of evolution. Even today a form of nontheological catastrophism survives in the controversial and dubious geological and astronomical theories of Immanuel Velikovsky.

While Marx and Darwin sought to bring mind as close as possible to matter in order to discern the laws operative in both realms, Hegel speculated from the subjective distance of mind alone. From his idealist pinnacle he concluded that evolutionary development could never be observed directly: that what we see are only its periodic results. He wrote, "To think of genera as gradually evolving out of one another in time is to make use of a completely empty concept."[7] Although this statement may appear to be a rejection of evolution, it amounts only to a denial of evolution the way we have come to regard it—as a gradual long-term transformation of living organisms in the sense elaborated by Darwin a half-century after Hegel.

Hegel's approach did not refrain from questioning biblical creation. In its place he substituted a chain of being or a hierarchy of developmental stages. He held that although each species is a unique and separate entity, there must be a deep creative unity underlying the chain as a whole: "The animal world is the truth of the vegetable world, which in turn is the truth of the mineralogical world."[8] The formation of each stage on Hegel's evolutionary ladder—*ladder* is as apt a metaphor for Hegel's evolutionary system as the branching tree is for Darwin's—becomes a struggle for what he called the "idea" to see the light of day at successively higher levels of organizational complexity. For Hegel the idea, or spirit, or the notion, as it is sometimes called, represents the line of self-reflective consciousness, of purpose, running from nature through prehistory, to the highest point in history (and the cosmos), his own Germanic civilization. Comprehending through his philosophical consciousness all that had preceded his existence in time and place, Hegel believed that he was the fulfillment of the idea up to the point in history that constituted his interpretive vantage point.

Each transformation by which the idea ascends is catastrophic, almost to the point of being a series of separate creations. The pageant begins in the sea, then moves to plants, fishes, land animals, and finally to human history where a new, more continuous kind of development takes place. The doctrine of *Natura non facit saltum*, that nature makes no leaps, does not hold; each shift is qualitative and sudden rather than the result of a quantitative buildings. The motive force behind the whole operation is teleological, almost mystical in conception; the idea struggles with matter in order to break through each successive level and establish itself on a higher plane. In his complex and often baffling manner, Hegel noted that each level always contains vestigal remains from the level that preceded it: "Matter involves itself into life and evolution is therefore also involution."[9] The highest stage is always the concrete unity of all those antecedent in time. The continuity is always between stages, or the properties of species as a whole, rather than through individual organisms. At one point Hegel almost sounds Darwinian when he declared that purposeful activity in nature is oriented toward self-preservation; however, nature as a whole always remains metaphysically and teleologically conceived: "To bring itself into the existence of spirit. . .constitutes the truth and ultimate purpose of nature."[10]

NATURE AND HISTORY

Despite the fact that Hegel's philosophy embraced both nature and history, he defined them as distinct spheres. It is history, he believed, that manifests the idea or spirit in its purest form, while nature represents the otherness of the idea or the idea in an estranged state. History for Hegel is inherently rational. Nature's reasonableness is not inherent but derives only from its inclusion into thought through man's philosophical consciousness. By contrast, in the writings of Marx and Darwin, nature constitutes an objectivity operating by a series of laws that in a number of instances can also be extended to humanity.

Thus the classical dualism of mind-body, nature-society (or history), or whatever other form it may take, while an essential aspect of Hegelian philosophy, is a component Marx rejected as a holdover from theological conceptions of the universe. René Descartes (1596-1650) was probably the most precise cartographer of this dualism. In the early seventeenth century he expounded the belief that mind is rational and free, while the body, synonymous with physical nature, operates by mechanical principles. As Marx and Engels pointed out, Descartes's theory of nature, by sacrificing physical motion to mechanical motion, led to the mechanistic materialism of the eighteenth century (*Holy Family*, 169-73). Mechanistic materialism, a perspective often and wrongly attributed to the writings of the later Marx and Engels, dispensed with notions of reason and freedom in human affairs, substituting instead a machine-like model deriving from Descartes's physics reinforced by Newton's clocklike model of the universe.

Hegel's approach resembles a Cartesianism set into historical motion. He held that the opposition between nature and history (equivalent to Descartes's body-mind separation) is one between determinism and freedom. Marx, by contrast, tried to pull the two extremes together with his belief that there is freedom and open-endedness in nature (which Darwin's theory reinforced) and determinism in history as a result of a compliance with various developmental laws.

In one respect, Hegel's concept of the nature-history dichotomy strikes an interesting contrast with the views of Marx and Darwin. For Hegel history, not nature, is a theater of perennial conflict. According to Hegel, history "does not present the harmless tranquility of mere growth as does that of organic life."[11] In Darwinian theory, nature exhibits constant struggle, usually of the organism against the environment (although owing to the "nature red in fang and claw" concept first propounded by Tennyson, subsequent generations would come to believe that Darwin viewed nature in terms of a day-to-day life-and-death struggle between individuals); in contrast, Hegel regarded nature as almost quiescent: "That development which in the sphere of nature is a peaceful growth, is in that of spirit in severe and mighty conflict with itself."[12] This belief, that in day-to-day activity nature is docile and unthreatening unless punctuated by a sudden catastrophe, was prevalent throughout the Enlightenment, where it survived as a holdover from biblical notions of the garden of Eden and the Deluge. It is also worth noting that the transition from the Enlightenment, and also the Hegelian perspective of nature as serene, to the Darwinian vision of continuing struggle was partly bridged by the romantic rebellion of the early nineteenth century. During this period artists, poets and musical composers began depicting nature as more ominous and threatening, a force capable of expressing a multifaceted temperament.

Hegel's *Philosophy of Nature* appears to have had little impact on subsequent generations. Darwin nowhere mentioned that he read it, and Marx, despite not having many scientific alternatives until Darwin, appears to have been unresponsive to this aspect of Hegel's thought. Since Immanuel Kant (1724-1804), science and philosophy have generally been parting company, a fact Marx found disturbing. Hegel's alliance with science was awkward at best, though it has been claimed in his defense that the reason his *Philosophy of Nature* lacks plausibility to subsequent generations results from the fact that the material he worked with became antiquated with dramatic suddenness.[13] Marx admired the encyclopedic range of Hegel's erudition and the logic of his method, but when it came to dealing with nature he seems to have been more partial to Hegel's great poetic contemporary, Goethe (1749-1832); Denis Diderot (1713-1784), the eloquent philosopher of the French Enlightenment; and Ludwig Feuerbach.

Goethe's opinion that natural science and the study of man and history were compatible, along with his questioning of previous historical approaches—"How much does even the best historical study give us of the real life of a people"[14]—formed a deep, if generally unheralded, influence on Marx. Diderot was a materialist not in the mechanistic sense, as were a number of his contemporaries, but in the open-ended manner of Marx and Engels. He strongly endeavored to shatter the mind-body, nature-society dichotomy at every turn: "If you admit that the difference between the animal and yourself is merely one of organization you will be showing good sense and reason."[15] Diderot attacked notions put forth by Descartes, and even Rousseau (the latter a close personal friend) that held animals to be naturally ordained machines, a criticism echoed by Marx and Engels in *The Holy Family*. In a Victorian parlor game when Marx was asked to name his favorite poet, he listed Goethe; he then went on to nominate Diderot as his favorite prose writer.[16]

Part II
THE HUMAN-THEORETICAL FRAMEWORK

4

Human Nature: Marx's Anthropological Assumptions

> The most useful and least advanced of all human knowledge seems to me to be that of man.
>
> —Jean Jacques Rousseau

Any critical perspective dealing with the human situation presupposes, if not a formalized theory, at least a set of what can be called anthropological assumptions regarding human nature. When, as in the case of Marx's early writings, these assumptions are extensively elaborated, the enterprise may be called a philosophical anthropology.

Although Marx's reputation derives primarily from his theory of history, economic analysis of the capitalist regime, and revolutionary socialism, these topics are linked to anthropological assumptions depicting a generic framework for human nature. This human-theoretical framework is not directly elaborated in the more well-known and influential historical writings such as *Das Kapital*. As a result it has been contended that the tradition following from Marx has sought to attack concepts of an innate basis for human nature, substituting instead the contention that man is a creature primarily shaped by his environment.[1] This has been the dominant trend in institutionalized Marxism behind the Iron Curtain where a tabula rasa concept of human nature, maximizing malleability and ignoring specific biopsychological foundations, prevails. The result of such a stance has been a series of prominent scientific biases. Until recently, modern genetics was deliberately suppressed, as was any dialogue with a psychology not predicated on an environmentalist or a stimulus-response model.[2]

The situation with respect to Marxist scholarship in the West is somewhat different, although equally frustrating.[3] Marx has recently been analyzed in considerable depth, and this has served to reveal anthropological assumptions of considerable significance. Psychologist Erich Fromm is not alone in his declaration that Marx believed in a concept of human nature biologically and psychologically and therefore cannot be labeled a sociological relativist.[4] Despite this declaration, there has been a tendency on the part of Fromm and others to abstract Marx's ideas on human nature from the rest of his theories, presenting him as a humanist to an American public traditionally hostile to his writings.[5] This trend has resulted in considerable recent exposure being given to the early Marx, most notably his *Economic and Philosophical Manuscripts of 1844*, where the subject of human nature is profoundly discussed in a language of baffling complexity and continually shifting nuances.

This concern with the early Marx is both healthy and revealing; however, almost all contemporary Western writers who deal with the subject fail to recognize that although Marx is speaking as a philosopher and in a philosophical language that verges on being poetic, he is pleading a scientific case.

One basis for life and another basis for *science* is *a priori* a lie. The nature which develops in human history—the genesis of human society—is man's *real* nature; hence nature as it develops through industry, even though in an *estranged* form, is true *anthropological* nature....

...History is a *real* part of *natural history*—of nature developing into man. Natural science will in time incorporate into itself the science of man, just as the science of man will incorporate into itself natural science: there will be *one* science....

...*Man* is the immediate object of natural science. [*Paris Manuscripts*, 143]

In spite of the many recent efforts to see the early Marx as a humanist and even an existentialist, trends undeniably present, a strong case can be argued for the possibility that he believed the opinions he put forth on human nature had scientific legitimacy, if not in conjunction with the science of his day certainly with respect to the unified natural and human science of the future that he so eloquently predicted.

The writings produced from 1840 to 1846 extensively elaborate the anthropological assumptions. Soviet Marxism and its kindred traditions have either ignored or downplayed these efforts as impressionistic sketches of only passing interest when compared to the major scientific formulations of the so-called mature Marx. The fact that scientific contentions can be derived from the early writings has not been dealt with by Soviet Marxists, probably because they would be averse to the aspects of science relevant to such an undertaking. The mistake on the part of several writers in the West has been to exalt the early writings, and at the same time to sever them completely from any scientific affiliation. This is largely in reaction to the stigma on the link between Marxism and science, deriving from Soviet-based interpretations of his "mature" work. The "mature" work, however, is not exactly devoid of anthropological assumptions. Any thorough study of the later writings will reveal that Marx consistently worked out his historical perspective and economic analysis with reference to human-theoretical parameters.

In both the early and the later writings, man is not seen as a passive, infinitely malleable creature. He is held to be an active agent possessing characteristic life forces. Although this position is blatantly stated in the early writings, it does not disappear altogether in *Das Kapital*; instead it becomes an implicit, rather than an explicit, point of reference. Since Marx worked out his vision of human nature early, and apparently for the purpose of self-clarification—neither the *Paris Manuscripts* nor many of the ideas in them were published during his lifetime—he felt no need to restate the results of this research in *Das Kapital*. In any case, a number of his formulations necessitated reassessment in light of new scientific knowledge, and after he moved to London in 1849 he barely had time enough to deal with the economic issues.

It would be inaccurate to describe Marx as having a unified or formal scientific theory of human nature; rather he made a series of related theoretical assumptions. In addition to being expressed in the *Paris Manuscripts*, these assumptions appear in several of the other early works: the *Critique of Hegel's Philosophy of Right*, *The Holy Family*, and most notably in *The German Ideology* where naturalism and humanism marry a new materialism. These works are now essential if we are to grasp his thought in its entirety and understand the full implications of his major contribution, *Das Kapital*. Although *Das Kapital* is first and foremost an economic treatise, it was conceived with reference to man, a creature whose labor produced an intricate web of economic relationships that ultimately entrapped him. To want to change the world by overthrowing the capitalist regime, as Marx did, required the belief that the system does not properly reflect human nature and that other arrangements can be more consonant with the fundamental and authentic parameters of the species. Marx perceived this early in life. He also came to realize that the major contribution he could make toward this end was not in the realm of a unified human science—the vision of the *Paris Manuscripts*—still lacking theoretical underpinnings, but in a practical, social scientific demonstration of the inner workings of the exploitative system. Materials for the analysis were all around him, and *Das Kapital* became the culmination of this critical labor.

When Marx deals with human nature in his early texts, formal exposition of the subject is lacking; hypothetical conjectures abound; catchy phrases reveal sharp insights; promising leads evaporate; diverse concepts are juxtaposed; and there is a strong sense of improvisation, of mind in process. The major contributor to this state of affairs is perhaps the fact that much of the early writing was composed for the purpose of clarifying his own thinking on a number of topics.

During their later years, when confronted with the possibility of having some of the early texts published, Marx and Engels showed little interest. This does not imply a rejection of the ideas contained in these works but rather an embarrassment over the lack of conceptual precision, especially considering the great changes that had taken place in nineteenth-century science. However, in the case of *The German Ideology*, composed in 1845-1846, which contained important reflections on human nature as well as the first elaboration of the materialist conception of history, Marx and Engels tried to get the book published as soon as it was written. When the publisher balked because of the radical implications of the work, the two authors, who by then were immersed in further studies, took his reaction in stride. Their comment reveals a commitment to scholarship and intellectual integrity rarely paralleled: "We abandoned the manuscript to the gnawing criticism of the mice all the more willingly since we had achieved our main purpose—self-clarification" (*Critique*, 22).

In elaborating the formulations of influential thinkers from the past, one has a tendency to impose an order and development that reflects the concerns of present inquiry. In the case of Marx, it is just as apparent in this study as it is in those of numerous other writers. When dealing with the problem of human nature, Marx ranged widely and was often ambiguous and contradictory. My intent is to group sets of related concepts together and to reveal what I contend are significant directions in his thought. From this effort a frame of reference will emerge—one that has been continually overlooked by subsequent interpreters of his work: Marx's assumptions about human nature, though pre-Darwinian in inspiration, are strongly biological and psychological in orientation; they provide thorough philosophical and scientific definition of the human species and its relationship to nature.

These observations on human nature become more significant when Darwin's later work on the same subject is considered, despite the fact that Marx derived his assumptions from philosophy and Darwin from the evolutionary biology he established almost singlehandedly. True, Marx abandoned his quest for a unified science of human nature in favor of economic theory; nevertheless, should anyone wish to elaborate and update this aspect of his legacy, as a number of recent writers seem to want to do, the tradition of Darwin is the necessary marriage partner— the fulfillment of the promise-prophecy of the natural science of humankind outlined in the *Paris Manuscripts*.

FEUERBACH

Like Rousseau, the Scottish moral philosophers,[6] and a host of other writers in the century preceding his own, Marx began his philosophical and scientific odyssey with an attempt to discern the nature of human nature. He believed that to comprehend fully the social and historical architecture created by the human species, he must first analyze its organic building blocks, the raw material of human nature. Although influenced by many sources in this endeavor, two are particularly noteworthy: Hegel and Feuerbach.

From Hegel, Marx derived an understanding of process and a sense of history. However, he found Hegel's perspective too abstract, too removed from the salient realities of man's physical and sensuous nature. Ludwig Feuerbach (1804-1872), a philosophical contemporary who rose to prominence in the 1840s, provided the logical complement. Feuerbach stressed the corporeal aspects of human nature. Throughout his writings he relentlessly attacked theological and idealistic conceptions of human nature, and Marx lauded him for this effort on a number of occasions. Feuerbach's criticism of Hegel was particularly devastating and a delight to Marx and Engels. Nevertheless, Marx's commitment to Feuerbach's intellectual position was never total. He noted that the latter was too much concerned with nature and too little with politics and that his naturalism failed to relate human nature to its historical realizations.[7] In the first of the famous eleven theses on Feuerbach (written in 1845), Marx stated:

THE chief defect of all hitherto existing materialism—that of Feuerbach included—is that the object, reality, sensuousness, is conceived only in the form of *object* or *contemplation* but not as human sensuous *activity*, *practice*, not subjectively. [Quoted in *Feuerbach*, 82]

The theses on Feuerbach are a criticism of the contemplative materialism expounded by that philosopher and the foundation for Marx's own materialist perspective. Engels referred to these theses as the first "document in which is deposited the brilliant germ of the new world outlook" (ibid., 8). Despite Marx's eventual historical and economic interests, he absorbed a good deal of Feuerbachian anthropology into his work. Incidentally, Feuerbach actually used the term *anthropology*; it signified a philosophical and scientific perspective aimed at the emancipation of man through an understanding of human nature. It is clear from the *Paris Manuscripts* as well as *Das Kapital* that the following programmatic statements issued by Feuerbach in the 1840s profoundly influenced Marx:

The new philosophy makes *man, together with nature* as the basis of man, the *exclusive universal*, and *highest object* of philosophy; it makes *anthropology, together* with *physiology*, the *universal science.*[8]

Philosophy must again unite itself with natural science, and *natural science with philosophy.*[9]

Although the methods and the content may have differed, this plea for a unified science converged remarkably with that Marx propounded in the *Paris Manuscripts*.

The contemporary French Marxist philosopher, Louis Althusser, has claimed that there is a division between an early Marx, dominated by the "problematic" of Feuerbach, and a later more mature Marx who broke with and rejected such concepts in favor of a more scientific historical approach.[10] The shift in focus is undeniable, but rather than breaking with Feuerbach's vision, it would be more accurate to say that Marx transformed it and assimilated it into his new materialist perspective. Although Feuerbachian ideas about human nature are not directly in evidence in *Das Kapital*, there is a concern with the organic nature of man underlying history that represents his continuing influence: "The productiveness of labour is fettered by physical conditions. These are referable to the constitution of man himself" (*Capital*, 1:512).

It is significant that as late as 1888 Engels would not let the legacy of Feuerbach be forgotten. To preserve the memory, he wrote *Ludwig Feuerbach and the Outcome of Classical German Philosophy*, defending Feuerbach on a number of points. Engels pointed out that the link between philosophy and natural science that Feuerbach sought during his intellectual peak was impossible because the natural sciences at that time were still in a process of fermentation and that even though he lived to see Darwin's theory and a number of other major scientific discoveries, Feuerbach should not be blamed for his failure to assimilate them. This failure was caused by the repressive conditions in Germany that forced him outside of the mainstream of intellectual life (*Feuerbach*, 28-29).

It would seem to follow from Engels's line of reasoning that Marx's ideas on human nature and unified science, conceived shortly after Feuerbach's, faced the same immature body of natural science theory. Embarrassingly ahead of their time and lacking conceptual clarity, these ideas must still be seen as an attempt to generate what Marx hoped would be scientifically plausible formulations.

A THREEFOLD SCHEME OF INTERPRETATION

Marx approached the subject of human nature from a number of different directions. Three interrelated frames of interpretation appear to me to be useful repositories in which to group his various assumptions. Although the insights belong to Marx, their order and manner of presentation reflects a perspective inspired by Darwinian theory and modern anthropology, a perspective that should help both to clarify the original context of his work and highlight its continuing relevance.

1. Continuity is established among man, nature, and history. Man is viewed as a part of nature to counter the rift opened up between the two realms by traditional theologies and the Western metaphysical tradition of Descartes, Kant, and Hegel.

2. Man is seen as possessing a network of species characteristics distinguishing him from the rest of creation. Nevertheless these characteristics are said to have a naturalistic basis.

3. The natural capacities of the human species interact with external nature through labor to produce the constantly changing economic, social, and ideological situations—culture in the modern sense—in which man defines himself and his human nature.

Throughout this triadic scheme runs a major Marx concept, alienation: man's estrangement from his species nature through the consequences of his labor. A good deal of insightful contemporary Marx literature has been devoted to this topic.[11] The complexities of the problem, and the urgency to explicate on a new biosocial level Marx's ideas on generic man, preclude the present study from examining the alienation question as well. Nevertheless, in Marx's writing, discussions of human nature and alienation constantly interpenetrate, and I will elaborate this relationship where appropriate without engaging in an extended analysis.

Continuity with Nature

According to Marx, the life of any organic species is typified by a primary dependence on the products of nature. Even man's distinctive mode of living must derive from the same basic products— plants, animals, and sunlight—that give nurturance to other life forms. Marx referred to this relationship as one that makes nature man's "*inorganic* body—both inasmuch as nature is (1) his direct means of life, and (2) the material, the object and the instrument of his life activity" (*Paris Manuscripts*, 112). *Inorganic body* is used as a metaphor to indicate continuity between man's obvious organic body and the earthly world that gives sustenance to it. Nature is perceived in this way because human existence necessitates a continuous exchange with it. While these reflections appear to be obvious and fundamental, we must remember that previous philosophy, notably the German idealist tradition immediately preceding Marx, ignored the earthly aspects of man in favor of the spiritual. In Marx's approach, as Engels noted, nothing exists apart from nature and man, and nature remains the foundation upon which human beings develop whether or not philosophy chooses to recognize it (*Feuerbach*, 18). In 1844 without hesitation or ambiguity, Marx openly proclaimed this relationship: "That man's physical and spiritual life is linked to nature means simply that nature is linked to itself, for man is a part of nature" (*Paris Manuscripts*, 112).

The continuity between man and nature stressed by Marx in 1844 represents a vision Darwin tried to establish with scientific precision nearly thirty years later. However, although man and nature are inextricably entwined in Marx's early philosophical anthropology, there is no historical sense of nature developing into man as we later find in *Das Kapital* (as a result of Darwin's influence); the two realms simply coexist in an integral relationship. Any attempt to trace man back through successive generations to the point when the first man emerged from nature is condemned as high-order speculation. By implying that there was a time in past history when man was nonexistent, Marx believed that we only further abstract him from nature (ibid., 145). In 1844 he regarded an evolutionary line of reasoning as unsupportable by reliable scientific evidence. He linked it to notions of special creation holding that an alien being in existence above nature and man must be responsible for their first creation. Although he did not recognize evolution in the organic realm, he did hold it to be an attribute of the earth's inorganic history. He accepted the work of Lyell in geology and believed it demonstrated that the earth was self-generating, therefore disproving any idea of creation (ibid., 144).

In summary, then, the young Marx saw the three earthly realms of geology, biology, and human history as separate in that transformation from one to the other was deemed impossible without invoking an external hand, yet also linked because at any given moment in time the three are in constant interaction with one another. With the advent of Darwin's theory in 1859, Marx reaffirmed his earlier belief in the continuity between man and nature, although he did reject his belief in its nontemporal character by recognizing the historical component of nature and the gradual emergence in an unbroken trajectory of man and human history out of nature. In his later scientific writing, Engels extended the parallel between the development of the Marxian world view and nineteenth-century science by discussing the plausibility of various theories pertaining to the emergence of life from inorganic matter, a topic Marx would have thought absurd in 1844.

In *Paris Manuscripts*, Marx described his approach as a "naturalism," differentiating it from both the idealism of his philosophical precursors and the mechanical materialism of the tradition following from Descartes physics, including the French physiocrats of the previous century. During this period he demonstrated a deep concern with human nature and only a passing interest in history: "Only naturalism is capable of comprehending the act of world history" (ibid., 181). In other words, only through an understanding of human nature can the full implication of its historical consequences be weighed. A year later the point of focus shifted. In *The German Ideology*, an understanding of the productive relations governing history became the central task. Nevertheless, the earlier view was not completely abandoned; it was relocated in a new context. Instead of being the only arbiter of history, human nature is now the primary point of departure for a more inclusive vision: "The first premise of all human history, is of course, the existence of living human individuals. Thus the first fact to be established is the physical organization of these individuals and their consequent relation to the rest of nature" (*German Ideology*, 31).

Totally caught up in his new fascination with the historical process, Marx nevertheless reiterated the importance of human nature to the enterprise but admitted that he was in no position to provide a complete assessment of it. Perhaps he sensed that the *Paris Manuscripts* might have been an overly ambitious effort and that his new scientific-historical role necessitated more caution when dealing with a topic as elusive as human nature. By 1845 the critique of the materialism of the previous two centuries, his naturalism, and the new interest in the dynamic of the productive forces had given birth to the approach he termed *the materialist conception of history*, the intellectual stance that remained with him throughout his life. For Marx *materialist* referred not only to the economic relations of production, the generally accepted position, but to the organic constitution, the biological and psychological makeup of man himself and his relationship to external nature.

In his early writings, Marx viewed nature and human nature as coexisting forces. They interpenetrate to such a degree that many of Marx's observations can be easily accommodated to a framework that sees this reciprocal relationship resulting from man's emergence out of nature, although he adhered to no theory of biological evolution at this time. Marx referred to man as a *"natural being"* actively endowed with *"natural powers of life"* that exist in the form of "tendencies and abilities—as instincts" (*Paris Manuscripts*, 181). These are phrases that one usually associates with descriptions of animal behavior. Marx insisted that there is nothing divine or mysterious in man rendering him above nature (this is Feuerbach over Hegel). These traits coupled with his corporeal and sensuous being make man "a *suffering*, conditioned and limited creature, like animals and plants" (ibid.). Even though man may think that he exists apart from nature, the thoughts that give rise to this belief have their origin in human nature's inextricable bond to organic nature: "Life is not determined by consciousness, but consciousness by life" (*German Ideology*, 37-38).

In arguing for the unity between nature and human nature in the Marxian texts, a crucial problem of interpretation arises. Marx stated that "taken abstractly, for itself—nature fixed in isolation from man is *nothing* for man" (*Paris Manuscripts*, 191). Did he believe in a concept of nature apart from man? Several of his recent philosophical interpreters have taken the position that his method is applicable only to history and that his apparent interest in nature (even after Darwin) is only incidental.[12] There is some truth to this perspective if we confine it to the early writings. However, as Marx's ideas developed in conjunction with nineteenth-century science, intellectual reasonableness necessitated his acceptance of a concept of nature separate from man and history.

There is evidence to indicate that any concept of nature apart from human nature would have been regarded during the 1840s as a needless abstraction. Since nature at that time had yet to be conceived historically in a scientifically convincing way, Marx, as a result, saw nature as inseparable from its coexistence with man. Therefore, nature extricated from this context, nature without reference to human nature, held little interest for him. With the emergence of Darwinian theory, the relationship of nature to human nature took on new and increased significance in Marx's eyes. But in accepting Darwin totally, as evidence indicates he did, Marx had to accept a belief in the existence of a nature that was also prior to and separate from man. This position is clearly stated by Engels and doubtlessly acquiesed in by Marx: "Nature exists independently of all philosophy" (*Feuerbach*, 18). After 1859 Marx emphatically believed that an analysis of natural processes in and of themselves, apart from man, could contribute to human understanding. In *Das Kapital*, he used a model of speciation, admittedly deriving from Darwin, to explain the formation of several human institutions. He then cited Darwin specifically for the inspiration provided by his history of "Nature's Technology" (*Capital*, 1:340, 371).

Man's Species Nature

For Marx man is a natural being possessing various species traits that set him apart from other organisms. The most obvious one is his physiology, which was of great concern to Feuerbach. But Marx was more interested in the dynamic aspects of human nature—the behaviors that result in visible life activity. He insisted that such phenomena, no matter how abstract they seem to be, are intrinsically bound to organic processes related to those found throughout the natural world. These ideas appear in his early writings and predate Darwin. The source might conceivably be the early Greek conceptions of pantheism, naturalism, and materialism.

Marx referred to these organically grounded distinctively human proclivities as man's "species-character" or his "species-being." In elaborating them his immediate source of inspiration was Feuerbach, who employed similar terms. Marx extended the list to include "species-life" (*Gattungsleben*), "species-activity" (*Gattungstatigkeit*), "species-spirit" (*Gattungscharakler*), species-relationship" (*Gattungsbewusstsein*), and "species-powers" (*Gattungskrafte*). Through the employment of these concepts in the works written prior to 1845, Marx discussed man in terms of his subsistence activity, creative capacity, and sex and social relationships. The result can be viewed in modern biological perspective as a species-specific model of human nature. In his early writings, this model forms the foundation upon which Marx elaborated historical relations.

Despite the many characteristics affirming the link between man and nature, the human species nonetheless has a fundamental uniqueness: "Man is not merely a natural being: he is a *human* natural being. That is to say, he is a being for himself" (*Paris Manuscripts*, 182). Marx was aware that man shares many life functions with other animals—eating, drinking, and procreating are given as examples of what he calls "animal functions." But they are also taken to be human functions when they are discharged in the sphere of all other human activity. Since man is more than the sum of his life functions, his full expression, or individuation, is contingent on these functions not being turned into "sole and ultimate ends" as they are when his relation to the products of his labor becomes alienated or estranged:

This relation is the relation of the worker to his own activity as an alien activity not belonging to him; it is activity as suffering, strength as weakness, begetting as emasculating, the workers *own* physical and mental energy, his personal life indeed, what is life but activity?—as an activity which is turned against him, independent of him and not belonging to him. [Ibid., 111-12]

Marx's vision of human nature is tightly woven to his concept of alienation, one result of the perspective whereby man is regarded as being partly animal and partly his own unique creation. Marx was critical of two situations that deny human nature its full expression. For making the animal or life functions an end in themselves through a reduction in the human potential of the laborer, the capitalist system of production is condemned; and, in a more intellectual vein, for exalting the uniqueness of man and downplaying his natural capacities, theology and philosophy are called into question.

Marx used the difference between what is unique in man and his animal-linked life activity to understand the full dimension of human experience. The influence of Feuerbach is important here. Nevertheless, although Marx initially accepted certain of his assumptions, he eventually made some distinctive modifications. In Feuerbach's philosophical anthropology, the crucial division between man and animal is consciousness. In manifesting consciousness, man becomes aware of himself as a species, of his "being" in the world. When this understanding is expressed through science, man becomes the object of his own systematic thought: "Science is the consciousness of the species."[13] While other animals, according to Feuerbach, cannot conceive beyond the limited realm of their respective biological worlds, man is capable of making the whole of nature the object of his thought.

The dualism in man between consciousness and his animal nature, propounded by Feuerbach and accepted by Marx in 1844, differs significantly from the classical mind-body dualism of Descartes that became a mainstay in idealist philosophy. As Hanfi points out, following Heidegger, Feuerbach's concept of consciousness is not metaphysical but an "existential characteristic belonging to the ontological constitution of man."[14] Unfortunately, even though Feuerbach's concept of consciousness had biological foundations, there was no way to demonstrate this using the scientific resources available during the early nineteenth century. This is one possible reason why after 1845, Marx felt increasingly uncomfortable with what he called Feuerbach's "contemplative materialism." Had Feuerbach at least taken his concept of consciousness out of the arena of pure philosophy and applied it to actual human situations, Marx might have been more receptive to it.

By 1844 Marx developed further but had not as yet transcended Feuerbach's basic insights. Like Feuerbach, he held the distinguishing feature of the human species to be "free conscious activity." This was deemed essential for both the maintenance of physical existence through productivity and the procreation of fresh life (*Paris Manuscripts*, 113). He followed Feuerbach in noting that while animals are "immediately one" with their life activities, man can make these activities the object of his will.

Through conscious activity, man can transform organic nature to human ends. He therefore interacts with a world of objects. In elaborating a difficult train of thought, Marx used the concept of objects in a dual sense: to draw man into closer proximity with nature and as an indicator of human uniqueness. Man is said to have instincts like other animals and consequently "the *objects* of his instincts exist outside him, as *objects* independent of him; yet these objects are *objects* that he *needs*—essential *objects*, indispensible to the manifestation and confirmation of his essential powers" (ibid., 181). Marx noted that any being that does not have a need for things external to it is not a natural being and therefore plays no part in the "system of nature." As an example, he cited hunger in man as a natural need requiring an external object for its satisfaction.

While the need for external objects is a common denominator between man and the rest of nature, the manner in which these objects are transformed and rendered adequate to the human sensibility reveals the uniqueness of our species:

Therefore, *human* objects are not natural objects as they immediately present themselves, and neither is *human sense* as it immediately *is*. . . . Neither nature objectively nor nature subjectively is directly given in a form adequate to the *human* being. [Ibid., 182]

By being conscious of his needs, man transforms external nature. In a perceptive aside thought, Marx added that animals can effect similar alterations of their external circumstances. Bees, beavers, and ants can build nests and dwellings that change their natural surroundings and express their species nature. However, he insisted that the animal produces only "one-sidedly," what "it immediately needs for itself or its young," while man is capable of producing even when he is free of immediate physical need. Through consciousness he can produce in anticipation of a future need. The animal's product belongs intrinsically to its physical body. It is a continuing replication of the unvarying standard of the species, while man, by contrast, "freely confronts his product" (ibid., 113).

Several of these ideas were taken up later in *Das Kapital* in a manner suggesting that Marx sought to elaborate and qualify, rather than abandon, his early anthropological assumptions. This situation can lend further evidence for continuity in his thought. In *Das Kapital*, these assumptions leave the realm of philosophical speculation and enter Marx's systematic historical perspective. He remarked that while animals tend to be at one with their life activity, man has the ability to distinguish himself from his life activity and to act back on it. Using the modern philosophical terminology, we may say that man becomes conscious of his intentionality. Labor, a marriage of consciousness and practical activity, assumes prime significance. Through the labor process man starts, regulates, and controls reactions taking place between himself and nature:

He opposes himself to Nature as one of her own forces, setting in motion...the natural forces of his body, in order to appropriate Nature's productions in a form adapted to his wants. By thus acting on the external world and changing it,...he...develops his slumbering powers and compels them to act in obedience to his sway. [*Capital*, 1:177]

In contrast to the *Paris Manuscripts*, the concept of labor is now strongly emphasized. In the *Manuscripts*, consciousness is primary; labor is secondary. History is regarded as the "conscious self-transcending act of origin" (*Paris Manuscripts*, 182), and consciousness is linked to knowledge as opposed to action: "Knowing is the sole act" (ibid., 183). Labor and productive life are held to be aspects of man's species-character only insofar as they are the direct emanations of his consciousness. This emphasis on conscious, or knowing, undoubtedly resulted from the lingering influence of Hegel, in particular, *The Phenomenology of Mind*.

In *Das Kapital* Marx still viewed man as a transformer of nature, but through labor directly rather than through consciousness as a first cause. Instead of being epiphenomenal to consciousness, labor has subsumed it, and the two taken together now define man. In *Das Kapital*, Marx abandoned the interesting terminology he employed in the early writings, which included phrases such as *species-being and species-character*. Labor, a more practical and operationalizable concept, now becomes the primary natural human force, the necessary condition for effecting the exchange of matter between man and nature: "It is the everlasting Nature-imposed condition of human existence, and therefore is independent of every social phase of that existence, or rather, is common to every such phase" (*Capital*, 1:183-84). Labor, therefore, is not a result of convention, consent, or external circumstances but a deeply rooted panhistorical, pancultural endowment of the species.

Although Marx assumed labor to be a generic capacity, it is not taken to be a simple reflexive response of the human organism to the environment but part of an intricate reaction taking place between external nature and the biological and psychological nature of man, with the most essential aspect of human nature, the brain, acting as mediator. The brain accounts for the unique stamp in man, differentiating him from other animals. Again using analogies from the animal world as he did in the *Paris Manuscripts*, Marx observed that a spider conducts operations not unlike a weaver and a bee not unlike an architect, but the crucial distinction between an architect and a bee is that the "architect raises the structure in imagination before he erects it in reality" (ibid., 178). Although this may appear to be a return to Hegel's notion of the idea as first cause, there are significant differences. The imagination Marx referred to is not an autonomous or spiritual phenomenon; it is the psychological consequence of the material (here synonymous with biological) functioning of the human brain, an organ engaged in a constant dialogue with the exigencies of a real physical environment.

In an important passage in the preface to *Das Kapital*, Marx alluded to the nature of mind in order to distinguish his approach from Hegel's:

To Hegel, the life process of the human brain, i.e., the process of thinking, which, under the name of "the idea", he even transforms into an independent subject, is the demiurgos of the real world, and the real world is only the external, phenomenal form of "the idea". With me, on the contrary, the ideal is nothing else than the material world reflected by the human mind, and translated into forms of thought. [Ibid., 119]

The crucial word in this quote is *reflected*. Is Marx implying that the images in our brain are direct reflections of the material world? Lenin thought so.[15] Recent Western interpreters deny that Marx was so simple-minded, yet they have no hesitancy in attributing the reflection hypothesis, or copy theory as it is sometimes known, to Engels, from whom it is said Lenin derived the inspiration. The weight of evidence against Marx's holding the reflection hypothesis has been drawn primarily from his earlier writings where the influence of Hegel, self-consciousness, and free will predominate. While this line of argumentation is valid, to use it as several writers have in denying that Marx had a materialist perspective on mind (in other words that he believed it functioned in accordance with natural laws—a view in no way incompatible with the belief in self-consciousness and free will) does an injustice to his theoretical imagination.

Marx's contention that there is a material world subject to various laws and a human mind comprehending it also subject to various laws is illustrated by his remarks that the material world is not merely reflected by the human mind but is *translated* into forms of thought. In this process of translation, the unique laws of mental functioning are to be found. Marxist-Leninism has taken its conception of human nature and mind solely from reflection, leaving out translation and all that it can imply. These implications might include a psychology devoted to understanding the development of the brain using evolutionary theory in the sense that Darwin, and to a degree Freud, used it, and also perhaps a perspective delineating the operations of mind underlying cultural processes, an enterprise not unlike what is being done today in certain quarters under the banner of structuralism.[16]

While it is fairly clear that Marx never conceived a psychology—

Darwinian, Freudian, structuralist, or otherwise—to go with his vision of man and history, evidence indicates that Engels had some leanings in a number of these directions. In 1888 he emphasized the importance of the brain in initiating behavior by pointing out that everything that sets men acting finds its way through it: "The influences of the external world upon man express themselves in his brain, are reflected therein as feelings, thoughts, instincts, volitions—in short, as 'ideal tendencies', and in this form become 'ideal powers' " (*Feuerbach*, 30). For Engels, like Marx, the reflection of the world by the mind is not a direct mirroring activity. It is mediated by a repertoire of distinct biopsychologically grounded processes. Engels's list of active human traits is strikingly similar to the one elaborated by Marx in the *Paris Manuscripts*. This is ironic considering recent commentaries putting the early philosophical Marx and the later scientific Engels at virtually opposite intellectual poles.[17] Even more ironic is the similar terminology employed by Engels. He used *instinct*, *volitions*, and *powers*, terms that rarely appear in the writings of the later Marx.

There are two related reasons why Engels may have resurrected the concepts and terminology of the early Marx. First, they are useful at the level of biological and psychological description; second, Darwin had provided a method whereby these and similar assumptions could now be assessed with greater scientific certainty. Engels was aware that Darwin's theory was not limited to explaining how the various species in nature came into being. He recognized that it provided a basis for understanding the development of mind itself, "for following all its various stages of evolution from the protoplasm, simple and structureless yet responsive to stimuli, of the lower organisms right up to the thinking human brain" (*Feuerbach*, 67). He added, and Marx would have undoubtedly concurred, that without this kind of scientific legitimation, the existence of the thinking brain must remain a miracle. Unfortunately the path to understanding man's species-nature based on definitions propounded by the early Marx, and the scientific approach provided by Darwinian theory, was only glimpsed by Engels. The possibilities that could derive from this synthesis have been overlooked, both in subsequent Marxism—East and West—and by the Western social science tradition.

Self-Creation Through Labor

Establishing continuity between nature and human nature and highlighting the repertoire of species traits that define man were useful steps in Marx's world view. Since labor and productivity define man, to comprehend fully the resultant implications for history they must be grasped in the active sense through the process of self-creation whereby man effects the changes in his social and ideological situation that provide the context for self-definition. The work launching this concern was *The German Ideology*. Earlier in the *Paris Manuscripts*, Marx acknowledged labor and productivity for the part they play in the maintenance of the species, but he did so in a static sense, as the handmaidens of consciousness and outside of history. In 1845 this view is set into historical motion:

Men can be distinguished from animals by consciousness, by religion or anything else you like. They themselves begin to distinguish themselves from animals as soon as they begin to *produce* their means of subsistence, a step which is conditioned by their physical organisation. By producing their means of subsistence they are indirectly producing their actual material life. [*German Ideology*, 31]

In 1844 man was seen as a being who could freely confront the products of his labor; now, in 1845, he is engaged in an ongoing dialogue with these products. As a result, he becomes the consequence as well as the cause of his own life activity. His natural human capacities act upon external nature, effecting transformations in this sphere having direct social repercussions.

Through labor, man mediates his natural needs to conform to what is distinctive by his own nature, and he does this to a greater extent than does any other organism. By producing his means of subsistence, as Marx noted, man distinguishes himself from animals and the rest of the natural world. He effects what the contemporary anthropologist Claude Lévi-Strauss has so often referred to as the passage from nature to culture. For Lévi-Strauss one index of this movement is the act of cooking, where the raw product of nature is transformed to the human sensibility. He also contends that the nature-culture transformation is a recurring theme in much of primitive mythology.[18] Although Marx did not use the term *culture*, which was defined in its modern anthropological sense by Edward Tylor in 1871, he did work with a number of premises that we have come to attribute to that concept.[19] However, while for Lévi-Strauss the passage from nature to culture is predominantly conceptual and of no historical importance, Marx regarded it as a significant indicator of the degree of development of the productive forces at the point in time where animal consciousness is displaced by human consciousness—the dawn of history.

With the commencement of history, the generation of social forms and self-conceptions becomes directly linked to the way in which labor is deployed in productive activity. The particular expression that the life activity of a given human group takes, what we would today refer to as its social and cultural organization, is referred to in *The German Ideology* as "a definite mode of life." Marx described the reaction in the following manner: "as individuals express their life, so they are. What they are coincides with what they produce and how they produce. The nature of individuals thus depends on the material conditions determining their production" (*German Ideology*, 32). As men produce through labor,

The phantoms formed in the human brain are also necessarily sublimates of their material life process, which is empirically verifiable and bound to material premises. Morality, religion, metaphysics, all the rest of ideology and their corresponding forms of consciousness, thus no longer retain the semblance of independence. They have no history, no development; but men, developing their material intercourse, alter along with their real existence their thinking and the products of their thinking. [Ibid., 37-38]

There is a paradox that emanates from these observations, —one that has continually made the resolution of Marx's concept of human nature complicated. If man is what he produces and if human nature results from the material conditions determining productivity during any given epoch, as Marx seems to suggest, then fixed generalizations about human nature, which he continually makes, must invariably lead to interpretive contradictions.

The view that human nature is in flux appears elsewhere in Marx's writing. The following passages are well known: "All history is nothing but a continuous transformation of human nature" (*Poverty Philosophy*, 147), and, "By thus acting on the external world and changing it, he [man] at the same time changes his own nature (*Capital*, 1:177). Understanding Marx's intent is difficult. It requires a degree of interpretation from the vantage point of the present and the demarcation of concepts that in his case had no clearly defined parameters. It would not be inaccurate to assume that Marx's use of the phrase *human nature* had two implications. In one sense he referred to it in terms of generic universal and unchanging attributes; in another it is said to be comprised of social and ideological conceptions, information historically acquired.

In the *Paris Manuscripts* and even *Das Kapital*, Marx made reference to universal unchanging aspects of human nature. He did not believe that there have been any significant physiological changes during history, and similarly, the various instincts, volitions, tendencies, and the labor process itself are attributed to man in every historical epoch. If this were not the case, the concept of alienation would not be possible. If each stage of history produced a requisite form of human nature, then there would be no conflict between what man is and his external circumstances; the capitalist mode of production would produce a harmonious blend of capitalist and worker human nature. Marx devoted a good deal of his energy in showing that this is not the case and that the products of history, although made by men and the basis of man's ideological conception of himself, during certain periods have acted as an alien power impeding the full expression of the universal recurring elements in human nature:

this consolidation of what we ourselves produce into an objective power above us, growing out of our control, thwarting our expectations, bringing to naught our calculations, is one of the chief factors in historical development up till now. [*German Ideology*, 45]

Within the capitalist system all methods for raising the social productiveness of labor are brought about at the cost of the individual laborer; all means for the development of production transform themselves into means of domination over, and exploitation of the producers; they mutilate the laborer into a fragment of a man, degrade him to the level of an appendage of a machine, destroy every remnant of charm in his work and turn it into a hated toil; they estrange from him the intellectual potentialities of the labor process [*Capital*, 1:645]

The second citation provides strong evidence that the alienation concept, usually associated only with Marx's early writings, retained significance in *Das Kapital*.

The alienation question has been the subject of considerable recent interest in Western intellectual circles. If man in capitalist society is alienated, what is he alienated from? Marx provided a number of answers in the concept of human nature in the *Paris Manuscripts*. In *Das Kapital*, man in capitalist society is still said to be estranged from his essential nature; however, rather than reelaborating why this is so, Marx was more concerned with demonstrating how the system creating the situation operates. Capitalism is not regarded as consonant with human nature. The negation of capitalism, communism, is held to represent humankind's full flowering. In part this belief was inspired by romantic conceptions of the communal nature of primitive society— later supplemented with considerable ethnological information.

When dealing with human nature, Marx wanted to delineate two domains that appear to be in conflict: a concept of human nature based on universal unchanging traits and one that is historically acquired. When referring to the generic or universal human traits, his writing often lacks clarity, probably because he was aware that the enterprise was suggestive of idealism. Not until the twentieth century, with the emergence of modern genetics and the extensive cross-cultural studies by anthropologists, could scientific credence be lent to this belief. Marx was on much firmer footing when he connected human nature to the social and productive apparatus of a given historical period. However, he never did this in an absolute sense, despite several statements that make it appear otherwise. When Marx wrote that human nature changes during the course of history as a result of changing productive circumstances, he did not mean intrinsic biological nature but the social and ideological conceptions that form the basis of a people's identity. However, he did tend to blur distinctions between the two. Today we recognize that they are separate but related domains. Humankind creates and is created by history and society, but to this process it brings a distinctive repertoire of behaviors that underlie all historical periods and contemporary societies.

Evidence that Marx held both a generic and a historical conception of human nature, and that they were compatible, can be drawn from his position on slavery. In his early writings, he was a strong believer in universal natural rights as a justification for freedom. He lauded Fourier's assertion that the right to hunt and fish is an innate right of all men (*Holy Family*, 118). In *Das Kapital*, human equality is a repeating motif. Looking back to the Greek society of Aristotle's day, Marx remarked that it had for its "natural basis" an organization of labor predicated on slavery. This was a result of the social conditions of the period— not an expression of any innate differences in human nature between slaves and slaveholders. Underlying the observed inequalities was a common and equal humanity that Aristotle was prevented from discovering, although he was brilliantly able to discover relations of equality in the value of commodities because of the "conditions of the society in which he lived" (*Capital*, 1:60). When speaking, as he did in this case, of the natural basis of a particular society, Marx was always referring to the dialogue between the mode of production and the natural environment, not to any innate biopsychological characteristics unique to the individuals in that society. Since biopsychological equality is a universal phenomenon, he believed that no one segment of society can justly emancipate itself until all members of the society as a whole are free, citing as an example the American situation prior to the Civil War: "Labor cannot emancipate itself in the white skin where in the black it is branded" (ibid., 1:301).

Despite his critical humanism, it was virtually impossible for Marx, in the nineteenth century, to have a clear idea of how the generic in man can be factored from its social and historical context or how the universal capacity of man to create a mode of life can be separated from the definition of man provided by the mode of life of a particular historical epoch. In a remarkable effort, he almost managed to comprehend this modern distinction, but the effort is full of ambiguity, blurred distinctions, imprecise concepts, and the intellectual illusiveness that often accompanies daring theoretical ventures.

With the intricate problem of the generic and the historical in Marx's vision of human nature now clarified, if not satisfactorily resolved, we can turn again to the master concept integrating the two domains: labor. The products of labor are said to shape the changing social circumstances in which man finds himself during the course of history. Tools become labor's primary agent in forging human destiny. Marx subscribed to Benjamin Franklin's definition of man as a tool-making animal (ibid., 1:179). Tools are seen as fabrications of the human will as it seeks to appropriate from nature. His definition of tools as "*organs of the human brain, created by the human hand*; the power of knowledge objectified" (*Grundrisse*, 706), is unsurpassed even in light of contemporary anthropological formulations.[20] In the manufacture of tools, the earth itself becomes the instrument of labor. It supplies the materials that are transformed into railways, telegraphs, and other artifacts of industry.

The increasingly complex historical interaction among tools, labor and productive circumstances results in technological development. Rooted in the level of technology are socioeconomic relations and their ideological rationalizations. To gain insight into the historical basis of these relationships, Marx insisted that we study the bygone instruments of labor in a manner comparable to the way that we study "fossil bones for the determination of extinct species of animals" (*Capital*, 1:180). It was his belief that prehistoric or archeological remains indicate the degree of development that labor attained in the past and its requisite social conditions. They therefore establish that man prior to history existed in fully human form as a laborer producing his means of subsistence. Consequently any assessment of Marx's historical perspective or any extended Marxian-inspired study of history must take into account his interest in prehistory. As early as 1867 he was attuned to discoveries in this area, being fascinated by stone, bone, and shell tools, the products of labor in its earliest stages. He believed that the implements providing the richest information about the characteristics of any given epoch are "those of a mechanical nature, which taken as a whole, we may call the bone and muscles of production" (ibid.). Included in this category are hunting implements, traps, nets, weapons, tools for agriculture, and those that provide a source of energy. All are expressions of human nature as it interacted with the natural environment to produce a particular mode of life.

Through the use of tools, man creates the technological environment that provides the framework for his ideological creations. One of the most enduring and essential of these ideological creations is art. According to Marx, various artistic conceptions flourish only insofar as they explain phenomena that technology has not yet been able to control. In a perceptive and eloquent passage noting the connections between the natural and social relations portrayed in Greek art and Greek mythology, Marx asked whether the Greek imagination is possible at all in the face of railways and the telegraph:

What chance has Vulcan against Roberts & Co., Jupiter against the lightning-rod and Hermes against the Credit Mobilier? All mythology overcomes and dominates and shapes the forces of nature in the imagination and by the imagination; it therefore vanishes with the advent of real mastery over them. What becomes of Fama alongside Printing House Square? Greek art presupposes Greek mythology, i.e. nature and the social forms already reworked in on unconsciously artistic way by the popular imagination. . . .

From another side: is Achilles possible with powder and lead? Or the *Illiad* with the printing machine. Do not the song and the saga and the muse necessarily come to an end with the printer's bar, hence do not the necessary conditions of epic poetry vanish? [*Grundrisse*, 110-11]

While Marx admitted that the Greek arts are bound to certain forms of technological and social development to which we can never return, he was acutely aware that they continue to give us artistic pleasure. He referred to the Greek epoch as the "childhood of humanity" and its expressions, with all their naiveté are regarded as truths well worth reproducing at a "higher stage" (ibid., 111). In these passages he suggested that the artistic impulse is a component of human nature finding expression in every historical period. It is the result of free conscious activity and an aesthetic faculty; however, the particular forms that are created in any given period are an outgrowth of the relevant productive circumstances.

Whether in conjunction with the mythology of an age or its forces of production, man must have a vehicle to communicate his intentions and coordinate his social activities. Language serves this purpose, Marx referred to language as "practical consciousness that exists also for other men" and claimed that it is as old as consciousness itself, having arisen from "the need, the necessity, of intercourse with other men" (*German Ideology*, 42). Language as an individual creation he declared to be an impossibility. Its origins are said to be in the context of community where it is both the "product" and the "presence" (*Grundrisse*, 490). In Marx's scheme, language mediates between the individual, his thoughts and feelings, and the social necessity. Since language is produced by men, Marx implied that it must be the result of some natural capacity—an aspect of human nature. As a universal capacity, it has properties linking it to labor and a molder of human destiny. Like labor, language moves through historical time, changing in conjunction with the change in social and productive relationships. Created through need and human interaction, it acts back on its producers, helping them to create an identity and a definition of themselves.

Labor, consciousness, language, and the various other species traits postulated by Marx combine to form a human-theoretical framework. Since the inspiration for this endeavor came prior to Darwin, the concern was not for the origins of man but with comprehending him as the creator and end product of history. Yet, Marx believed, a knowledge of history alone would never result in adequate human understanding. History is made by conscious men, a unique collection of beings who are at the same time organic creatures bound to nature and natural processes. The recognition of human necessity upon which we must base future action must derive from an assessment of both of these possibilities.

A number of Marx's observations on human nature predate and parallel those elaborated by Darwin, despite the fact that the two men came out of totally different traditions and had dissimilar goals. Although most of Marx's insights on human nature were formulated prior to the establishment of evolutionary theory, their biological cast is so pronounced that whatever his intentions may have been, he invariably tells us something about human origins. This mode of intellectual inquiry, whereby a thorough comprehension of present circumstances yields insight into their possible sources, was poignantly noted by Feuerbach in 1844: "Where does man come from? First ask: 'What is man?' Once his essence is clear to you, you will also know his origin."[21]

Human Nature: Darwin's Giant Leap

Human nature is the only science of man; and yet has been hitherto the most neglected.

—David Hume

Looking back at the nineteenth century from our own position, it seems almost inevitable that Darwin would want to deal with the nature and origins of humankind. Although his work in this area constitutes an enormous contribution to the fields of biology and anthropology, the decision to publish was not taken lightly, and very nearly could not have occurred at all. Unlike Marx, Darwin came to the subject of human nature late in life. In 1871 he published *The Descent of Man and Selection in Relation to Sex* and in 1872 *The Expression of the Emotions in Man and Animals* —major works overshadowed by the impact resulting from *The Origin of Species*. Michael Ghiselin has referred to Darwin as the Newton of biology and the Galileo of psychology. What is illuminating about this statement is not the appropriateness of comparing Darwin to either Newton or Galileo but the fact that Darwin's contribution has such breadth and significance that it can be compared to the work of two other highly definitive thinkers.

I believe there were three great biological problems to be resolved in the nineteenth century:

1. Generating a plausible theory and marshalling adequate supporting evidence for evolution—not simply affirming it as a fact of nature the way Lamarck, Robert Chambers, Herbert Spencer, and others had done prior to Darwin.

2. Using all of the scientific resources available to assess man's place in the natural scheme of things.
3. Formulating a viable mechanism of inheritance.

Darwin dealt with the first to such a degree that the theory we use today still bears his name and if that were not enough, he went on to do more than any other thinker to put us on the right track for the second; amazingly he attempted briefly to deal with the third, and failed. The principles of inheritance, which along with Darwin's theory of natural selection have given us the modern synthetic or neoDarwinian theory of evolution, were discovered by Gregor Mendel in 1865. Unfortunately, these principles remained unknown until they were rediscovered along with Mendel's research on the problem by Correns, Tschermak, and De Vries at the turn of the century. Interestingly enough, Darwin had access to Mendel's work shortly after it was published, but he failed to recognize its significance. His own attempt to discern the mechanisms of heredity, through what he called the theory of pangenesis, was one of his least insightful contributions.[1]

HUMAN EVOLUTION

The Origin of Species exploded into public prominence in 1859. Darwin's first work on the human species, *The Descent of Man*, appeared in 1871 with an impact that was considerably less dramatic. Unlike *The Origin*, *The Descent* never became a cause célèbre. Considering Darwin's established reputation, it is surprising that the publisher, Murray, brought out so few copies the first year, but Murray had little confidence in the work; he also had the same feelings regarding *The Origin*, which he nevertheless published. Darwin did not help matters when, with his usual hesitance and reserve, he wondered "whether the book is worth publishing" (*Life*, 3: 131). Here then was the most up-to-date and thorough scientific treatise on human nature yet conceived, its author one of the most original and controversial thinkers of the age, and not only were its eventual repercussions minimal, the author himself seemed to be less than enthusiastic about the venture.

On closer scrutiny answers to this paradox begin to appear. The position Darwin took in *The Descent* regarding man's kinship with brute creation was one he had already been criticized for a number of times. During the latter part of the nineteenth century, many people believed that *The Origin*, despite the fact that it did not directly discuss human antiquity, implied that links between man and prehuman primates had scientific legitimacy. Although Darwin deliberately refrained from discussing human evolution in *The Origin*—he certainly had enough to handle in arguing for organic evolution—this did not prevent numerous discussions on the ape-versus-angel status of man from taking place, and they were, of course, directly inspired by Darwin's researches. The most notorious of these debates took place in 1860. The primary antagonists were Bishop Samuel Wilberforce and Thomas Huxley (at this time Huxley was rapidly becoming known as Darwin's bulldog for his staunch defense of the theory of evolution).[2] By 1871 it is conceivable that both the scientific and lay public had wearied of the controversy, and as a result Darwin's statements about human phylogeny, which would have been shattering in 1859, appeared anticlimactic.

Ironically the subsiding of public interest may have been a crucial factor in Darwin's decision to publish. He noted that he had refrained from discussing man earlier despite having a keen interest in the subject because he did not want to invoke any more prejudice against his views (*Descent*, 1). Apparently by 1871 Darwin believed that further prejudice would be inconsequential to his argument, or perhaps he felt that his evolutionary views were securely enough established by then that there would be little risk in extending them to include the discussion of human antiquity in a public forum. Hesitancy and delay typified almost all of his endeavors. One wonders how long the publication of *The Origin* would have been stalled had not the 1858 letter from Alfred Wallace, also outlining natural selection, spurred Darwin into action.

Darwin's giant leap occurred in 1871 when he began publishing his ideas on human evolution. A wealth of evidence indicates that he had been reflecting on the problem for a number of years previous. A glimmer of this thinking surfaced briefly in *The Origin* when he wrote that in the future, "much light will be thrown on the origin of man and his history (*Origin*, 483)." This passage is somewhat cryptic. He was probably hoping that someone other than himself would pick up where he left off and deal with the subject, but the confidence expressed implies that Darwin himself might be willing to undertake the venture. Fortunately for posterity Darwin decided to fulfill his own prophecy, though at the time this does not seem to have been his immediate intention.

Darwin had been thinking about the subject of human nature for as long as he had been working on the problem of organic evolution. As early as 1837 he pondered in his notebooks about the ultimate bearing that his work might have on man: "My theory would give zest to recent Fossil Comparative Anatomy: it would lead to the study of instincts, heredity, and mind heredity, whole of metaphysics...causes of change in order to know what we have come from and to what we tend" (*Life*, 2:4). This quote is representative of the many possibilities flowing through Darwin's mind during his formative years. Recently a number of materials dating from this period have been made accessible, in particular two notebooks illustrative of the way he grappled with various issues that he referred to as man, mind, and materialism.[3] From these notebooks a comparison and contrast with Marx emerges. While Darwin's best-known human-theoretical contributions derive from the later writings that comprise a formal scientific treatise on the subject, Marx's ideas on human nature are located primarily in the early philosophical sketches that constitute the *Paris Manuscripts*.

At least on the surface, Marx's work, because its probable intent was to clarify his own thought rather than to be published, invites comparison to the informal anthropological assumptions that abound in Darwin's early notebooks drafted six to eight years previously. Both thinkers discussed the human nature question. Marx attempted to define the phenomenon in terms of an organic rather than a theological locus. He held that science must be brought to bear on the problem. Although he did not pick up this train of thought again, a concept of human nature deriving from these early impressions underwrites his later historical and economic studies. Darwin also believed that human nature is a biological reality, and he tried to chart the various ways in which scientific discovery could illuminate the question. He abandoned this quest temporarily in favor of dealing with the theory of evolution in general, but returned to it in earnest during the later years of his life. Marx's *Paris Manuscripts* and Darwin's early *Notebooks* depict the dialogue with self of two great intellects endeavoring to focus on related concerns. Each work reflects the particular cast of mind and temperament of its youthful author. While Darwin was scientifically imaginative, yet cautious, Marx was philosophical and speculative.

Darwin divided the presentation of his materials on humankind into two books, *The Descent of Man and Selection in Relation to Sex* and *The Expression of the Emotions in Man and Animals*. *The Descent* is really a twofold work. The first part, aptly called "The Descent or Origin of Man," deals with the evolution of man's body and mind and can easily stand alone as a self-contained treatise. The second part, "Sexual Selection" is an essay on that subject and its relationship to natural selection. It is twice as long as the first part and in typically Darwinian fashion filled with examples. It is the section on human evolution, however, that I will primarily be concerned with.[4] *The Expression of the Emotions in Man and Animals* originally started out to be a chapter of *The Descent*, but materials and ideas came to Darwin in such abundance that he decided to render it as a separate work. In *The Expression* Darwin grappled with the entire range of behaviors found in man and animals, pointing to continuities where present and the crucial points of divergence.

It would have been understandable if Darwin had confined his analysis of the human species solely to a comparison of the physical continuities between Homo sapiens and other animals. In dealing with behavior, morality, and mind, he showed considerable intellectual boldness for one so allegedly timid. As the anatomist of this century, Wilfred LeGros Clark has pointed out, considering the controversy stirred up by *The Origin*, to publish a book as daring as *The Descent* must have required great moral courage on Darwin's part.[5] To say that in bodily form humankind is part of the order of nature as Darwin did in *The Descent* was not such a heretical proclamation; the taxonomically oriented natural scientists of the previous century often said as much with reference to the great chain of being. Nevertheless, lending up-to-date evolutionary credibility to this position served to make a number of people uncomfortable and hostile. However, to go on as Darwin did and state that the relationship between man and nature included links of gradation in terms of mind and behavior was unequivocally heretically and a belief not shared by a majority of the members of the scientific community of Darwin's day.

Perhaps the most interesting dissident was Darwin's friend and colleague, Alfred Russel Wallace. Wallace revered Darwin to the point where he even wrote a book expounding Darwinian theory;[6] but although Wallace was a co-discoverer with Darwin of the principle of natural selection, he was hesitant to use it to explain the evolution of mind. Also disagreeing with Darwin on the relationship of mind to nature was Samuel Butler, a well-known literary figure. Butler expressed the affront to the human sensibility posed by the theory of natural selection applied to man when he stated that Darwin had banished mind from the universe. Answering Butler nearly 100 years later, anthropologist Robin Fox has remarked that far from banishing mind from the universe, Darwin gave us a basis for explaining how mind got into the universe in the first place.[7]

As in all his other endeavors, Darwin's motive for writing *The Descent* and *The Expression* was the furtherance of human knowledge. Unlike Marx, he was not a crusader, and controversy frightened him. Yet Darwin's withdrawn personality harbored one of the most daring and revolutionary thinkers of any age. What Copernicus did in the sphere of astronomy, Darwin did for biology and potentially also for the human sciences. In demonstrating that the earth is not the exalted center of the universe, Copernicus created a paradigm receptive to a whole new series of observations and ideas.[8] In viewing humankind not as the purpose of creation but as part of creation, Darwin gave new meaning to the biological sciences. His perspective can apply equally to the human sciences, yet they continue to defy his influence.

In writing about humankind, Darwin established through weight of evidence and scientific reasoning what the early Marx could only hope for and speculate philosophically about: that the true study of man is not theology or philosophy but an anthropology dealing with man in terms of his relatedness to nature and natural processes. Although this modus operandi was not taken up by the social sciences during the twentieth century, it was central to the concept of anthropology as outlined by its modern founder, Edward Tylor. In 1875 Tylor stressed that

anthropology (*the science of man*) denotes the natural history of mankind. In the general classification of knowledge it stands as the highest section of zoology or the science of animals itself the highest section of biology or, the science of living beings. . . . Not only are these various sciences (anatomy, physiology, psychology, sociology, etc.) concerned largely with man, but several among them have in fact suffered by the almost entire exclusion of other animals from their scheme. It is undoubted that comparative anatomy and physiology by treating the human species as one member of a long series of related organisms have gained a higher and more perfect understanding of man himself. . . . it is regretted that hitherto certain other sciences—psychology, ethics, and even philology and sociology—have so little followed so profitable an example.[9]

EVIDENCE LINKING MAN TO NATURE

In *The Descent of Man*, Darwin sought to establish that man evolved from some preexisting form. He also put forth several admittedly hypothetical constructs to illustrate the manner of this development. Having already done so much in *The Origin* to convince the scientific and lay public that evolution is a relentless fact of nature, *The Descent* became an unparalleled attempt to subsume man's physical and psychological nature under the same canopy: "man is variable in mind and body; and the variations are induced either directly or indirectly, by the same general causes, and obey the same general laws, as with the lower animals" (*Descent*, 46).

With his usual modesty, Darwin noted that he was far from being the first to champion the antiquity of man, pointing out as worthy forerunners Lamarck, Lyell, Haeckel, and Lubbock. He also cited the archeological work of Boucher de Perthes, Lyell, and Lubbock as evidence for a lengthy human genealogy; however, as the skeptics of his day frequently noted, archeological remains constitute only indirect evidence. With the exception of one Neanderthal find, its validity highly suspect at the time, Darwin worked without benefit of direct fossil evidence for the existence of prehuman ancestors. It is not surprising that when reliable fossil remains, such as Java Man (referred to at the time as Pithecanthropus erectus), were unearthed over a dozen years after Darwin's death, the argument regarding human ancestry was rekindled in both public and scientific circles.

Without a fossil sequence to guide him, Darwin tried to demonstrate human evolution by making a series of morphological (physical structure) and behavioral inferences from man to other animals. He undertook a speculative reconstruction of the appearance and habits of our early ancestors, a daring exercise even in light of today's knowledge. Darwin's contention was that if a plausible case could be made for kinship between man, mammals in general, and primates in particular, it follows that at some point in the distant past there must have been common ancestry. In a series of anatomical comparisons, Darwin showed that man and other animals share a similar diversity of physical types within a given species. He then went on to deal with the phenomenon of vestigal organs in man; examples include reduced canines, molars being absent or abnormal, and muscles that move the scalp and ears. These are regarded as clues to the possibility that at some prior time in his biological existence, man differed from his present self. Darwin also compared man with other primates in terms of susceptibility to a number of diseases and the facility with which both can acquire certain habits.

What is surprising today about this aspect of Darwin's inquiry is that it is again coming to the fore among students of physical anthropology and human evolution. After Darwin's death, his comparative perspective was supplanted by a concern with the prolific fossil materials recovered during the first half of the twentieth century. However, the past several years have shown that there are practical limits to what fossil records can tell about human evolution. An increasing number of those interested in the subject are now turning again to the kind of cross-species morphological and behavioral inferences that Darwin made, only at a much more detailed level of analysis.

Not content to let the question of man's nature and origin rest on physical evidence alone, Darwin put even greater stress on the continuities between man and other animals in terms of behavior:

As man possesses the same senses as the lower animals, his fundamental intuitions must be the same. Man has also the same few instincts in common, as that of self-preservation, sexual love, and the love of the mother for her new born offspring, the desire possessed by the latter to suck, and so forth. But man, perhaps has somewhat fewer instincts than those possessed by the animals which come next to him in the series. [*Descent*, 64]

Nevertheless on a number of occasions he granted that there are considerable differences between man and other animals, although these differences are always seen in terms of degree. In both *The Descent* and *The Expression*, he piled observed facts of behavior one upon the other the same way that he piled up the facts relating to the physical structure of nonhuman life forms in *The Origin*. In making argument for continuity in behavior, Darwin totally obliterated the mind-body, nature-society dichotomy. On one end, he dragged man down to the level of the beast, and this is what most of the protest was about. On the other end, he had a tendency to exalt and anthropomorphize animals. While man with his passions, sensations, and facial expressions is placed in proper though extreme zoological perspective, Darwin found traditional notions regarding the animal as a kind of hydraulic machine governed by blind instinct seriously wanting (Marx and Engels in their criticism of eighteenth-century mechanistic materialism were of the same opinion). From numerous anecdotal material, as well as firsthand observations made both in the field and at the zoo, Darwin concluded that animals are to a degree capable of reason, learning, and a number of human-like emotions. Arguing from animals to man became as important to him as arguing from man to animals in the struggle to reduce the gulf between opened up by previous religious and intellectual traditions.

Although Darwin held that man indisputably is a creature of reason, having that capacity in far greater abundance than any of his nonhuman relatives, he believed that the human species retains aspects of an earlier instinctual legacy. The concept of instinct first intrigued him in *The Origin*, where he devoted a whole chapter to it. He deliberately refrained from a definition of instinct because he found too many exceptions to any attempt to frame the concept precisely. Using *instinct* in a general sense to indicate a number of behavioral predispositions, both flexible and inflexible, he went on to show that it is as important to a species as aspects of bodily structure and is subject to variation and natural selection. In this manner he saw complex instincts arising when natural selection operated on simpler instinctive actions. He also insisted that no instinct is ever produced solely for the good of another species and that if someone were to locate such an instinct, it would be fatal to this theory. In *The Descent*, Darwin continued the discussion by observing that the higher one moves up the animal scale, the fewer the instincts. As an example he cited chimpanzee nest building. Usually attributed to blind instinct, Darwin noted that since chimpanzees stand so close to man on the natural scale, it is not impossible that such behavior is the result of human-like reason. One of his major contentions was that instinct and reason are not in opposition but form a continuum, grading into one another. However, he did not elaborate this notion in any detail, and we are left with some interesting unresolved possibilities.

He made his main argument for an instinctive residue in man in *The Expression of the Emotions*. This work, it must be remembered, is an outgrowth of *The Descent*, and it is the two taken together that comprise Darwin's complete treatise on human nature. In *The Expression*, Darwin took quiet satisfaction in pointing out such animal-like behaviors in man as baring the teeth in rage and the bristling of the hair in terror. Darwin looked at a great range of expressive behavior and nonverbal communication in man and animals with an eye to discerning aspects of continuity. In examining actions, such as weeping, laughter, anger, and fear, he drew from a multitude of sources: observations of the insane; studies of children, including a number of observations he made of his own offspring; an analysis of the expressive behavior depicted in works of art; ethnographic information from cultures around the world, not only from the usual sources, published accounts of missionaries, explorers, and travelers, but also from an elaborate questionnaire that he compiled and sent to a number of far-flung locales; and, in a surprisingly modern methodological instance, he showed photographs of various expressive behaviors to informants and tried to elicit interpretations— one of the first attempts to use photography as a tool of scientific research. Darwin concluded that the expression of the emotions is an integral aspect of social communication in both man and animals and a forerunner of more stylized gestures and language; that the continuities of expression between man and animals give evidence of related origins; and since expressive behavior found in all races of man is so uniform, something he immediately perceived, the races must comprise one species.

Although *The Expression* is a pioneering effort in both cross-specific (looking comparatively at different species) and cross-cultural methodology, it is not without shortcomings. As in most of Darwin's other work, fact is heaped upon fact to such a degree that the reader often loses sight of the initial argument. Also in attacking the theological and philosophical separation of mind-body, nature-society, or whatever form it happened to take, Darwin exhibited a dualistic bent of his own; he placed instinct and reason, if not in opposition, at least at opposite ends of the behavioral spectrum. He equated instinct in man almost solely with the expression of the emotions. In addition, it was Darwin's belief that as one moved up the scale toward man, instincts became fewer and habitual learning more determinant. Today it seems limiting to confine instincts, or similar generalized innate response mechanisms in man, to the domain of immediate emotional expression. Could they not govern other realms and be exceedingly complex? If the formulations of generative transformational linguistic theorists, such as Noam Chomsky, are correct, this could be the case. They have suggested that a unique, innate, and exceedingly complex language acquisition capacity exists in the human species.[10] Although Darwin never considered this notion, his theory certainly has the inclusiveness to accommodate it as a possibility.

Darwin helped establish that just as each species has a distinctive morphology in terms of bones, teeth, and other bodily structures, each has distinctive characteristics in terms of behavior patterns, and man is no exception. We achieved our current

status not through divine intervention but through an elaboration of traits found in our prehuman ancestors. Our primate
cousins all exhibit powers of memory, curiosity, observation,
and intelligence, traits greatly developed during the course of
our own evolution. These traits were extended and amplified
through the development of the erect posture, bipedalism, tool
use and manufacture, language, and the extension of our social
capacities. Darwin saw sociability rather than a life and death
struggle between individuals as the crucial factor in human evolution: "[Man] owes his immense superiority . . . to his social habits,
which lead him to aid and defend his fellows" (*Descent*, 47). In
this, as in other aspects of human evolution, intelligence and
not mere strength played a central role. Just as natural selection
operated to improve structural efficiency in organisms throughout nature, so it operated on cerebral efficiency in the human
line: "The individuals who were the most sagacious, who in-
vented and used the best weapons or traps and who were best
able to defend themselves, would rear the greatest number of
offspring" (ibid., 125).

Like most other theorists who ponder the problem of human
nature, Darwin inevitably came around to the question of language, its characteristics and possible origins. Only man, he
observed, is capable of fully articulate verbal communication.
However, this uniqueness must be seen in terms of degree because human language has roots in the communication systems
and various emotional gestures and facial expressions found in
other animals. He perceptively noted that language is not an
instinct in the strict sense because each language requires learning; nevertheless, there must be some kind of instinct-like basis
to explain a phenomenon so general. To support this contention
he cited the babbling of children as evidence of an innate predisposition to speak, a contention subscribed to by a number of
linguists today. Darwin then lapsed into his typical reductionistic mode of argument, which is far less effective in dealing with
language than it is in other areas. Language, he held, owes its
origins to "the imitation and modification of various natural
sounds, the voices of other animals, and man's own instinctive
cries aided by signs and gestures" (ibid., 84). He then invoked
sexual selection, showing how man's early ancestors developed

their vocal tracts through the various musical cadences used in courtship: "It is, therefore probable that the imitation of musical cries by articulate sounds may have given rise to words expressive of various complex emotions" (ibid., 85). As the voice was used more and more, he believed, the vocal organs would develop through the inherited effects of use, and this would have fostered a feedback between language development and the brain in general.

Modern thinking tends to see language as having an arbitrary nature and therefore as evolving out of a purely conceptual rather than from an emotional substrate. Syntactic behavior, the increasing separation of conceptual activity from the sensory environment, now appears to be a more revealing place to look for language origins than the emotional and imitative domain that Darwin focused on.[11] In seeing language from the particular angle that he did, Darwin had a worthy precursor whom he seems to have been unaware of. In the middle of the eighteenth century, Jean Jacques Rousseau, in his *Discourse on the Origins of Inequality* and later *Essay on the Origin of Languages*, put forth the notion that human language evolved directly out of the emotional cries of nature and that song and poetry represented the first human languages. This appeal to the emotions is a typical aspect of Rousseau's romanticism. However, in Darwin's case it serves to show that he was not the cold, soulless materialist that some of his critics depicted.

In dealing with language, Darwin did not give primary emphasis to natural selection, although the concept still retained significance. He followed Max Müller in believing that a struggle for existence goes on among the grammatical forms and words in each language as shorter, easier, and better forms and pronunciations eventually gain predominance. He also noted, following Von Schlegel, that the language of a primitive people often exhibits a high degree of complexity, more so than many civilized tongues, and he used this as further evidence for his belief that all mankind constitutes a single species. On the whole Darwin's ideas on language, like the other aspects of human nature he examined, became colored by the attempt to link these phenomena to their alleged precursors in the animal world. Working out the full details of any problem always remained subordinate to the overall thesis: establishing man's relatedness to nature. In the case of language the interesting possibilities it posed for Darwin's method has to remain subordinate to the argument establishing it as one of a number of natural facts: "Nor as we have seen, does the faculty of articulate speech in itself offer any insuperable objection to the belief that man has been developed from some lower form." (*Descent*, 89).

Viewing human nature as part of natural history was and is highly revealing. The vision represents Darwin's major contribution to the study of humankind, yet at times it caused him to give simple answers to complex questions, and this is particularly obvious with respect to his ideas on language and mind.

TYLOR, MORGAN, AND DARWIN

The possibility unveiled by Darwin of using evolutionary theory to explain certain fundamental aspects of human behavior was largely ignored by the social sciences in the century following his death. Yet during his own lifetime, Darwin influenced a number of highly regarded scholars who were concerned with the subject of human nature—scholars who cannot justly be labeled social Darwinists. One example is Sir Edward Burnett Tylor (1831-1917), a contemporary and countryman of Darwin and a figure many hold to be the founder of the modern discipline of anthropology. Although apparently unresponsive at first, Tylor eventually had a conversion experience regarding Darwin's researches.

In one of his early and major works, *Primitive Culture*, written in 1871, Tylor expressed the belief that "the history of mankind is part and parcel of the history of nature."[12] He argued that in the sphere of history and culture, as in the case of nature, evolution has occurred in the form of a gradual and cumulative development. He examined all manner of cultural (the modern definition of culture is generally attributed to him) phenomena with the assumption that they are subject to laws similar to those found in nature. Although the influence of Darwin would appear to be pronounced, Tylor, in the preface to the 1873 edition of *Primitive Culture*, stated that he came to his formulations independently. He presented a case for parallel development between his own and Darwin's work that, given Tylor's reputation for integrity cannot be suspect. In fact, Tylor's perspective, dealing as it often did with independent invention (that is, parallel responses to similar needs taking place in different areas), could be used to explain his own and Darwin's appropriation of the evolutionary perspective.

The conversion experience happened some time shortly after 1873 when, with Darwin's work becoming more widely known, Tylor fully absorbed and acknowledged the influence. Not only did Tylor undertake a thorough study of Darwin's work, the two men began a correspondence of mutual admiration. In 1881 Tylor published another major work, *Anthropology*, the first modern interdisciplinary text on that subject. In outlining the scope of the discipline and the most rewarding methods that it should adopt, he stressed Darwin's contribution at every turn.

In *Anthropology*, Tylor followed Darwin in emphasizing the relationship that man's morphology and anatomy bears to other animals, most notably the primates. He remarked on the importance of tools in defining human physiological and cultural evolution. In this context, he stressed the reciprocal feedback, through the use of tools, of the development of the hand, language, culture, social organization, and the highest intellectual faculties. This was a trend that Darwin began elaborating in *The Descent* and Engels continued in his *Dialectics of Nature*. Although there are a number of similarities between Tylor, and Marx and Engels regarding the continuities between nature and history, their points of focus were different. Marx and Engels dealt primarily with economics and social organization, while Tylor was more concerned with ideological phenomena that included customs, religion, art, and myth. To the best of my knowledge there is no available evidence indicating that Tylor had a familiarity with the writings of either Marx or Engels.

Tylor also followed Darwin by contending that human nature is not an autonomous and divinely inspired phenomenon. For Tylor man's behavior is not a negation of the behavior patterns found in other animals but an extension and elaboration. He argued against Locke's notion that the difference between man and beast is that man is capable of forming abstract notions by insisting that animals are fully capable of rudimentary generalizations. Today Gestalt psychology and ethology (the biological study of behavior) lend considerable support to this assertion.[13] The one characteristic in which Tylor believed man differs from animals is speech. He held that the faculty of articulate speech enables man to be far more self-conscious than any other animal. Nevertheless, in language, as well as in a number of other areas, Tylor believed that man is guided by both learned experience and the natural proclivities that both he and Darwin labeled instincts, even though they were both aware of the imprecise nature of this concept. Tylor, in founding the empirical tradition in modern anthropology, shared the emphasis present in Marx and Darwin of regarding human nature as remarkable and unique but nonetheless continuous with nature and natural processes.

Jointly given credit along with Tylor for establishing modern anthropology is the American, Lewis Henry Morgan (1818-1881). His most famous work, *Ancient Society* (1877), exerted a tremendous influence on the thinking of Marx and Engels regarding primitive society. However, Morgan's intellectual horizon extended beyond the bounds of ethnology, a fact rarely recognized by contemporary social and cultural anthropologists who cite him as a founding father.

Like Tylor, Morgan was concerned with one of the great nineteenth-century questions: man's place in nature. He adhered to the view that human behavior and animal behavior are related phenomena. Of particular concern to him was establishing the concept of reason across species lines and of disavowing all notions that regard animals as machines regulated by blind instinct. In 1843 he expressed his interest in animal behavior by publishing an article stating that man is in error if he claims to possess exclusively the thinking principle. He attacked the concept of instinct as it was then being applied to the animal kingdom in terms of the mind-instinct dichotomy. Morgan held that animal behavior differs from human behavior only in degree and that the concept of instinct prevalent during his day was a "fraud upon the animal races...a vague fictitious invention of those metaphysicians for the purpose of retaining the chasm between man and the animal, which leaves the phenomenon unexplained.[14]

Morgan set out to test his ideas in a field situation. Although his fieldwork on American Indian groups, in particular the Iroquois, is well-known anthropological history, he also did noteworthy research along somewhat different lines. In 1868 he published *The American Beaver and His Works*, a superb naturalistic study of the behavior of that species and the culmination of years of travel and careful observation. The book is kind of a nineteenth-century forerunner of the recent and well-known attempts to study various animal species in the wild rather than in captivity.[15] It concluded with a plea, largely unheeded until recently, for further systematic accounts of the comparative behavior of animals in their natural habitat.

In *The Descent* Darwin gave Morgan's book on the beaver high praise, although he was puzzled by such an insistant and unyielding attack on the concept of instinct. The difficulties present any time instinct was used for explanatory purposes—it is a concept that can be used to signify a wide range of behavioral responses—were as obvious to Darwin as to Morgan, but Darwin wanted to retain the concept and strive for a more precise and accurate usage while Morgan sought to abolish it. Morgan held that reason is an essential element of both animal and human behavior. Darwin agreed and, approaching the problem from the other direction, noted that instinct is also an integral component of both animal and human behavior. Each in his own way endeavored to fracture the mind-body, nature-society separation. What makes Morgan's effort remarkable is that when his early work on animal psychology and the beaver was undertaken, he did not believe in the evolution of species. Instead he placed his faith in the concept of the great chain of being whereby each species was separately conceived by a creator who made the differences among them of degree rather than kind. Therefore, just as it is possible to be an evolutionist without being a Darwinian, for example, by substituting cataclysmic successions, the inheritance of acquired characteristics, or a number of other notions in place of natural selection—so it is possible to believe in the unity between humankind and nature without being an evolutionist, as Morgan demonstrated. Eventually, however, at some point in the mid-1870s, Darwin's arguments made a convert of Morgan. At the time he came to accept Darwin's theory of evolution, Morgan was preoccupied with ethnological problems, and he never again addressed himself to naturalistic or philosophical issues.

Although two of anthropology's major founders, Tylor and Morgan, showed in their own way the emphasis present in Marx and Darwin of regarding human nature as a logical extension of organic nature, later anthropology tended to follow the direction of the other social sciences in confining what is human to a separate plane of understanding. There are several factors responsible for this change in direction. Any explanation of human behavior that derived from biology was invariable linked in the ideology of the disciplines involved with social Darwinism and racism. Since one of the major concerns of early twentieth-century anthropology was establishing the psychic unity of the various races, it became expedient to view what was human, the capacity for culture, as existing on a level qualitatively removed from the natural world. Anthropologists of the period, such as Franz Boas, Robert Lowie, and Alfred Kroeber, established that all that is human, from grass hut to ivory tower, is fully human, that the mental capacities of the various races are equal, and that no racial group is closer on the evolutionary scale to our early ancestors.

It is conceivable that this major intellectual achievement could have been accomplished without reestablishing the mind-body dichotomy in its new garb; nature-culture—a dualism that has been reinforced by the separation of the human from the natural sciences during the twentieth century. For example, both Darwin and Tylor regarded humankind as a single species and would have agreed with most of the conclusions of the later anthropologists. An alternative perspective might have been built around a Darwinian model of culture as a species-specific characteristic having an evolutionary foundation. This could have been tied to the evidence demonstrating that generic culture, a species—wide given, can be variably expressed around the world, yielding specific cultures, the lifeways of a given social group, without there being any relevant biopsychological differences between these groups. This viewpoint, not any form of social Darwinism or racism, would be the primary consequence of connecting a Darwinian model of human nature to the empirical revelations of twentieth-century social science.

Fortunately anthropology, unlike a number of other disciplines, did not dispense entirely with the natural sciences. Although the anthropologists did not use Darwinism or biological explanations in the area of cultural analysis, they retained biology, along with linguistics, archeology, and the cultural realm, as one of the four basic building blocks of the discipline. Humankind's physical evolution and place in nature were recognized and accepted, and it was believed, or hoped, that some day a unified human science would emerge from this foundation. However, the trend today in the discipline is that when material from one sector of anthropology, the biological, is used to help explain what is transpiring in another sector, the cultural, the operation is disclaimed, not because it fails to constitute the anthropoligical possibility but because the discipline is said not to be ready for a synthesis of its subfields. This attitude is symptomatic of the obsession with specialization, and the academic security accompanying it, that has fragmented and trivialized the human disciplines during the twentieth century.[16]

The Social
as Natural: Marx

> For society to exist at all the individual must bring into it a
> whole group of inborn tendencies; society therefore is not self
> explanatory; so we must get down to life, of which human
> societies...are but manifestations.
>
> —Henri Bergson

Several academic disciplines have claimed Marx as one of their
own, among them philosophy, economics, political science, anthropology, and sociology. Marx is a figure of such range and
insight that he lends himself to this state of affairs, and also the
diversity of concerns in his writing on various subjects yields the
possibility that within the context of a particular discipline, more
than one Marxian-inspired perspective is possible. Sociology is a
case in point; Marx has made vast and multiple contributions to
its subject matter. One area, however, has been virtually unacknowledged: his formulations on the nature of society.

Probably the most widely accepted of Marx's contributions to
modern sociology is his analysis of the way in which social
forms constrain the collective beliefs (ideology) and political actions of human groups. The well-known passage in his writings
exemplifying this approach comes from the preface to his *Critique of Political Economy*: "It is not the consciousness of men that
determines their existence, but their social existence which determines their consciousness" (*Critique*, 21). The sociology of
knowledge is one sector of modern sociology that has drawn
sustenance from this viewpoint. It has used Marx's thesis that
consciousness in man is a social product to examine political
ideologies and intellectual currents in a wide historical sense[1]

and to scrutinize, in a more immediate manner, the social constructions of everyday life.[2]

Although the sociology of knowledge draws significant methodological inspiration from Marx when dealing with the social basis of human action, it has tended to ignore his assumptions on the nature of society and their relationship to human nature, preferring in this area to accommodate other sources, notably the views of sociologists Emile Durkheim (1858-1917) and Max Weber (1864-1930). The result has been a separation of the social from the natural in the twentieth-century sociological tradition. Durkheim set society apart from the organic realm in order to discern its unique nonnatural regularities and to define it as an autonomous sphere of inquiry. Weber was less concerned with regularities than he was with meshing a historical and humanistic dimension to social analysis. Both disavowed the link between the natural and the human sciences that Marx held to be a cornerstone of his approach, and subsequent sociology has, for the most part, followed this precedent.

A number of related areas within the discipline of sociology take the importance Marx gave to social relations and apply it to a wide range of phenomena. The result has been a series of perspectives stressing the primacy of the social used to analyze subjects that include religion, mass communications, political development, and modernization. Nevertheless, it must be remembered that although Marx held that collective belief and action is a consequence of the social order, this order must be regarded as the outcome of constraints exerted by the infrastructure— the totality of relations of production. Combining a Marxian approach with the conceptions of Durkheim and Weber, recent sociology, in addition to accepting the separation of the social from the natural, has tended to downplay Marx's insistence on the importance of economic factors. This tendency is not entirely unwarranted. It has served to correct an imbalance in Marxian analysis created by Soviet-inspired interpretations, particularly in the writings of Lenin, whereby the ideas and institutions of society, what Marx referred to as the superstructure, are taken to be a direct reflection rather than a translation of the economic relations.

The preface to *Critique of Political Economy* is probably the most succinct statement of Marx's method to be found anywhere in his writings. In it, he differentiates the economic conditions of production that "can be determined with the precision of natural science" from the "social forces of production" and both from "the general process of social, political and intellectual life" (*Critique*, 20-21). He goes on to state that changes in the economic foundation invariably lead to transformations in the superstructure. Rephrasing the argument to a degree, we can say that the economic infrastructure relates to the ideological superstructure not directly, by reflection, as it does in the copy theory, but only insofar as it is mediated or translated through the social process. For Marx, society is not viewed as a transparent medium through which the economic relations pass en route to framing political and ideological structures, nor is it held to be, as in the case of Durkheim, the ultimate or final arbiter, determining all human relations and institutions. In the Marxian scheme the social exists as one of a series of levels of constraint affecting human activity.[3] It is an integral component in a process that begins with the appropriation of organic nature and leads ultimately to self-creation through labor at a particular historical moment.

The social for Marx is both generic and historical. Human beings are not simply born tabula rasa into a particular historical milieu. They bring with them certain tendencies predisposing them to the social mode. This generic legacy does not determine the character of an epoch; rather it interacts with the traditions handed down by past generations. The resultant interaction mediates or translates the given circumstances of production into new historical relations, which in turn constrain the next generation. Therefore, if a comprehensive view of the Marx legacy is to be sought, the Marxian conception of society should be understood in both its generic (the biological, what the individual brings to the world) and historical (the encountered traditions) dimensions.

The social process that results from the active encounter of the generic and the historical elements constitutes an interface translating between various levels of constraint. In the copy theory and related misinterpretations of Marx, the social is seen only as a space through which relations of production pass on their way to being reflected by the dominant ideology. Elsewhere I have called this situation the periscope effect and its practitioners periscope theorists.[4] Although a number of self-avowed Marxists hold such views, the source derives from crass empiricism and vulgar materialism rather than from the materialist conception of history as outlined by Marx.

In Western sociology, the combined approach of Marx, Durkheim, and Weber has been a useful tool of analysis, but it has failed to yield an inclusive perspective on the nature of society, one capable of drawing the social and natural sciences into greater proximity. This is an aspect of Marx's legacy still awaiting consummation. While Marx placed considerable importance on the historical reaction taking place between social relations and the resulting institutions, society was not regarded as being only the outcome of this reaction. Underlying the entire operation is the bedrock of Marxian social theory: a belief that the capacity to be social is a deeply rooted biological given, the most important manifestation of human nature. Marx thought, as did Darwin, that "man is, if not as Aristotle contends, a political, [he is] at all events a social animal" (*Capital*, 1:326). His observations on the social nature of humankind are widely spread throughout his writings, though the focus is more pronounced in the early texts. Nevertheless, interpreters in both the East and West seem to be unaware of these formulations. Even recent writers concerned with the concept of human nature as expressed by the early Marx have failed to acknowledge his attempt to define the naturalistic foundations of society, preferring instead to stress individual attributes. The analysis that follows will attempt to remedy this state of affairs and, in conjunction with the later survey of Darwin, will illuminate the possibility of a science of the social capable of drawing from a number of disciplines.

EARLY INFLUENCES

The argument regarding the social nature of the human species, particularly as it is expressed in Marx's early work, is inseparable from his total conception of human nature. Marx regarded the social as an integral aspect of man's organic, psychological, and historical being. However, because the social conceptions are so extensive and crucial to understanding other segments of his work, it will be useful to identify and study them in a separate context; nevertheless, this exercise must be seen as continuation of the earlier analysis dealing with his human-theoretical framework.

Marx showed little curiosity regarding the question of social origins, a topic destined to be of primary interest to Darwin. Marx's foremost concern, as it was with the other aspects of human nature that he dealt with, was to define in a philosophical though not unscientific manner the properties of the phenomenon under scrutiny. This effort, although heavily concentrated in the early writings, is still a significant aspect of *Das Kapital*, which is laced with assumptions on the social as natural that are direct echoes of what appeared in the *Paris Manuscripts* and *The German Ideology*.

In both the early and later writings, Marx speculatively anticipated a number of conclusions relevant to human natural history that would be outlined by Darwin in 1871. It must have been gratifying for Marx to see in Darwin's late writings an attempt to substantiate scientifically some of his own independently conceived earlier notions. Unfortunately, we have no written documents to verify that Marx ever read this aspect of Darwin.[5] Although Marx wrote most of his social analysis too early to have been influenced by Darwin, he did not derive his ideas on the subject in a vacuum. In contrasting ways that he tried to render complementary, Hegel and Feuerbach provided Marx with the insights he needed to lay the foundations of his social theory.

From Hegel, Marx derived a belief in the collective reality of the social. Hegel believed that society is more than the sum of the behavior of the individuals comprising it. It constitutes instead a separate order of phenomena—a supraindividual system. Marx accepted this, but he was forced to reject the mystical and theological argument that Hegel used to rationalize the position. Briefly stated, Hegel thought that any set of social relations represents only a "moment" or temporal segment of the idea or spirit. The forms and institutions of society as they develop historically are regarded as episodes in the struggle whereby the idea strives to embody itself in the state, its highest expression. The various divisions of the social world of his day were held to be direct expressions of the power of the idea. In Hegel's scheme, the state, as the political arm of the idea, determines the nature of social processes and institutions, which in turn determine the activities of human individuals. In the *Critique of Hegel's Philosophy of Right*, written between 1841 and 1843, Marx accused Hegel of deriving society from theology when it should in fact derive from anthropology, the study of human relationships.

Rather than being an idle philosophical exercise, the critique of Hegel is a vehicle of constructive criticism whereby Marx tried to replace flaws in Hegel's social architecture with some of his own formulations. In attacking Hegel, Marx was simultaneously attacking the social and political order of the constitutional monarchy in Germany at that time, an order ideologically legitimated in Hegel's writings. The tendency in Hegel's philosophy, and German politics, was to subordinate the laws and interests of the family and civil society to the dictates of the state. Marx pointed out that in Hegel the family and civil society take on an abstract quality, representing only moments of the idea. At this point in his intellectual development, history had a twofold aspect for Marx. The realm of the state and the political ideology emerging therefrom he referred to as the *esoteric* side, while the concrete social fabric, the family and civil society, the arena in which the individual discharges his life activity, he referred to as the *exoteric* side. For Marx, "The real development proceeds on the exoteric side" (*Critique Hegel*, 8). In emphasizing the esoteric, Hegel presupposed "the separation of civil society and the political state (which is a modern situation) and developed it as a necessary moment of the 'idea'" (ibid., 73).

In Marx's analysis, society is not the consequence of the idea but its cause. The foundations of society are the family, the natural group in which man is nurtured; and civil society, a conjunction of families and individuals based on a natural recognition and an exchange of mutual needs. In this particular context, Marx used civil society in a manner not unreminiscent of later sociological conceptions of community. He went on to criticize Hegel for looking at individuals as political agents of the state apparatus rather than as corporeal beings whose activities led to given types of political organization. For both thinkers, man reduced to his essential nature is a social being, not the self-seeking individual organism conceived by classical political economy. While the social for Hegel is a collective expression of the abstract idea, for Marx it is a collective expression of natural qualities residing in the human species itself:

The nature of this particular person is not his beard, his blood, his abstract physics, but rather his social quality, and the activities of the state, etc., are nothing but the modes of existence and operations of the social qualities of men. [Ibid., 22]

. . . As human nature is the true communal nature, or communal being [*Gemeinwesen*] a social being [*gesellschaftiche Wesen*] which is no abstractly universal power opposed to the single individual, but is the nature of being [*Wesen*] of every single individual, his own activity, his own life, his own spirit, his own wealth . . . men as actual, living, particular individuals, not men considered in abstraction, constitute this being. [Ibid., xiii]

The family, civil society, and the state result from qualities that are both inherent in particular individuals and part of a universality common to all men; they constitute "the actualization and objectification of man's essence" (ibid., 40).

In contrast to Hegel, who used a theology, Marx tried to base his social insights on a naturalistic anthropology.[6] He accepted Hegel's belief that social and political expressions are not merely the sum of individual expressions. Yet, he reasoned, society cannot be divine. Somehow it must be connected to the organic qualities of the individuals comprising it. Since no reliable body of scientific data could lend support for this presupposition, Marx turned again to philosophy and its most earthy exponent, Ludwig Feuerbach.

Feuerbach countered the entire Western metaphysical tradition with a humanism based on naturalism. He rose to prominence during the 1840s when Marx was just beginning to generate serious theory, and he had a great influence on the early Marx. Like Marx, Feuerbach had to confront the awesome power and influence that Hegel had bequeathed to the intellectual climate of the day. In Feuerbach's opinion, Hegel's principal error in trying to understand man derived from his use of a theology separating man from nature instead of an anthropology capable of drawing the two spheres into proper harmony:

Just as theology *dichotomizes* and *externalizes* man in order to then identify his externalized essence with him, so similarly Hegel *pluralizes* and
splits up the *simple, self-identical essence* of nature and man in order to
bring together forcibly what he has separated forcibly.[7]

Partly on his own and partly deriving from the influence of
Feuerbach, Marx found the same flaws in Hegel's argument.

It was Feuerbach's belief that the essence of man is tangible
and earthly, not spiritual, and that it is most vividly expressed in
the social link between men, in community, a fact that he believed should become a fundamental building block for future
human science:

The single man *in isolation* possess in himself the essence of man neither as a *moral* nor as a *thinking* being. The *essence* of man is contained
only in community, in the *unity of man with man*. . . .

. . .The *Trinity* was the *highest mystery*, the *central point* of the *absolute
philosophy* and religion. But the secret of the Trinity. . .is the secret of
communal and *social* life. . .*truth* and *perfection* are only the union and
unity of beings that are similar in essence. Hence the highest and ultimate principle of philosophy is the *unity of man with man*.[8]

The influence this vision exerted on Marx cannot be underestimated. Nevertheless, he did not appropriate all of Feuerbach's
thinking. Marx accepted the belief that the social gives man his
uniquely human quality and that it is organically grounded, but
he was critical of Feuerbach for conceiving man's social nature in
a contemplative manner. Feuerbach's conception of the social
bond, cemented by ties of love and friendship, remained too
abstract for Marx because it omits history and the relationship of
real men to their productive forces (*German Ideology*, 59). Marx's
concept of society is always active and rooted in individuals
producing, no matter at what level of prehistory or history. This
productivity in turn is attributable to an exchange with "nature
on the part of an individual within and through a specific form
of society" (*Grundrisse*, 87).

THE NATURALISTIC FOUNDATIONS OF SOCIETY

Although the words and phrases Marx chose to describe the
nature of society changed, his overall perspective on it remained

fairly constant throughout his writings. In the early period he saw the social as an irreducible aspect of human nature. After 1845, it was coupled with labor to provide the framework for history. In both cases there was no formal discussion of society as a phenomenon separate from the tendencies of the individuals comprising it. In Marx there is also no sociology existing apart from his economics, history, and anthropology. Nevertheless, the basis for a sociology is there—in the philosophical and scientific assumptions and in the historical method. This foundation contributes to an academic discipline that did not exist in his day, sociology, and clarifies Marx's thought as a whole.

Society for Marx was generic to and synonymous with being human. Every relationship in which man finds himself "is first realized and expressed in the relationship in which man stands to other men," and following from this his relation to himself in turn "only becomes for him *objective* and *actual* through his relation to other men" (*Paris Manuscripts*, 115-16). Marx remained convinced that there was never an early prehistoric phase where only isolated individuals existed, producing on their own independently of all social ties. Despite the lack of historical evidence for this belief, it was given scientific status thirty years later when Engels, following Darwin's lead, hypothesized that man's primate ancestors must have been gregarious.[9]

In Marx's opinion, the autonomous individual hunter-fisherman of David Ricardo and Adam Smith belonged to the imagination of an epoch that saw Robinson Crusoe as the prototype of the natural man (*Grundrisse*, 83). In an early example of the sociology of knowledge, he observed that "as every society has its own peculiar nature, so does it engender its own peculiar natural man" (*Early Texts*, 32). This statement implies that previous epochs derived their views of the fundamental nature of man from their prevailing ideologies. Hence in Marx's time, and the 150 or so years preceding it, the categories of bourgeois Christian thought, economically, socially, and historically conditioned, projected into a theory of human nature, yielded the autonomous resourceful individual. Robinson Crusoe, a figure from the literary imagination of the period, became the archetype of the natural man. In *Das Kapital*, there is a delightful analysis of Crusoe complete with his watch, ledger, pen, and ink: "a true-born Briton" (*Capital*, 1:77). Crusoe has all the social forces of the era at his disposal; however, they were attributed to the powers of reason that emerged from him as an individual, while Marx contended that they derive from social elements within him that had already undergone development. Capitalist society as conceived by the political economists of the day was held to be the sum of a multitude of Robinsons, consenting and exchanging as independent individuals.

The view that society results from an agreement between individuals was not limited to the classical political economists. Radical philosophers like Rousseau had similar beliefs.[10] Although Marx held Rousseau in high regard, he was critical of the theory of society expressed in Rousseau's *Discourse on the Origin of Inequality*. It assumed that prior to history, man was a highly individual creature, though in Rousseau's case natural man was far from being bourgeois or Christian. In Rousseau's model natural man emerged out of the state of nature (this state is not synonymous with primitive society, nor is natural man ever described by Rousseau as a noble savage), communed with his comrades through agreement and consent, and thereby established the social contract. In enunciating this bit of conjectural history, Rousseau polarized nature and society. Nature was seen as a self-regulating, machine-like contrivance in which no development or change occurred, not an unusual stance to take in the eighteenth century when writing prior to Darwin and Lamarck. Perfectibility, synonymous with the capacity for development— not necessarily to the good—was confined to historical occurrences set into motion after society was first formed.

Like Rousseau, Marx conceptualized the prototype of the social as the cooperation of several individuals engaged in a given task under given conditions. But with Marx there was more operative than consent or contract. The unity of man expressed in group behavior results from capacities inseparable from his organic being. Marx did not resort to historical or evolutionary explanations to deal with how this may have come about; he accepted it a priori. Social bonds at their most fundamental level are said to exist as an expression of two primary life processes: the production and maintenance of life through labor and the generation of fresh life through procreation (*German Ideology*,

41). These are not viewed as conscious conventions but as expressions of anthropological nature.

The social experience derives, Marx contended, from a deep-seated need humans have to associate with other individuals. The biological character of this is apparent in that Marx referred to it as an "instinct" and used the metaphor "as animal as social life itself" (ibid., 42). He went on to remark that although human society has its own distinctiveness in that the social instincts become conscious, it has its roots in the gregarious propensity found in the lower animals. This is the same argument that Darwin placed in an evolutionary context approximately thirty years later.

In *Das Kapital*, Marx still adhered to the belief that collective activity in man has an organic basis. Nevertheless, the complexities that abound in the labor organization of industrial society can hardly be assumed to result from a direct instinctual expression. Instead the social activity necessary for this organization precipitates

an emulation and stimulation of the animal spirits that heighten the efficiency of each individual workman. Hence it is that a dozen persons working together will, in their collective working-day of 144 hours, produce far more than twelve isolated men working 12 hours, or than one man who works twelve days in succession. The reason for this is that man is, if not as Aristotle contends, a political he is at all events a social animal. [*Capital*, 1:326]

The productive power of social labor in industrial society results from the way in which its social institutions are able to harness the raw urge to cooperate present in all men: "When the labourer cooperates systematically with others, he strips off the fetters of his individuality, and develops the capabilities of the species" (*Capital*, 1:329). While Marx never denied man individuality, he held it to be an aspect of existence bound to man's situation in society: "The human being is. . . not merely a gregarious animal, but an animal which can individuate itself only in the midst of society" (*Grundrisse*, 84).

It is no accident that throughout his writings Marx often described man as an animal or in terms usually applied to animals.

It was his way of striking back at the theological and metaphysical doctrines that located the source of human destiny outside of man. In constantly referring to him as an animal, Marx wanted to show that man is both the source of social life activity and the only agent to whom the consequences of this activity are accountable. When Darwinian theory drew man and animal closer together, Marx exuberantly welcomed the revelation. To him this was the death blow to all of the suprahuman determinisms proffered by theology and idealist philosophy.

Writing in the *Paris Manuscripts,* with reference the natural basis of society, Marx noted that man's mind and senses serve as organs of appropriation and that their distinctive configuration results from the role they play as part of the social fabric. The fact that a given human eye or ear can be receptive to variations in stimuli in a manner beyond what it would be capable of in a crude state led Marx to refer to them as "social organs." These social organs in effect comprise the active patterning of relationships that take place among the external world, physiology, the senses, and mind.[11] This process, always dynamic and having no fixed ratio, becomes an avenue "for *expressing* my own *life* and a mode of appropriating human life" (*Paris Manuscripts*, 140). In Marx's analysis, the social organs can be seen as a psychological interface between the generic, the inherent social capacities, and the historical traditions that confront particular societies.

The concept of the social organs, at least as elaborated in the *Paris Manuscripts*, illustrates that Marx did not adhere to the belief that the material world is directly and objectively transposed into thought, as the copy or reflection theory asserts. The social capacity, social organs, social powers, or whatever term he chose to use in the kaleidoscopic prose of the *Manuscripts* transforms the distinctive way in which the external world is perceived and appropriated:

The manner in which they [external objects] become *his* depends on the *nature of the objects* and on the nature of the *essential power* corresponding *to it*, for it is precisely the *determinate nature* of this relationship which shapes the particular, real mode of affirmation. [Ibid., 140]

Unfortunately there is not always a clear separation between what we would today call the innate social capacity and the externally derived traditions. As a result, distinct levels of analysis are sometimes blurred. Nevertheless, Marx was unambiguous on one point: whatever exists in man as social colors the way he comprehends the world. He does not do it solely with the individual senses in isolation.

The way Marx uses terms like *social organs* and *social ·powers* must not be confused with the concepts of the social organism and the superorganic elaborated by later theorists.[12] With Marx, the social is never a force over and above man constraining his behavior as it is in Durkheim, nor is it the sum of individual decisions in the manner postulated by utilitarianism. It exists, rather, as the collective realization of each individual's natural proclivity to exchange with other members of his species his intellect, sense experience, and labor powers:

Since human nature is the true communal nature of man, men create and produce their communal nature by their natural action, they produce their social being which is no universal power over and against individuals, but the nature of each individual, his own activity his own life. [*Early Texts*; 193-94]

Throughout the early writings, Marx related man's social tendencies to the role played by his other organs. In so doing, he anticipated a fundamental principle of Darwin's theory, elaborated in the twentieth century in a number of biological traditions.[13] This principle states that the basis of human sociality is as much a part of man's phylogenetic legacy as are his various morphological traits. They both evolve in similar ways, as Darwin demonstrated, through the process of natural selection.

Of all the distinctive traits marking man as a social species, Marx believed that the capacity to exchange is one of the most, if not the most, fundamental. *Das Kapital* is steeped in examples, ranging from the basic exchange of labor in everyday activities to a complex analysis of the flow of commodities between various sectors of capitalist society expressed in terms of an intricate economic algebra. Although he described exchange as "the social metabolic process" (*Critique*, 86), he did not see it as an aspect of society residing outside man's organic being:

. . . exchange or trade is the social species act. [*Early Texts*, 196]

Exchange, both of human activity within production itself and also of human products with each other, is equivalent to species-activity. . . whose real being . . . is social activity. [Ibid., 193-94]

Man as a social being is compelled to exchange. [Ibid., 184]

The *Paris Manuscripts* contains an extended discussion of the concept of exchange as it appears in classical political economy. Marx lauded the importance given to it by Smith, Ricardo, Say, Sorbek, and Mill. However, whether they stressed it solely as a quality of society or as a tendency inhering in individuals and expressed in society, they attributed it to egoism and self-interest. Each man, according to the political economists, perceives through reason the common advantage to be gained by sharing differences in aptitude and activity. This view presupposes that society is an aggregation of particular individuals, the result of a primal contract, rather than an essential expression of human nature:

Division of labor and *exchange* are the two *pheomena* which lead the political economist to boast of the social character of his science, while in the breath he gives expression to the contradiction in his science—the establishment of society through unsocial, particular interests. [*Paris Manuscripts*, 163]

In retrospect the political economists, with their limited notion of individual self-interest underwriting society and fostering exchange, appear to be on more solid, and more limited, ground than Marx. Marx's a priori assumptions about society were, in 1844, considerably abstract, owing more to philosophical principles than to the kind of methodological rigor typical of the political economists. Disregarding the provisional nature of his formulations at the time, Marx's critique of the classical political economists was nonetheless well put. Support for his contention that society is not merely a collection of individuals can be found in the writings of Darwin and Durkheim. In *The Descent of Man* Darwin leveled a similar critique against the classical political economists and their philosophical comrades, the utilitarians. His social theory, being both collective, in that it was based on the assumption that society is anterior to specific individuals, and a totality that is more than the sum of its parts, and organically grounded, strikingly parallels Marx's. The major difference is that Darwin was able to reason his argument within the context of natural history, while Marx utilized a naturalistic philosophy. Durkheim, the staunchest collectivist of all, directed the same kind of criticism at utilitarian and related individualist theories of society, but his strategy of attack differed considerably from that propounded by Marx and Darwin. In establishing the collective quality of the social, Durkheim severed it completely from the biological (and the psychological) and therefore rejected the possibility of using natural history, or human nature, as an explanatory aid.

It is not inaccurate to note that for Marx and Darwin, man is held to be a social being while for Durkheim he is only a socialized being. A social being, although born into society, nevertheless brings with him certain traits predisposing him to the social mode.[14] A being who is only socialized is social because of the alleged external objective power of society that becomes the sole agent accountable for his particular behavioral repertoire. For Marx, man is not passive in the face of society. He is an active agent, a carrier of social tendencies that nevertheless can be realized only in community with other men, and in this sense they are likened to language (*Grundrisse*, 84). Just as language has to be collectively developed through individuals living together and talking to one another, so must man be reared in society in order to express his social tendencies. As a consequence, some aspect of the social affects every facet of human experience. In the sixth thesis on Feuerbach, Marx states that "the human essence is no abstraction inherent in each single individual. In its reality it is the *ensemble* of social relations" (*Feuerbach*, 84). These social relations in turn act back on man and color the activity he does as an individual:

When I am engaged in activity which I can seldom perform in direct community with others—then I am *social*, because I am active as a *man*. Not only is the material of my activity given to me as a social product (as is even the language in which the thinker is active): my own existence *is* social activity, and therefore that which I made of myself for society and with the consciousness of myself as a social being. . . .

Above all we must avoid postulating "Society" again as an abstraction *vis-à-vis* the individual. The individual *is the social being*.

His life, even if it may not appear in the direct form of *communal* life in association with others—is therefore an expression of and confirmation of *social life*. [*Paris Manuscripts*, 137-38]

There is give and take in this model. While Durkheim studied social traditions apart from the nature of humanity creating them, Marx held the two to be inseparable.

In Marx's opinion, it is the social qualities per se, not the rationalizations of politics and religion, that bind men together through constantly altering historical circumstances. He stressed this point in the seventh thesis on Feuerbach: "Feuerbach. . .does not see that the 'religious sentiment' is itself a *social product*, and that the abstract individual whom he analyzes belongs in reality to a particular form of society" (quoted in *Feuerbach*, 84). He went on to describe this social cement as a "materialistic connection" of men with one another based on their innate tendencies and the given mode of production (*German Ideology*, 41). By "materialistic connection" Marx not only referred to economic determinants but to the physiological and psychological factors that also help define human distinctiveness. In the sense that these factors can be scrutinized by the methods of natural science, he implied that human social behavior can be partly receptive to such treatment.

For Marx, man is first and foremost a creature, who is, as French philosopher Henri Bergson would later remark, prefigured by nature to be social.[15] This notion is crucial to his world view, yet it is often bypassed in more subtle analyses of his work. The open-ended and inherently interdisciplinary nature of Marxian social theory makes dialogue with later discoveries in biology and psychology potentially revealing. Marx emphatically believed in a human inquiry that regards the social as inextricably linked to the natural:

The *human* essence of nature first exists only for *social* man; for only here does nature exist for him as a *bond* with *man*—as his existence for the other and the other's existence for him—as the life-element of human reality. Only here does nature exist as the *foundation* of his own *human* existence. Only here has what is to him his natural existence become his *human* existence, and nature become man for him. Thus *society* is the unity of being of man with nature—the true resurrection of nature—the naturalism of man and the humanism of nature both brought to fulfillment. [*Paris Manuscripts*, 137]

PRIMARY AND SECONDARY SOCIAL RELATIONS

Throughout his writings, Marx handled the concept of society in a twofold manner. This not always obvious dichotomy can be referred to as the primary and the secondary social relations. The primary relations comprise the fundamental human cement. They derive directly from man's organic and psychological being and include a number of the natural tendencies actualized in concrete social situations; these include the various forms of the family and the basic interpersonal bonds like those residing at the root of cooperative labor. The secondary social relations comprise the complex historical network of productivity and exchange. They reside at various levels above the primary relations; examples include civil society, feudalism, the modern state, and their derivative associations.

Although the primary relations bind humans together at the interpersonal level in all societies, they are more obvious and play a greater role in social productivity in the earlier phases of history:

The more deeply we go back into history, the more does the individual, and hence also the producing individual, appear as dependent, as belonging to a greater whole: in a still quite natural way in the family and in the family expanded into the clan [*Stamm*]; then later in the various forms of communal society arising out of the antitheses and fusion of the clans. [*Grundrisse*, 84]

The primacy of the family as the original social tie between human beings is also emphasized in *Das Kapital*. However, accompanying the extensive anthropological (ethnographic) studies that preoccupied Marx before his death came a change in perspective.[16] Engels documented this change in a footnote to the third edition of *Das Kapital*, pointing out that these anthropological studies eventually caused Marx to conclude that it was not the family that developed out of the tribe but the tribe as a primary social relationship that eventually gave rise to the varous types of family structure: "The tribe was the primitive and spontaneously developed form of human association on the basis of blood relationship, and that out of the first incipient loosening of tribal bonds, the many and various forms of the family were afterwards developed" (quoted in *Capital*, 1:351).

Regardless of whatever order of priority existed between the family and the tribe, Marx believed that the kind of cooperative social labor and exchange evidenced in primitive society and in prehistory arose spontaneously out of natural human relationships. He noted that at the dawn of history this mode of existence was strongly evident in those groups who lived by hunting, citing Linguet to the effect that hunting may have been the first form of cooperative social labor (ibid., 334), thus remarkably anticipating some recent anthropological speculation.[17] He went on to describe the situation in such groups and also in primitive agricultural communities as one in which social and natural relationships coincide,[18] where the ownership of the means of production is in common and individuals are integrally wedded to the group. Recasting the argument somewhat, we can say that in the tribal societies envisioned by Marx, primary social relations and the organization of society as a whole are more congruous than during any later social epoch. This tribal nexus Engels described as being "the real starting point of history" (*Anti-Dühring*, 298).

Eventually through elaboration of the division of labor, exchange between groups, and conquest, the primary relations that characterize human nature in tribal societies become subsumed under the subsequent relations that arise from the advent of civilization (coterminous with the state) and its historical expansion. Marx meticulously described this process:

Division of labour in a society, and the corresponding tying down of individuals to a particular calling, develops itself, just as does the division of labour in manufacture, from opposite starting-points. Within a family, and after further development within a tribe, there springs up naturally a division of labour, caused by differences of sex and age, a division that is consequently based on a purely physiological foundation, which division enlarges its materials by the expansion of the community, by the increase of population, and more especially, by the conflicts between different tribes, and the subjugation of one tribe by another. On the other hand, as I have before remarked, the exchange of products springs up at the points where different families, tribes, communities, come in contact; for, in the beginning of civilisation, it is not private individuals but families, tribes, etc., that meet on an independent footing. Different communities find different means of production, and different means of subsistence in their natural environment. Hence, their modes of production, and of living, and the products are different. It is this spontaneously developed difference which, when different communities come in contact, calls forth the mutual exchange of products, and the consequent gradual conversion of those products into commodities. Exchange does not create the differences between the spheres of production, but brings what are already different into relation, and thus converts them into more or less inter-dependent branches of the collective production of an enlarged society. In the latter case, the social division of labour arises from the exchange between spheres of production, that are originally distinct and independent of one another. In the former, where the physiological division of labour is the starting-point, the particular organs of a compact whole grow loose, and break off, principally owing to the exchange of commodities with foreign communities, and then isolate themselves so far, that the sole bond, still connecting the various kinds of work, is the exchange of the products as commodities. In the one case, it is the making dependent what was before independent; in the other case, the making independent what was before dependent. [*Capital*, 1:351-52]

In the shift from the production of the means of subsistence for the group to the production of commodities for exchange (having exchange value) between groups, the new relations of production, taken together, comprise the specific form of society, ancient, feudal, bourgeois, at a given point in history (*Wage Labour*, 28). The history of humanity must therefore, according to Marx, be approached and treated with respect to the social relations deriving from the history of industry and exchange (*German Ideology*, 41). From this base emerges a corresponding social constitution (*Poverty Philosophy*, 180). The social mechanisms that produce and are produced by these circumstances can be viewed as natural in that they reflect man's proclivity to cooperate and exchange, but they lack the spontaneity and immediacy that he believed characterized the primary social relations. As secondary social relations ramify historically, they tend to ensnare man in situations that work against basic human interests. The formation of the state has been the major consequence of this trend.

With Marx it is not society that constrains men, as is the case with Durkheim, but the state, a complex imposition over the natural mode of the primary social relations. The state evolved historically as subsequent social relations, based on exchange between groups, led to the expansion of communities, an increase in population, conflict between groups, and the subjugation of one group by another. In early society, labor, as part of the appropriation of nature, is simply exchange between individuals through primary social relations; later, exchange takes place between communities, resulting in the production of commodities having various values affixed to them; this is eventually elaborated into larger networks based on slavery and serfdom (*Capital*, 3:177). The state becomes the ideological power fabricated by society for the regulation of these exploitative interests. Marx endeavored to show that although the state is the logical outcome of social development, it served to work against the primary social relations that he believed comprised the bedrock of human nature. He was not alone in this criticism. During the eighteenth and nineteenth centuries, it was shared by several thinkers of differing intellectual persuasion.

A generation before Marx, the German culture historian and philosopher J. G. von Herder (1744-1803) attacked the state along quite similar lines. Herder's critique forms an interesting bridge in the history of radical social thought between the perspectives of Rousseau and Marx. He saw the state as an artificial imposition over the natural-social mode of life. This mode, he believed, consists of units in which men actively cooperate and share a common culture. Herder saw culture and language as inextricably entwined.[19] He remarked that millions of people lived without states in kin and extended kin relationships; "What the state can give us is an artificial construction...it can...rob us of ourselves."[20] During Marx's lifetime the state was just as vociferously attacked (the attack, like Marx's, was in part leveled at Hegel) from quite different quarters by the Danish philosopher and forerunner of existentialism, Sören Kierkegaard (1813-1855). Unlike Marx who saw salvation in man reaffirming primary social ties, Kierkegaard looked toward the individual, who he believed should pledge allegiance to his inner spiritual qualities not the dictates of the state or any other social arrangement. This tradition was continued later in the century in the writings of Friedrich Nietzsche (1844-1900), who in his exaltation of the individual attacked the state as the very devil.[21]

In formulating his critique of the state, Marx took aim at Hegel. For Hegel the state existed as a grand abstract idea with a life and will of its own. The various forms of the family and civil society were seen as mere embodiments of this idea. Marx sought to realign the priorities. He saw civil society and the various social and productive relations that derive from it giving rise to the state, and not vice-versa. It was the economic interests and conflicts that arise in developing communities that necessitated the fabrication of the state to regulate and impart order to the whole. Engels expressed the argument succinctly:

The state is therefore by no means a power imposed on a society from without; just as little is it "the reality of the moral idea," "the image and the reality of reason," as Hegel maintains. Rather, it is a product of society at a particular stage of development; it is the admission that this society has involved itself in insoluble self-contradiction and is cleft into irreconcilable antagonisms which it is powerless to exorcise. But in order that these antagonisms, classes with conflicting economic interests, shall not consume themselves and society in fruitless struggle, a power, apparently standing above society, has become necessary to moderate the conflict and keep it within the bounds of "order"; and this power, arisen out of society but placing itself above it and increasingly alienating itself from it, is the state. [*Origin Family*, 229]

In 1884 Engles tried to demonstrate the conflict of interest between state organization and primary social relations, using the extensive ethnographic and comparative sociological texts that proliferated during the second half of the nineteenth century. Marx, however, had pointed in this direction in the 1840s in an effort that lacked empirical foundations, although it did have the grandeur capable of inspiring a more rigorous elaboration. In his essay, "On the Jewish Question," written in 1844, he described how the state puts the "species life of man in opposition to his material life," causing him to thrust the values he holds as a member of a natural community against the forces compelling him to treat other individuals as a means, thus degrading his humanity and rendering him the plaything of alien forces: "In the state [man]...is an imaginary participant in an imaginary sovereignty, he is robbed of his real life and filled with unreal universality" (*Early Texts*, 93-94). The real universality in man rests in his social-communal nature. Through convention, consent, and sometimes force, a separation of social and political powers is effected through the formation of the state.

It was Marx's belief that the state would eventually wither and that primary social relations would reassert themselves in the communist society of the future as a result of the triumph of the proletariat. This has not happened in any society proclaiming Marxist affiliation, or any modern society for that matter. Conditions Marx never visualized have arisen and ensured the survival, at least for the present, of the state apparatus. Yet the persistence of the state and the new conditions in which it functions can still be the subject of a conscientious Marxian-inspired analysis.[22]

There is much of contemporary worth in Marx's ideas on the nature of society. His fundamental assumption that society has a naturalistic basis in itself can expand theoretical horizons by drawing the biological and social sciences into greater proximity. This avenue has not gone unrecognized. It was elaborated by several thinkers at the turn of the century. Nevertheless social science orthodoxy failed to acknowledge the possibility. It is worth reexamining in light of the recent developments in biology and anthropology that shed considerable new light on the foundations of human social life.

The Social
as Natural: Darwin _____

Mankind has always wandered or settled, agreed or quarrelled, in troops and companies.

—Adam Ferguson

The systematic study of the biological basis of social behavior is currently being explored by ethology, physical anthropology, comparative psychology, and sociobiology. Under the impetus of a number of researchers crossing the study of animal behavior with the modern evolutionary theory, these disciplines have emerged as recognized contributors to natural science inquiry and controversial, suspiciously regarded adjuncts to the social sciences. One of their primary assumptions is that a cross-specific methodology can, if properly employed, be used to gain insight into the biological basis of social behavior in any species, including humankind.[1] Darwin is unquestionably the major founder of this enterprise. In *The Descent of Man*, he applied the biological knowledge he derived from the empirical observation of animal and human behavior, together with evolutionary theory, to examine the phenomenon of social organization in a wide range of species. Darwin's approach has since been augmented by discoveries providing greater rigor and scientific certainty to this task. These include the development of genetics during the twentieth century and the birth of behavioral genetics, a field still in its infancy, the increased use of mathematical models in evolutionary theory, the emergence of the naturalistic study of animal behavior as a revealing zone of inquiry between biology and psychology, and the enormous potential neural science appears to be offering.

Despite the impressive array of contemporary resources that can be used when dealing with the biological basis of social behavior, the fundamental inspiration still remains Darwinian. In most cases we are dealing with the same problems that perplexed him, and we are using a similar research strategy, albeit with considerably more refined tools. While Marx affirmed intellectually what must have been obvious to his everyday sensibility— that human social organization is not divine or miraculous but part of a life activity continuous with nature and natural processes— Darwin sought to show why the phenomenon operates as it does and how it may have come into being. Marx linked the social to the natural through a philosophical argument steeped in a hoped-for scientific legitimacy. Darwin came to the social primarily from a scientific rather than a philosophical direction. He did this by continuing the argument he had already started in *The Descent of Man* regarding the kinship between nature and human nature.

It must be kept in mind as Darwin's efforts to define the biological basis of human social behavior are highlighted that this type of investigation is as controversial today as it was in 1871. Although the theory of evolution and the belief in humankind's physiological link to nature are now accepted by the academic establishment (even the Catholic church ceased regarding this as heresy after the papal encyclical on evolution was issued in the early 1950s), to hold that the social and cultural components of human behavior are subject to illumination by the discoveries of the natural sciences is to defend a heavily attacked position. While Darwin, in taking this stand, was chastised from various religious quarters, today those that follow his lead are liable to criticism from a body of knowledge as entrenched and unbending as nineteenth century theology: the contemporary social sciences deriving from Durkheim and Weber.

Another source of criticism that Darwinian theory applied to human social behavior has been subject to comes from several camps professing humanist affiliation. The recent attack on Edward Wilson's book, *Sociobiology*, is a major illustration.[2] The case against Wilson, although addressing itself to inadequacies is his argument, justified and unjustified, is in reality a disavowal of the sociobiological enterprise and, by extension, any attempt to apply models deriving from the natural sciences to human behavior. Sociobiology is attacked on the grounds that it will lead to social Darwinism and racism, a criticism that fails to comprehend fully the purpose of sociobiology, what it has so far discovered, and Darwin's initial quest for human understanding that first launched the venture. It is ironic to note, especially in light of the recent assault on sociobiology, ethology, and related biological attempts to deal with human behavior, that 100 years earlier, when Darwin applied his insights to humankind and established that the various races constituted only one species, the human species, his ideas were vehemently attacked by racist ideologues.

SOCIABILITY AMONG ANIMALS

Darwin sought to prove that human society has an evolutionary biological basis. The first prerequisite to establishing this was to show that elements of the social, often thought to be uniquely human, are present in animals both closely and distantly related to humankind. Social behavior for Darwin is an outgrowth of the moral sense that derives originally from what he termed the social instincts. The most fundamental of these instincts are parental and filial affection. In the state of nature, many species of animal, ranging from primates to birds and even insects, show evidence of social bonds of varying degrees of complexity. He noted that wolves hunt in packs, and a division of labor for defense can be observed in bisons, horses, and baboons. Reciprocal services such as grooming also take place among a number of species. A source of constant fascination for him was the phenomenon of animal sentinels who hover around the periphery of a group living in a constant state of risk in order that they might warn their comrades of danger. He also observed that many of these social traits, including food sharing and the defense of fellow captives, continue in captivity in modified form . These aspects of animal social behavior are not held to be blind impulses. They are by no means extended to all individuals of the same species, only to those of the same association (*Descent*, 95). Unfortunately, Darwin did not develop further this intriguing notion of an association within a larger species (what Marx might have referred to as a unit of cooperative social labor), applicable as it is to both human and animal social organization.

Although Darwin admittedly was in no position to explain how the first social instincts came into being, just as in 1859 he was in no position to deal with the origin of life, only its differentiation into species, he did argue that the feeling of pleasure many animals derive from living in social groups perhaps can be seen as an extension of parental and filial affection reinforced through habit but brought about primarily through natural selection:

> With those animals which were benefitted by living in close association, the individuals which took the greatest pleasure in society would best escape various dangers, whilst those which care least for their comrades, and lived solitary, would perish in greater numbers. [*Descent*, 102]

Here, and the notion is typically Darwinian despite the stigma surrounding his work created by the social Darwinists, we see natural selection acting in favor of cooperative behavior. It is easy to see why socialist theorists like Panneköek and Kautsky latched onto this aspect of his work and used it as a counterargument to the social Darwinist position. However, neither social Darwinism with its notions of individualism, selfinterest, and struggle, nor the Darwinian socialists who emphasized selfless cooperation, adequately reflected the intricacy of Darwin's position. Darwin held that the relationship between human society as a dynamic process and the individuals holding it together was permeated by conflicting interests at levels below generally observed social interaction. When describing this situation, I borrow a term used in association with Freud's work but also appropriate to Darwin's: instinctual conflict.

THE HUMAN SOCIAL IMPERATIVE

The social in man, according to Darwin, bears a direct relationship to the same phenomenon in the animal world: "In order that primeval men, or the apelike progenitors of man, should become social, they must have acquired the same instinctive feelings which impel other animals to live in a body" (*Descent*, 126). He speculated on how this may have come about:

A tribe including many members who, from possessing in high degree the spirit of patriotism, fidelity, obedience, courage, and sympathy, were always ready to aid one another, and to sacrifice themselves for the common good, would be victorious over most other tribes; and this would be natural selection. [Ibid., 129]

Darwin was not using the term *tribe* in the contemporary anthropological sense, but rather in a more flexible way to denote a hypothetical prehuman group undergoing behavioral evolution. Although cooperation is an essential component in this process, it is accompanied by aggressive encounters with other tribes of the same or a closely related species. This model, only partially developed by Darwin, can be described as ingroup cooperation versus outgroup conflict, and while today we often hold it to be typical of human social behavior, it has yet to be systematically elaborated in a biosocial manner.

Because our early ancestors were highly social creatures, we have retained what Darwin called an instinctive love and sympathy for our fellow man. Man, in general, he pointed out, dislikes solitude and is always searching for social liaisons beyond his immediate family. Although Darwin held the belief that all social tendencies arose out of a family structure in the distant past and that primeval man might have lived in single-family units, he did not believe that this situation, divorced as it is from wider social networks, is typical of contemporary human arrangements:

At the present day, though single families, or only two or three together, roam the solitudes of some savage lands, they always, as far as I can discern hold friendly relations with families inhabiting the same district. [Ibid., 105]

Like Marx, Darwin believed that any concept of an asocial state prior to history describing our ancestors as solitary individuals was out of the question. Therefore he opposed notions of a social contract carried over from the previous two centuries. Both Marx and Darwin believed the social in man to be a phylogenetic legacy—Marx intuitively and philosophically and Darwin through the support of his own biological observations.

In *The Descent* Darwin continually referred to man as having social instincts, although he was aware of the imprecise nature of the concept. Animals lower down on the evolutionary scale have what he called special instincts, ensuring social cohesion. Man, he claimed, has lost these special instincts but has retained a generalized impulse, which, accompanied by reason deriving from his improved intellectual faculties, results in social activity: "Thus the social instincts, which must have been acquired by man in a very rude state, and probably even by his apelike progenitors, still give impulse to some of his best actions (ibid., 106). These social proclivities provide the context for other activities essential to human evolution: imitation, reason, and the teaching and learning of the arts of survival.

Darwin believed that the social in man is accompanied by other impulses earlier in origin, notably selfishness and the desire for self-preservation. Although he gave self-preservation the status of an instinct (while again refraining from giving a precise definition of *instinct*), he noted that it can be overridden by altruistic acts that involve the risking of one's life, and he gave several examples: a savage risking his life to save a member of his own community, the frequency of altruistic maternal behavior, and instances where civilized man risks his life to save the life of a stranger. These acts indicate the strength that the social instincts exert—even in contemporary life.

Darwin recognized that hunger and self-preservation can significantly motivate human behavior. Nevertheless these powerful urges tend to be temporary, while the social and moral impulses are enduring and continuous. This led him to the assumption that the human species tends to obey more persistent and longterm impulses, even in the face of powerful immediate needs, a situation he believed constitutes one of the foundations of morality. Following the argument further steered Darwin into one of his rare exchanges with philosophy. In this instance, it was the ethical and moral aspects of utilitarianism, deriving from Jeremy Bentham (1748-1832), James Mill (1773-1836), and John Stuart Mill (1806-1873), that prompted his comments.

Darwin, like the utilitarians, was opposed to the notion that morality is founded on total selflessness, but he also argued that it does not derive from the greatest happiness for the greatest number principle conceived by the utilitarians. This principle, he pointed out, is only a standard, not a motive for conduct, it constitutes at best only a secondary guide. Underlying moral behavior in man (and animals) are deep-seated instincts and long-acquired habits. When a man risks his life to save another from fire or drowning, pleasure of happiness can hardly be a motive. Darwin claimed that such spontaneous behavior is instinctive in nature and part of a legacy man shares with a number of other animals. Social and moral behavior in man came about not for the general happiness of the species but for the general good: "The term general good, may be defined as the rearing of the greatest number of individuals in full vigor and health, with all their faculties perfect, under the conditions to which they are subjected" (ibid., 117). Although Darwin's political liberalism had much in common with the moral code of the utilitarians, he never accepted their empiricist individualist philosophical position as a guiding precept.

As the human species evolved, Darwin saw its social tendencies, inherited from previous generations through natural selection and acquired habit, being continually fortified through the development of reason. It did not matter that the social in man lost the instinctive force it had previously because the simplest reason, according to him, would teach each individual to extend his social inclinations and sympathy to other members of the same group or nation. Darwin's analysis is laden with beliefs typical of the progressivism, optimism, and rationalism of the eighteenth and nineteenth centuries. He held that as man evolved, the process caused small tribes to unite into larger communities, and larger communities into nations. Ultimately he believed that the recognition through reason of the social imperative would link all races and nations on earth. While his vision of social evolution is not totally misguided when used to describe particular liaisons that operate in and between small-scale societies, as a world-historical rationale it demonstrates considerable naiveté.

In addressing himself to a problem that also concerned Marx, social evolution within history, Darwin provided answers of a very different order. With his belief in the growth through reason of the social ideal (natural selection is still a factor though the inertia of reason diminishes its importance), his ideas resemble Hegel's formulations on the social. However, for Darwin, ideas are not disembodied spirits with a life of their own but a consequence of the biopsychological operations of mind. The problem is that he is still describing a process operating outside concrete social and historical contexts.

Darwin contended that social evolution in the human line resulted from what he referred to as a struggle between higher and lower desires. This process can be referred to as instinctual conflict, a term usually associated with Freud's work. For Darwin, the lower desires are older and equate primarily with self-interest and immediate self-gratification. This, of course, loosely parallels Freud's concept of the id (though as a thoroughgoing Victorian, Darwin refrained from discussing sexuality in this context) and refers to behavior that modern neuroanatomy would trace to the lower brain or limbic system. Darwin did not deal at all with the early evolution and adaptive logic of these lower urges. The higher desires are those relating to the social and moral. They are traits that resemble, but do not exactly parallel, Freud's concept of the superego. Biosocial evolution, as Darwin saw it, resulted from a struggle whereby the higher urges gradually overrode the lower, particularly when reason began to augment the higher urges in the human line. Eventually larger and more elaborate social arrangements developed out of this interaction.

In the conflict between social instincts and those of self-interest and self-gratification, the belief that virtuous tendencies acquired during an individual's lifetime could be inherited became central to Darwin's argument. Darwin also believed that malevolent tendencies are inherited in the same manner, yet the trend, he believed, was always for good to gain at the expense of evil. Here his "scientific" argument reflects aspects of Christianity, rationalism, and progressivism that he did not confront or acknowledge. In a related vein, his philosophical contemporary, Herbert Spencer, as thoroughly atheistic an intellect as Marx, adhered to a similar set of ideas. Spencer believed that man's social evolution was underwritten by a struggle between egoistic and altruistic tendencies.[3] As man became more perfect with the passage of history the altruistic tendencies gained at the expense of the egoistic. Spencer saw this as an inevitable and natural process of development, and consequently it did not require support in the form of social legislation, such as poor laws. These interventions would act only as impediments to the spontaneous and inevitable development of the morally just. This optimistic vision of social evolution as progressive and inherently good pervaded nineteenth-century thinking.

Marx, too, believed that the future would be better. But in explaining the development of society from antiquity to his nineteenth-century cultural present, he provided a method capable of standing apart from the optimistic spirit that helped bring about the inception of that method. While Darwin saw social evolution from prehistoric times to his own era as the result of a rapid, biologically based behavioral evolution strongly aided by the inheritance of acquired habits, Marx offered an explanation based not on the direct biological evolution of individuals but on the interaction of the forces of production, social organization, and ideology. Since Marx's approach has the advantage of being able to deal with social evolution in history without invoking any kind of significant biological or genetic changes, it has turned out to be more compatible with twentieth-century thinking on the subject.[4] Because Darwin's ideas on the social tendencies underlying history are invariably and wrongly linked with social Darwinism, his contribution has been almost entirely overlooked by sociology, history, and anthropology. What his approach can offer to these disciplines is an understanding of the universal social tendencies of the species, tendencies that become differentially expressed as they are constrained by particular historical circumstances.

In trying to explain the development of social and moral proclivities in the human species, an occurrence in which the inheritance of acquired habits was seen to play a large part, Darwin nevertheless did not completely abandon natural selection. However, recognizing that he was caught between the two modes of explanation caused him to ponder whether he had in fact painted himself into a corner. The following dilemma emerged. In the great struggle for existence engaged in by our ancestors, it is likely that the brave, noble, and self-sacrificing individuals perished more frequently than their less daring comrades. Since those who perish early tend to leave fewer offspring, how could these qualities be proliferated through natural selection? It would seem that the opposite would be the case if a strict selectionist argument is adhered to. Darwin was puzzled. The complexity of behavioral evolution did not cause him to abandon natural selection completely, a principle that worked so well for him in other areas; however, it did lead him to add a number of supplementary notions.

Some modern writers believe that the evolution of altruistic behavior, which on the surface appears to contradict the tenets of natural selection, can in fact be explained by those self-same tenets. In his *Sociobiology*, Edward Wilson summarizes this position:

The answer is kinship: if the genes causing the altruism are shared by two organisms because of common descent, and if the altruistic act by one organism increases the joint contribution of these genes to the next generation, the propensity to altruism will spread through the gene pool. This occurs even though the altruist makes less of the solitary contribution to the gene pool as the price of his altruistic act.[5]

It is a tribute to Darwin's intellectual legacy that the (possible) answer to this problem, although not the one he gave, derives from his method. Actually Darwin was not too far from a similar solution. In *The Origin*, when dealing with insects having worker castes, he asked, when calling into question Lamarck's notion of use and disuse and the inheritance of acquired characteristics, if worker castes leave no offspring, how could they have evolved? Darwin rescued his position by theorizing that in such instances natural selection was operating at the family rather than the individual level. Wilson points out that natural selection can indeed operate in this manner. In insect populations some individuals can be sterile but nevertheless are important to the welfare of their relatives: "With the entire family serving as the unit of selection, it is the capacity to generate sterile but altruistic relatives that becomes subject to genetic evolution".[6] Darwin, however, was unable to give this line of reasoning to appropriate modifications necessary to reapply it to the higher mammals, preferring instead to look for other processes.

In endeavoring not to abandon natural selection entirely when dealing with social and moral evolution, Darwin shifted its emphasis from individuals to groups. He noted that although high morality may not be particularly advantageous to each individual over others of the same tribe, an increase in the number of individuals so endowed in one tribe would give it an advantage over another, and this would be natural selection (*Descent*, 129). This concept, today known as group selection, lacks precision. Darwin never clearly defined his units of measure or explained how altruistic individuals could keep being produced in a given group (tribe) no matter how successful it would be in a struggle against others. Since he was probably aware that natural selection as an explanatory principle is more effective at the individual rather than the group level, he searched for an additional principle to explicate the tremendous development of sociability in the human line.

For Darwin the key factor in this development at its highest and most complex levels was reason. Each man, he surmised, would be aware that his aid to fellow men would result in return aid: "The habit of performing benevolent actions certainly strengthens the feeling of sympathy which gives the first impulse to benevolent actions" (ibid., 128). He also added another crucial factor, which he termed the "love of praise and the dread of blame." Members of a hypothetical primeval tribe would give praise to behaviors that appeared to be for the general good of the group and chastise what appeared to be detrimental. This could explain why a man would risk his life (assuming that a deep-seated instinct is not the cause) for the good of the group. He would be excited by glory, and Darwin believed that this attitude would be contagious and spread throughout the group. What Darwin was referring to in these illustrations frequently occurs throughout human society. Traditions and sanctions are acquired through learning, retained by the group, and passed to subsequent generations. They are components of our cultural legacy. Throughout human history, for perhaps as long as 100,000 years, culture has provided the variation necessary for further adaptation. Yet during that time, aspects of cultural evolution, such as increasingly complex social arrangements and the various sanctions regarding behavior mentioned by Darwin, occurred without any major changes in the biological nature of the species, a fact he would find difficult to fathom not having a knowledge of the way modern genetics has rendered the inheritance of acquired habits obsolete as a biological mechanism.

Social and cultural evolution, however, can still be regarded as biological adaptation. Variation and selection operate here, just as they do in the purely organic realm,[7] but in cultural evolution there is no gross change in the nature of the organism analogous to what happens in speciation. Darwin could not discern the process by which a Stone Age hunter-gatherer could become a proper Victorian in a generation. He invoked reason and the inheritance of acquired habit to explain what he concluded to be a modest biological transmutation. We now know that all peoples, no matter what their cultural affiliation, have the capacity to learn from a vast repertoire of behaviors. In any given situation only part of this repertoire can be utilized. If the situation changes, the new behaviors that result are not caused by biological changes in the organism, they derive from a vast generalized cultural capacity already present generically and in equal measure in all races of the human species.

No matter how man derived his social imperative, Darwin believed that it was a powerful force having consequences on a multitude of levels:

The aid which we feel impelled to give to the helpless is mainly an incidental result of the instinct of sympathy, which was originally acquired as part of the social instincts, but subsequently rendered, . . . more tender and more widely diffused. [*Descent*, 131]

Darwin believed that man's strong benevolent tendencies could be injurious to the species. He noted that in savage society, good health generally prevails as the weak are eliminated. In civilization we check the selective process through asylums, poor laws, vaccination, and similar measures. He drew an analogy with domestic animals by remarking that if survival of the weak is injurious to them, it might also be so with the human situation. But on a hopeful note he added that the feeble and weak might refrain from propagating their kind so as to prevent any escalation of this state of affairs. Despite this attitude and in stark contrast to social Darwinism, he emphasized that legislation for the less fortunate should continue, for we cannot "check our sympathy even at the urging of hard reason without deterioration in the noblest part of our nature" (ibid.). Darwin demonstrated an intellectual near-sightedness in this argument when he failed to note that even the feeble and weak can make contributions to society independently of their state of physical health and that fitness in society is relative; it is not identical to fitness in the state of nature.

Marx insisted that human society is inextricably linked to nature and natural processes, and this belief became part of the human-theoretical framework underlying his economic and political theory. Darwin, though he had a similar vision of the social as natural, tried in a more direct way to verify it by scientific weight of evidence. Not only was Darwin concerned with the properties of the phenomenon, he felt compelled to deal systematically with its origin and practical ramifications. His errors and his frequent naiveté are obvious. In *The Descent*, more than in his other writings, Darwin was guilty of being a child of his times. Yet he was always direct, honest, and disarming in the way he openly revealed evidence that might contradict his hypotheses.

With rare modesty, Darwin remarked that his formulations on man were highly speculative and that many would be proven erroneous. He was correct; he put forth ideas regarding the evolution of man's social capacity that have not stood the test of time. The inheritance of acquired habits and group selection are prime examples. True to the thrust of his work, he contributed a number of observations that have continuing validity; these include the generic nature of man's social faculties and the adaptive advantages of social behavior in a wide range of species. More importantly, he gave us the evolutionary theory against which his own and later formulations can be continually scrutinized. This perspective, updated by modern biological discoveries, has shown that in the realm of the social, natural selection has played a far larger part than Darwin could have believed possible. To say that Darwin's theory and method can be used today to disprove some of his own speculative assumptions is to pay him the highest tribute.

BRADLEY, TÖNNIES, AND KROPOTKIN

Marx and Darwin may have been the foremost theorists in the nineteenth century who elaborated the concept of the social as natural, but they were not the only thinkers to do so. This is notable in light of the fact that in the twentieth century, the concept of the social as it was employed in sociology, deriving primarily from Durkheim, became completely divorced from any naturalistic affiliation. Before the Durkheimian separation of the social from the natural occurred at the turn of the century, several thinkers who were influenced in part by either Marx or Darwin developed social philosophies in which concepts of a naturalistic foundation played a large part. The most notable were F. H. Bradley (1846-1924), Ferdinand Tönnies (1855-1936), and Petr Kropotkin (1842-1921). While not unknown in their respective fields for other accomplishments, Bradley was a moral philosopher, Tönnies a philosopher-sociologist, and Kropotkin a naturalist and political revolutionary; their ideas regarding the nature of society were destined to have little impact on the later social sciences.

It is a major contention of this book that the legacies of Marx and Darwin, particularly when both are taken together, represent an attempt to draw into close proximity the natural sciences and the study of humankind. Examining other thinkers of their age who shared this vision will serve to show that this enterprise has been and can be pursued in a number of quite different directions.

In 1876, when he was only thirty years old, F. H. Bradley published his *Ethical Studies*, a collection of essays showing considerable maturity in style and argument. As a British philosopher, Bradley was unusual in that he was one of the few idealists in a tradition that from Locke through Hume to Bertrand Russell has been dominated by empiricists. As an idealist, Bradley was influenced by Kant and to great extent by Hegel. What makes him interesting is that he perceived the significance of Darwin's researches and tried to draw them into his philosophical frame of reference.

In an essay in the *Ethical Studies* titled, "My Station and Its Duties," Bradley drew directly from Darwin in noting that "man has never been anything but social and society was never made by individual men."[8] Like Marx, he believed that human self-realization is attainable only through participation in community. For Bradley, man's identity is "cultural," a term he used in a sense that amalgamated social and natural. He held that the bedrock of human existence, human nature, consists in man's relationship to society: "Man is a social being; he is real only because he is social."[9] This train of thought recalls the early Marx of *The Paris Manuscripts*, particularly regarding the common influence Hegel exerted on both of their philosophies.

Like Marx, Bradley received inspiration related to the nature of social groupings from Hegel. Like Marx and Darwin, and unlike Hegel, Bradley did not view the social in opposition to the natural. Like Hegel and unlike Marx, Bradley drew no limits to what constitutes a viable human society. For Bradley all human arrangements—family, community, society, nation, state, and beyond—are equally authentic expressions of the social imperative. He assumed that during the course of history, human nature was undergoing transition from an incomplete to a complete state, and one indication of this was the great diversification of social roles. The social role, which he referred to as a station, took on biological proportions.

Since all manifestations of the social were seen as equally valid expressions of human nature, the morality of each historical epoch was justified. The result was confused integration of three inherently distinct concepts: biological evolution, history, and progress. Mixing these concepts became commonplace during the nineteenth century. For example, Bradley's contemporary, Herbert Spencer, also an apologist for progress, continually spoke of biological evolution and history as being the same process. Even Marx and Darwin believed that the three were continuous, but this belief was not essential to an application of their major analyses in the fields of history and evolution, respectively. Today we still have not extricated ourselves completely from conceptual blurring in this area. Although we know that history has transpired independently of major biological changes in the species and that biological evolution can not be equated with progress, we still cling to the belief that evolution and history are both progressive.

In his approach Bradley did not stop at the notion that man is social. He went on to contend that man is only social. In his denial of the importance of the individual, Bradley foreshadowed Durkheim, the primary difference being that for Durkheim the social is a phenomenon unto itself subject to its own unique laws, while Bradley linked it directly to the biological evolutionary context. Bradley projected this into the political realm by contending that the reduction of the individual resulting from the menial jobs of the industrial revolution was a valid expression of man's social potential. To say that man is social by nature, as both Marx and Darwin did, does not inevitably lead to Bradley's conclusion that all expressions of man's social potential are equally authentic. There are, as Marx's concept of alienation brilliantly illustrates, forces that take natural social arrangements and render them into unnatural distortions. This is a major point in his criticism of Hegel's belief that the state constitutes the highest and truest expression of the human social potential.

Bradley's social theory follows Hegel's quite closely. The social whole, no matter how large, abstract, or divorced from individual mediation it becomes, exists as a legitimate first cause reminiscent of Hegel's idea or spirit. Bradley updated this perspective by misguidedly trying to link it to the evolutionary possibility deriving from Darwinian theory. In retrospect, Bradley's belief that the social is an extension, not a negation, of the natural, and his interplay between philosophy, the humanities, and the natural sciences, demonstrates his perceptivity as a philosopher. It is unfortunate that failure to scrutinize critically the historical contexts that he analyzed, and the one in which he did his analysis, diminishes the significance of his contribution by making him another apologist for the nineteenth-century ideology of progress, class exploitation, and European chauvanism.

One theorist who believed in the social as natural and also that certain social arrangements are more natural than others was Ferdinand Tönnies. In 1887, he produced his major work, the sociological classic, *Gemeinschaft und Gesellschaft* [Community and society].[10] This text has yielded many insights that have been incorporated into the sociological tradition. However, the belief in the social as natural, fundamental to Tönnies's perspective, has not survived with the strength of his other contributions, in part because it was the subject of a direct criticism leveled at his work by Durkheim.

Tönnies insisted, and in this he followed the tradition of Marx and Darwin, that the social in man exists a priori: it is "a natural order...such an order exists by virtue of the organic nature of man before all human culture and history."[11] The norms relating to the social, according to him, are more universal than any particular system of legal obligations and must be studied in their own right. In making this contention, he tried to avoid what anthropologists call ethnocentrism: the belief that one's own social and cultural institutions are either superior to or the standard by which all others should be judged. In his quest for the universal aspects of social organization underlying all human societies, Tönnies recalled the early Marx, and in fact some of Marx's ideas did exert an influence on his thought. He also left social theory open to the inclusion of ideas deriving from the natural sciences, though he did not pursue this direction himself. Tönnies's main influences came from philosophy and the humanities rather than from the sciences and in addition to Marx include Aristotle, Hobbes, Rousseau, Goethe, Herder, and Maine.

In looking at human social arrangements, Tönnies came to the conclusion that man shares many segments of his being with organic nature and yet in a meaningful sense is also a unique being. To explain this apparent paradox, he postulated two fundamental and coexisting modalities of behavior in the human species: natural will and rational will. Natural will is comprised of life activity and includes the interplay of instincts and sensations. It is inborn in man in the same way that in other "species a specific form of body and soul is natural."[12] In making this contrast, Tönnies showed that in the mind-body, nature-society philosophical argument, he stood with romantics like Goethe, who claimed it was a false dichotomy, and not with the rationalists, following Descartes and Hegel, who insisted on the dualism.

Tönnies likened natural will to man's physical structure in that the various behaviors inherent in it grow and develop as the individual matures. He included among such behaviors facets of human interaction, such as the mother-child bond, the recipro-

cally binding sentiments that cause various kinds of social groupings, and language. Tönnies did not regard language as an invention. He believed instead that it is the result of an innate
biological predisposition tied to general aspects of communication shared with other animals.[13] These ideas are both ancient
and modern. Their modern grounding stems from Darwin's research linking processes human to processes natural through
the evolutionary perspective and the continuing exploration of
these regions taking place in the contemporary biological sciences. The origin of these ideas dates back to their first extrapo-
lation in the concepts of naturalism and pantheism developed
by the early Greeks. Tönnies's inspiration appears to derive from
these ancient and enduring beliefs rather than from the scientific
revolution of his day.

Rational will emanates from man's distinctive mode of thought,
his reason, and learned experience. It results in higher-level and
increasingly complex social arrangements and political ideologies. Rational will roughly approximates what we can refer to as
the culture of a people at any given point in history. The fact
that rational will is not directly connected to biology leads Tönnies
to some critical insights. During history, though external conditions may change and drastically affect man's living situation,
human nature (natural will) remains constant; however, its spontaneous expression can be severely thwarted by patterns of rational will, the imposition of the state being a prime example.
Tönnies did not confuse history with any kind of biological evolution despite having a biologically grounded view of human
nature. He also did not believe that progress is the inevitable
companion of history. As a consequence, he generated what
amounts to a concept of alienation not unlike that propounded
by Marx.[14]

It was Tönnies's belief that human fulfillment could be more
easily attained through a recognition of, and retaining a proximity to, what constitutes natural will. It was his opinion that
natural will receives greater expression in small-scale communities sharing a common language and intimate interpersonal group
structure than it does in large-scale civilizations with their vast
bureaucracies. Without doubt, *Gemeinschaft und Gesellschaft* is one
of the earliest systematic and certainly the most eloquent work

advocating the currently popular "small is beautiful" formula. Finally, it must be noted that because it was written after the advent of the Darwinian revolution, Tönnies's great book suffers from a failure to acknowledge what was transpiring in this area, information and evidence that would have supported many of his assumptions regarding human nature and society. As a result, his trenchant formulations exist as a sophisticated survival of the romantic rebellion instead of constituting a foundation for further research into a science of society.

In contrast to Tönnies, Petr Kropotkin, the Russian anarchist prince, strived to work directly from Darwinian sources. In *Mutual Aid: A Factor of Evolution*, he attempted to delineate the prehuman origins of man's social and moral faculties. The work grew out of a series of articles written between 1890 and 1900. Kropotkin's effort is noteworthy because he was, like Darwin, both a fieldworker and a theoretician. In the field, he did research both as a naturalist and as an anthropologist-sociologist. Early in his career (1862-1867), he traveled across Eurasia making careful observations on the behavior of a number of animal species and human groups, and these observations became the substance of *Mutual Aid*. Kropotkin's conception of society was very much in accord with Darwin's, and he was aware that Darwin's ideas held little resemblance to the interpretations of social Darwinism. Kropotkin extended several of Darwin's insights. He knew that in *The Descent of Man* the term *struggle for existence* is used in the widest sense to include the evolution of social and moral faculties, as well as the everyday battle for survival against the environment. Full of insight from his field experiences, Kropotkin elaborated in depth this previously unacknowledged aspect of Darwin's work. He saw sociability rather than a life-and-death struggle between individuals as typifying the animal world. Since Darwin had established continuity between man and nature through the theory of evolution, Kropotkin believed that the social in man must be located in processes similar to those operative in the zoological realm. In assessing this possibility, *Mutual Aid* became a pioneering work in cross-specific and cross-cultural methodology.

Kropotkin helped to entrench Darwin's contention that the social is not a secondary but a primary and deeply rooted aspect of human nature. He also realized that by stressing this belief he would be accused of denying the function of individuality. To counter this potential criticism, he gave a brief affirmation of the role of the individual in the social process, adding that it was the imbalance in human theory precipitated by social Darwinism that made it necessary for him to emphasize the social over the individual when dealing with the subject of human nature.

Kropotkin's anarchist politics, coupled with his human theory, led him to conclusions similar to those of Marx and Tönnies, and unlike those of Hegel and Bradley, regarding what constitutes an authentic and viable human society. He believed that the state is an unnatural imposition on the normal natural-social mode of human existence typified by fully cooperating small-scale communities like the peasant and tribal groups that he visited in his travels. In his "small is beautiful" philosophy, there are many parallels with Tönnies but no influence of either upon the other. Undoubtedly Kropotkin must have known about Marx because they were both in London during the early 1880s. Kropotkin, however, always remained an anarchist (in the respectable political sense) and a communalist. He never accepted communism and therefore was probably distrustful of large-scale labor organizations such as the International in which Marx and Engles had vested interests. Kropotkin was opposed to state socialism, and the feeling was mutual. Eventually the workers' communes that he conceived during the Russian Revolution of 1917 became suppressed by the Bolsheviks. While Marx's economic approach helped explain the differences in social and political organization in various historical epochs, Kropotkin did not attempt to assimilate it to his own point of view, which dealt in a more thorough manner than Marx with biosocial universals and their possible origins.

DURKHEIM AND BERGSON

The possibility of linking the social to the biological, which in their own way each of the previous thinkers was striving to do, came under direct attack from Emile Durkheim whose legacy has dominated the social sciences during the twentieth century. Why the social sciences opted for Durkheim and totally rejected

Darwin is a major problem in intellectual history and will be the subject of a forthcoming study by anthropologist Robin Fox.[15]

The Rules of the Sociological Method, first published in French in 1895, constitutes Durkheim's major programmatic statement. In it, he argued for the autonomy of sociology and social facts from the domains of biology and psychology. Social facts are, Durkheim stressed, subject to their own laws and not reducible to any other level of understanding. This led him to remark that although biology and psychology are useful enterprises and necessary to a complete science of society, they have relevance only to the study of the physiology and behavior of individual organisms respectively and can tell us nothing about the nature of society or its mode of operation. He therefore rejected outright the Darwinian conception of the social as an outgrowth of the biological. Society was defined as a phenomenon sui generis, a superorganic imposition external to individuals and exercising constraint over their behavior:

A social fact is every way of acting, fixed or not, capable of exercising on the individual an external constraint; or again every way of acting which is general throughout a given society while at the same time existing in its own right independent of individual manifestations.[16]

Society for Durkheim constitutes its own level of reality, and although individuals come and go, they function as the agents rather than as the creators of social patterns. This perspective does not require individuals to bring any inherent organizing principles into the social milieu into which they are born—only their raw and as yet undifferentiated sensations.

In Marx's sociology, society also helps to give man a definition of himself through its various traditions, but it remains a human creation in that individuals bring with them in each generation a social-creative capacity. The interaction between individuals actualizing this capacity and the preexisting circumstances that constitute its canvas form the essential dynamic of human history. In his belief that society shapes man's thoughts and actions, Marx has been justly compared to Durkheim; that branch of inquiry known as the sociology of knowledge has appropriated this aspect of both thinkers. The fundamental difference

between their respective social philosophies is that the reciprocal action by which human beings make society and society in
turn gives definition to its creators, central to Marx, is absent in
Durkheim. In Durkheim's case, there is no feedback; society
exists as a separate power, and man acts in accordance with its
dictates. An individual is born in a social milieu into which he
brings nothing save his senses: he is tabula rasa. Through the
collective representations of society, he acquires concepts of the
self, space, time, and perhaps the belief in an afterlife. For Durkheim
La Société, as an overriding almost mystical power, is similar to
Hegel's idea or spirit, although the French master's concept is
considerably more empirical. In The Rules of the Sociological Method,
social facts are deemed objective, observable, and subject to
statistical scrutiny in a manner comparable to the natural sciences.

The separation of the social from the natural in Durkheim's
writings reflects the influence of his philosophical forebears and
fellow countrymen, René Descartes (mind-body) and Jean Jacques
Rousseau (society-state of nature). It also foreshadowed the nature-
culture model definitively elaborated by his countryman of the
current generation, anthropologist Claude Lévi-Strauss.

Although society for Durkheim does not derive from an innate capacity in the sense elaborated by Darwin, neither does it
originate from a conscious agreement between individuals, as
postulated by the social contract theory of Hobbes, Locke and
Rousseau. If society is not the result of contract or a biological
urge, how does it retain its continuity? Without addressing himself directly to the question, Durkheim provided a partial answer in his conception of human nature. Man outside of society
(a state Marx and Darwin thought inconceivable, even hypothet-
ically, since society itself was seen to be an intrinsic expression
of human nature) would be a helpless animal dominated by
sensuous appetites and subject to impulse, whim, and fancy. As
a biopsychological legacy, Durkheim grants man only physiology and sensations. The generalized urges that emanate from
man's organic being are brought under control solely through
the reason of social institutions. There are congruencies here
with Freud's belief in the conflict between the id (self-seeking)
and the superego (social sanctions); but although the superego
is a rough equivalent of La Société, its locus for Freud is still in

individual human nature. Referring back to Marx's earlier observation that each historical era produces its own conception of human nature, we begin to see that for Durkheim natural man is wholly Victorian: a confused, potentially malevolent spirit brought into alignment through the sublime reason of society. Perhaps I can illustrate this more dramatically by taking an infamous and well-known statement from David Hume's *Treatise on Human Nature*; "Reason is, and ought to be, the slave of the 'passions,' " and after revising it in a manner appropriate to Durkheim, we might get, "The passions are, and ought to be, the slaves of societies' reason."

Durkheim's contribution is not without its brilliance. He combined a rationalist theory regarding the nature of society. The influence of Plato, Kant, and Hegel can be discerned, with an empiricist methodology for observing its operation, and the debt in this case is to the Scottish moral philosophers, Saint-Simon and Comte. Several of Darwin's contributions that could have helped Durkheim bridge these two vast intellectual islands went unrecognized. Durkheim was aware of Darwin, citing him a number of times in his first major work, *The Division of Labor in Society*, published in French in 1893. He even incorporated several evolutionary principles into his theory of society. However, it was the popular stereotype of Darwin deriving from *The Origin of Species*, emphasizing the brutality of nature and the struggle for existence, to which Durkheim subscribed. In developing his model of society, Durkheim tried to refute Darwin by showing that altruism and social solidarity, what he referred to as "moral life," can override the brute struggle of nature.[17] He did not realize that in *The Descent of Man*, Darwin elaborated the same belief at length by arguing that morality has a biological basis, as opposed to one that is contractual or socially separate.

In an interesting related case in intellectual history, Durkheim had a partial contemporary, also a Frenchman, Henri Bergson (1859-1941), who held almost the opposite position regarding the nature of society. Bergson, a philosopher, did not publish his ideas on society in full until he released *The Two Sources of Morality and Religion* in 1932, his last major work. Bergson agreed with Durkheim that to cultivate the "social ego is the essence of our obligation to society."[18] However, he also insisted that society remains inextricably bound to nature and natural processes:

"Everything, yet again, conspires to make social order an imitation of the order observed in nature."[19] Later in the book he wrote: "Nature, setting down the human species along the line of evolution intended it to be sociable, in the same way as it did the communities of ants and bees; but since intelligence was there, the maintenance of social life had to be entrusted to an all but intelligent mechanism; intelligent in that each piece could be remodelled by human intelligence, yet instinctive in that man could not, without ceasing to be a man, reject all the pieces together and cease to accept a mechanism of preservation. Instinct gave place temporarily to a system of habits, each one of which became contingent, their convergence towards the preservation of society being alone necessary, and this necessity bringing back instinct with it. The necessity of the whole, felt behind the contingency of the parts, is what we call moral obligation in general—it being understood that the parts are contingent in the eyes of society only; to the individual, into whom society inculcates its habits, that part is as necessary as the whole.[20]

Although Bergson appears to address his argument to Durkheim, he did not mention him by name or cite his work, preferring instead to make oblique references, as the following passage illustrates:

We are fond of saying that society exists, and that hence it inevitably exerts a constraint on its members, and that this constraint is obligation. But in the first place, for society to exist at all the individual must bring into it a whole group of inborn tendencies; society therefore is not self-explanatory; so we must search below the social accretion, get down to life, of which human societies, as indeed the human species all together, are but manifestations.[21]

These ideas on society and morality appear to echo in a more poetic manner what Darwin elucidated in *The Descent of Man*. Yet ironically Bergson was as critical of Darwin as he seems to have been of Durkheim. Again we encounter the misleading assumption that all that is representative of Darwinism derives from *The Origin of Species* and consists primarily in the struggle for existence. Compounding this, Bergson had the mistaken belief that Darwin's theory of evolution was completely mechanistic. To counter this alleged mechanism, he conjured his infamous *élan vitale*, or creative life force, which he claimed is the prime mover of evolution. Nevertheless, Bergson must be credited for being one of the few twentieth century thinkers who endeavored to link the social to the natural, but because the Durkheimian tide was flowing so strongly in the opposite direction, his influence on the social sciences has been negligible.[22]

Although Durkheim's analysis has yielded extraordinary insights, in seeking to make society accountable only to itself he defined limitations that preclude communion with other sciences. His position regarding the autonomy of the social, and the antireductionist posture he used to defend it, were not altogether unjustified at the turn of the century in the struggle to establish a new discipline, sociology, in an intellectual milieu essentially hostile to the project. Today this position strains to avoid confronting an enormous mass of information relevant to the study of society being turned up in the various biological sciences. It is now obvious that comprehending the social can no longer be the preserve of one discipline. It requires a cumulative cross-disciplinary effort that can break down or at least redraw some of the boundaries that have traditionally existed between the social sciences, the humanities, and the natural sciences. This does not imply a rejection of Durkheim. There are potentially many points of convergence between his ideas on society and biological processes, despite the fact that he conceived the two realms in opposition.

Part III

ETHNOGRAPHY AND HUMAN EVOLUTION

Primitive Society, Slavery, and Race

> Had my lot been cast among those peoples who are said still to live under the kindly liberty of nature's primal laws, I should I assure you, most gladly have painted myself complete and in all my nakedness.
>
> —Michel de Montaigne

The age of discovery, which opened up the New World for exploitation, created a confrontation of enormous economic and ultimately political significance: Western European colonists faced the otherness of themselves in the native inhabitants of the lands they sought to conquer. Despite accounts of indigenous peoples that often portrayed them as less than human, living an almost animal existence, they were nevertheless regarded as having souls worth saving in conjunction with the enslavement of their bodies and the plunder of their lands. The occasional enslavement of the aboriginal peoples of the New World never became an efficient operation. It was more expedient to bring over Africans, ripped from ties with their land, tradition, and families, to serve this purpose. On one end of the colonialist venture, native peoples were robbed and sporadically and systematically exterminated as Western Europeans spread throughout the Americas, and on the other end, a whole group of new inhabitants, the victims of cultural genocide, were relocated in various parts of the continent.

Slavery at the time of its inception was regarded as an economic necessity. However, by the early part of the nineteenth century changing technoeconomic conditions rendered slaveholding less viable than it had been in former generations. Also during this period news of atrocities committed by slave owners became widely publicized. Cries of moral outrage were expressed, and the issue became politically charged. On the conservative side of the debate, a number of thinkers regarded slavery and the extermination of native peoples as the inexorable result of progress—of a superior race displacing those of a lower order in the heroic struggle to tame the earth. Marx and Darwin disdained this attitude. Each in his own distinct way held that aboriginal peoples are unquestionably human, and therefore fully entitled to their land and lifeways, and consequently that slavery is morally reprehensible and constitutes a human violation of the highest magnitude. In addition to expressing an abolitionist sentiment, Marx and Darwin were concerned with the nature of primitive society as a contributor to an understanding of the human possibility. Their deep interest in these related subjects compels a comparative assessment.

While a number of nineteenth-century ideologues regarded aboriginal peoples as subhuman and their plight justified because of the inherently superior quality of the advancing civilizations, the previous two centuries had produced a number of significant thinkers who saw the primitive as something other than a distorted charicature of humanness.[1] In the late sixteenth century, Michel de Montaigne in his essay, "On Cannibals," created a portrait of primitive peoples that stressed the sublime reasonableness of their attitudes. This spirit of inquiry flourished during the Enlightenment with the concept of the noble savage inspired by Rousseau, although Rousseau never used the term so often attributed to him, nor was his idea of the state of nature synonymous with primitive society.

For Rousseau the state of nature is a hypothetical construct, a phenomenon "which no longer exists which perhaps never existed, which probably never will exist, and about which it is nevertheless necessary to have precise notions in order to judge our present state correctly."[2] Although the contemporary savage did not, according to Rousseau, live in the state of nature, he was closer to this condition of primal innocence, and primary human nature, than so-called civilized man. Rousseau took great delight in parts of *A Discourse on the Origin of Inequality* in pointing out the contradictions and superfluous aspects of Western civilization when seen through the critical eyes of the aboriginal. A similar technique was employed a generation earlier by Montesquieu in *The Persian Letters* and also by Rousseau's contemporary, Diderot, in his *Supplement au Voyage de Bougainville.*

Marx and Darwin both showed a keen interest in the nature of primitive society, believing that here were living replicas of the manner of life that characterized our early ancestors. They thought that an understanding of this period of social development could provide invaluable clues to the roots of our humanness. When Darwin regarded primitive peoples by drawing from his own experiences on board the *Beagle* and the anthropological writings of his contemporaries, Tylor and Lubbock, he was compelled to conclude, "Such were our ancestors" (*Descent,* 613).

Unlike Darwin, Marx did not have firsthand encounters with primitives. When referring to them in his early writings, he appears to have been influenced by the noble savage concept as it was expressed in romantic literature and by Rousseau's formulations. In his later work, just as he thoroughly assimilated the discoveries of nineteenth-century science, he absorbed the increasing number of new anthropological insights that began to proliferate around mid-century through the writings of Maine, Mclennan, Morgan, Tylor, Lubbock, and a number of lesser figures. The *Ethnological Notebooks,* composed shortly before his death and used as a resource by Engels in *The Origin of the Family, Private Property, and the State* (1884), are a testament to Marx's belief in the importance of comparative anthropology and his diligence in studying it.

For Marx, man "was a savage after he had ceased to be an ape" (*Critique Gotha,* 4). In this savage state, he became fully human for the first time, producing his means of subsistence through hunting and gathering in cooperating social groups. Marx and Darwin believed that many phenomena contained within their structure the vestige of past states of existence, and human nature is a prime example. Because we were once primitive, we still carry with us this quintessential humanness, and therefore studying man at all levels of history and prehistory can give us vital clues to understanding him as he now is, a perspective that has been central to modern anthropological inquiry.

The ideas of Marx and Darwin with regard to the position of

primitive peoples on the historical scale are representative of a nineteenth-century tradition known as social evolutionism. Despite the label *evolutionism*, this perspective did not originally owe its genesis to theories of biological evolution. In the previous century, it had able proponents in Rousseau, Turgot, Condorcet, and the Scottish moral philosophers Adam Ferguson, John Millar, and Adam Smith. They saw man evolving (*progressing* was the term often used) through a series of economic, social, and/or intellectual stages. The infamous "savagery," "barbarism," "civilization," typology had its origins during this time. In the nineteenth century Spencer, Maine, Lubbock, Tylor, Morgan, and Marx became heirs to this legacy. Darwin's inroad to the problems dealt with by social evolutionism did not come from insights provided by these intellectual precursors but through his own independent biological researches. These researches converged on a number of points with conclusions that were being formulated by more sociological and historical writers.

The social evolutionists (not to be confused with the later social Darwinists who espoused crude notions of social development based on a loose application of concepts taken from *The Origin of Species*) took a paternalistic attitude toward indigenous peoples, and Marx and Darwin were no exception. The non-European races were held to represent the childhood of the species. However, almost all of the social evolutionists shared a number of humanistic assumptions regarding non-Western peoples. They regarded them as fully human and believed that their seemingly bizarre behaviors had a logic in terms of the circumstances to which they were adapted. It was also held that if left to their own devices, primitives would eventually develop civilization, a contention that had been disputed by Rousseau who, in *A Discourse of the Origin of Inequality*, gave a number of critical reasons for primitives not desiring the civilized state. Following these criteria, a number of the social evolutionists declared that it is immoral to enslave primitives, pillage their land, or tamper with their way of life, an edict nineteenth-century imperialism completely disregarded.

The social evolutionist position, by regarding primitive culture as the first fully human stage in an inevitable ascent to civilization, paternalistic as it may have been, served to counter the contention that these people were remnants of a higher level of social order who had fallen from grace, which had been elaborated by degenerationist theorists such as Louis de Bonald, Joseph de Maistre, Richard Whately, and the duke of Argyll. The degenerationist or degradationist position was often used to justify an everlasting position of inferiority for the darker-skinned races, and Marx and Darwin had little patience with it.

DARWIN'S ETHNOGRAPHY

Unlike Marx, many of Darwin's conclusions regarding indigenous peoples derived from firsthand encounters. It may not be accurate to say that Darwin's writing in this area comprises an ethnography (an anthropological term referring to a descriptive account of a given people, usually non-Western) in the true sense, nevertheless he was among the first Europeans to observe a number of aboriginal groups, and the description of their lifeways contained in *The Voyage of the Beagle* constitutes a precious early record. Darwin's ethnographic work took place in the same context as his naturalistic observations. From December 1831 to October 1836, he undertook his monumental voyage around the world on the *Beagle*. The *Beagle* touched upon lands where the geology, flora, and fauna became the subject for research. Since native inhabitants were often found in the regions he visited—many of these natives had never seen a white man, firearms, or a ship—they became an inevitable source of curiosity and comment.

In his descriptive ethnography, Darwin exhibited several varying attitudes. In a most obvious manner, the raw humanity exhibited by primitive peoples, so alien to the European sensibility, never ceased to give him culture shock:

It was without exception the most curious and interesting spectacle I ever beheld. I could not have believed how wide was the difference between savage and civilized man: it is greater than the difference between a wild and domesticated animal, inasmuch as in man there is a greater power of improvement. . . . .

. . . .

. . . near Wallaston Island we pulled alongside a canoe with six Fuegians. These were the most abject and miserable creatures I anywhere beheld.... Viewing such men, one can hardly make one-self believe that they are fellow creatures and inhabitants of the same world. [*Voyage*, 205, 213]

These remarks reveal a bourgeois Victorian sensibility that would have amused Marx and Engels. The impact of his first encounter with the Fuegians stood rooted in Darwin's mind throughout his entire life. In the final page of *The Descent*, he remarked that he would as soon be descended from a heroic little monkey or the old baboon whose altruistic behavior he cited, as from a savage who commits torture, offers up sacrifices, and partakes in superstition. I believe that Darwin was expressing his ultimate preference for the morality of nature over not only savage society but the whole human race. The atrocities perpetrated in the name of civilization were as painfully obvious to him as were the actions of native peoples.

The eye Darwin had for discerning the logic in natural processes seems to have been impeded by a prudish sensibility that prevented him from grasping the logic in alien human behavior. His failure to deal with human beings on a level commensurate with his abilities as a naturalist has been noted by biographers on several occasions.[3] Darwin was a brilliant naturalist who, when confronted with an extraordinary and exotic ethnographic situation, produced a response that was short of being outstanding. Nevertheless, in comparison to other accounts rendered during that era, most of them unsystematic and impressionistic, Darwin's ethnography does not appear quite so inept. Perhaps it is because his insights into geology and biology were so astute that his ethnography seems shallow in comparison. This is not to say that he did not commit a number of blunders. His observations were sometimes superficial, as was his use of informants. In one instance, he incorrectly concluded from a limited survey that the Fuegians practiced cannibalism. He also described their language as being "scarcely... articulate" (*Voyage*, 206), echoing an observation Cook had made a number of years earlier.

Darwin's indignant attitude toward primitives was steeped in a subjectivity rarely found in his purely scientific writings, although he did have a tendency to anthropomorphize animals. This subjectivity was nevertheless accompanied by the belief that groups like the Fuegians must not be as "miserable" (a frequently used adjective) as they appear:

There is no reason to believe that the Fuegians decrease in number; therefore we must suppose that they enjoy a sufficient share of happiness of whatever kind it may be, to render life worth having. Nature in making habit omnipotent, and its effects hereditary has fitted the Fuegian to the climate and productions of his miserable country. [Ibid., 217]

Darwin realized that a human group like the Fuegians, having endured through time despite their impoverished circumstances, must be doing something right in order to be adapted to so harsh an environment. But, why they chose to leave the rich areas to the north to settle on the bleak tip of South America puzzled him.

With reference to his observation that the Fuegians are not decreasing in number, we must remember that although contact eventually led to their extermination directly, and indirectly through disease, this was not yet apparent during the 1830s. Nevertheless Darwin did observe such processes taking place among other indigenous groups and expressed deep lament over the situation: "I think there will not in another half century be another wild Indian northward of the Rio Negroe. . . .It is melancholy to trace how the Indians have given way before the Spanish invaders" (ibid., 104). Darwin saw indigenous cultures as unique and precious species experiments, their equilibrium upset not by a failure to adapt to a natural situation but through contamination by the alien and overwhelming power of civilization.

Although Darwin's attitude toward non-European races may have been ethnocentric and naive, it was also laced with a compassion that made apparent the noblest aspects of his nature. It is a tribute to his powers of reasoning that despite the affront they caused to his prudish sensibility, he believed them to be fully human. This is nowhere more obvious than in the outrage he expressed in his narrative at the extermination of aboriginal peoples throughout South America, and in his vehement and unyielding opposition to slavery. He adhered to these views throughout his life. They resurfaced significantly in his assessment of the race question in *The Descent* and subsequent conclusion that all of mankind comprises one species. In these writings, Darwin spoke as a humanist and moralist, aspects of his personality history has tended to overlook.

The Voyage of the Beagle chronicles the extermination of native peoples wherever Darwin encountered it, either through first-hand experiences or by information provided through European informants who regarded the procedure as nothing reprehensible and were more than willing to discuss it. Darwin recounts several such incidents in detail, and it is surprising that his message did not have more impact on European audiences. He reacted to one massacre with the comment, "Who would believe in this age that such atrocities could be committed in a Christian civilized country?" (ibid., 103). Darwin's most readable book, *The Voyage of the Beagle*, an apparently innocent travel narrative intended for a wide audience, is in fact one of the most telling documents on the subject of genocide produced in the nineteenth century.

Darwin's outrage was directed primarily at Spanish colonials in South America. He believed the situation in the British colonies was considerably better, and in those British colonies that he visited, particularly in the Pacific, there were significant differences. However, it must be remembered that the *Beagle* did no research in Africa, or Darwin might have been less laudatory of the British effort. In the colonial skirmishes that he carefully chronicled in the *Beagle* narrative, Darwin's sympathy was always on the side of the natives. On a number of occasions, he commented on the gallant resistance of the natives in a manner expressing admiration for their actions. The following is typical:

To avoid the shots, the Indian rode in the peculiar method of his nation; namely, with an arm around the horse's neck, and one leg only on its back. Thus hanging on one side he was seen patting the horse's head, and talking to him. The pursuers urged every effort in the chase; the Commandant three times changed his horse, but all in vain. The old Indian father and his son escaped and were free. What a fine picture one can form in one's mind—the naked, bronze-like figure of the old man with his little boy, riding like a Mazeppa on the white horse, thus leaving far behind him the host of his pursuers! [Ibid., 105]

No moral and political issue caused Darwin to be more outspoken than the case against slavery. Throughout his life he was an ardent abolitionist. He supported the North in the American Civil War with an ardor matching that of Marx and Engels. Slavery was rampant in Brazil when he visited it: "On the 19th of August we finally left the shores of Brazil. I thank God I shall never again visit a slave-country" (ibid., 497). He regarded what he saw in Brazil as moral debasement in the extreme. In grim detail, he told of tortures, beatings, and the cruelty inherent in breaking apart families to sell individual members to different owners: "And these deeds are done and palliated by men, who profess to love their neighbors as themselves, who believe in God, and pray that his Will be done on Earth" (ibid., 498). On one occasion he intervened in order to prevent the beating of a slave from continuing. He frequently expressed outrage at the way escaped slaves were hunted down. The very fact that slaves would risk their lives to escape impressed him considerably. With an air of respect he recounted one instance where a woman jumped from a mountain to her death rather than be led back again into slavery: "In a Roman matron this would have been called the noble love of freedom: in a poor negress it is mere brutal obstinancy" (ibid., 20).

Darwin's disdain for slavery was of such magnitude that on one occasion it put his situation on the *Beagle* into jeopardy. Fitz-Roy, the ship's captain, a proponent of slavery and an ardent fundamentalist as well, sought to convert Darwin to the pro-slavery position. He told him of a Brazilian slaveowner who assembled his slaves and asked them if they wished to be free; all answered in the negative. Darwin's response to FitzRoy was that a slave's answer in the presence of his master was of dubious worth (ibid., xv). FitzRoy, a volatile and unstable man, became enraged, accusing Darwin of doubting his character and banishing him from the captain's mess. Had FitzRoy not apologized to Darwin shortly afterward, the voyage might have terminated prematurely or have been considerably uncomfortable for the young naturalist.

Later in the expedition, several people spoke to Darwin of slavery as a tolerable evil, pointing out the gaiety exhibited by many Negroes. Darwin commented in his journal that the belief in the gaiety of the slave generally derives from those who observed domestic slaves from upper-class houses. The situation is much grimmer, he noted, among field slaves attached to the less-prosperous lower class. Darwin added that it would also be in a slave's own best interests to give a positive assessment of his situation when asked: "The slave must indeed be dull who does not calculate on the chance of his answer reaching his masters ears" (ibid., 497). That the attack on slavery was of paramount importance to Darwin is illustrated in the fact that he restated his position with renewed emphasis in the conclusion to the *Beagle* narrative.

The polemic against slavery notwithstanding, *The Voyage of the Beagle* is essentially an engaging literary account of Darwin's observations of natural phenomena and alien cultures. As a source of ethnographic information his work cannot be disregarded. During the nineteenth century, formal anthropological accounts were rare, and the usual travelers' tales and missionary accounts were often unreliable. Some of the best anthropological field-work at that time was done by figures who, like Darwin, were more renowned for other accomplishments. Herman Melville spent several months on a South Pacific island, and this experience was incorporated into his novel *Typee*. Robert Louis Stevenson's *In the South Seas* was the culmination of much traveling and observing in that region. Darwin's account of the *Beagle* voyage contains passable ethnography biased by the bourgeois attitudes of his era and social class. The book also reveals the spark of a talent for writing that flourished only sporadically in his other works.

When Darwin first saw the Fuegians, he felt as if he had been transported back into prehistory. These nearly naked inhabitants of the southern tip of South America lived primarily through hunting and fishing in a land where temperatures hover near freezing year round and winds and rain pound mercilessly. He gave a useful description of their life situation, but it remained colored by his initial awe at the starkness of their circumstances. He commented on their customs and behavior with some objectivity; however, when it came to dealing with their language, political organization, and religion, he was considerably less thorough. He concluded that they scarcely possessed articulate speech, had no government, and were lacking any semblance of religious worship. Their ability to withstand the cold, wearing hardly any clothes, was a constant source of amazement to him and probably one of the main reasons why he classified them as the most primitive of all human groups. He evaluated the Fuegians against the Eskimos, who he contended were more skillful in the arts of life; the South Sea islanders, who were "comparatively civilized"; the tribes of southern Africa, who were "sufficiently wretched"; and the Australian aborigines, the people who he believed come nearest to the Fuegians in primitiveness, although their ability to manufacture the boomerang, spear, and throwing stick give them a slight edge (ibid., 231).

Darwin observed aboriginal groups only from a distance. He never lived among them for any length of time or attempted a thorough study of their culture. Nevertheless, he did have a firsthand acquaintanceship with three Fuegians—two males, York Minster and Jemmy Button, and a female, Fuegia Basket—who had been brought to England by FitzRoy on an earlier voyage. His plan was to civilize them, convert them to Christianity, and then release them among their own people in the hope that they would transmit these enlightening qualities to fellow tribesmen. The plan failed completely, for upon being returned to their countrymen they quickly reverted to their native ways. Darwin appears to have been unable to extract much information from the three, although he did note that they were quick to learn a number of skills while on board the ship. They all spoke and understood a good deal of English, and when Fuegia Basket spent time ashore in Rio de Janeiro and Montevideo she easily acquired some Portuguese and Spanish as well. Clearly the favorite of the three was Jemmy Button:

It seems wonderful to me, when I think over all his many good qualities, that he should have been of the same race, and doubtless partaken of the same character, with the miserable, degraded savages whom we first met here. [Ibid., 208]

It is impossible to overestimate the importance of Darwin's contact with the three Fuegians when considering his concept of human nature. They were individuals from a desolate part of the earth exhibiting a way of life only fractions away from what he believed to be an animal state, and yet the improvement they demonstrated in learning over so short a span of time astounded him. Although he never did regard them as the full psychological equals of Europeans, the fact that in a few years they almost attained "civilized" status caused him to infer that the human species was so modifiable that even the lowest savage, given favorable circumstances, could become fully civilized in a generation or two. Human nature, even though hierarchically cast among the various races, was, in Darwin's opinion a mutable phenomenon.

Several years later, Darwin's friend and colleague, A. R. Wallace, pondered the same problem from a different angle: "The more I see of uncivilized people, the better I think of human nature, . . . and the essential differences between civilized and savage men seem to disappear."[4] He noted that the mental capacities of savages were hardly inferior to those of civilized men, and this caused him to question natural selection as the crucial factor in the evolution of mind. Wallace believed that man's intellectual development had reached a high level in the prehistoric past, perhaps through the intervention of some higher intelligence.[5] For Wallace a group's learned repertoire of behavior, its culture, could vary greatly and independently of the innate capacity of mind. Wallace held that mind, or mental potential, is fairly constant throughout the species, a modern notion that we can now explain through neo-Darwinian evolutionary theory and modern genetics.

Wallace's separation of mind from the evolutionary continuum disturbed Darwin: "I hope you have not murdered too completely your own and my child" (*Life*, 1:211). Darwin would have none of Wallace's recourse to an external agent. His own experiences with savages led him to conclude that there are a number of differences between savage and civilized man in terms of mind and a crucial similarity: the force of habit and the inheritance of acquired habits. Darwin said very little about the inheritance of acquired characteristics when dealing with plants and animals; however, because man is capable of learning so much in such a short space of time (the capacity for improvement among savages providing vivid evidence for this), he invoked the inheritance of acquired habits as a distinguishing feature of the human species. Wallace was critical of this tendency in Darwin, though he offered no alternative when dealing with mental development in the species save a recourse to the intervention of higher intelligence.

Although several nineteenth-century theorists grappled with the culture-human nature problem, Edward Tylor came closest to approximating the modern position. In his *Anthropology* (1881), Tylor saw the capacity for culture arising through Darwinian processes. To this universal foundation he added a concept of culture that conceived the phenomenon in a cumulative and historical sense. Cultural evolution became explicable in terms of its own patterns and processes and by selectionist principles but without recourse to any mental-genetic evolution. For Tylor, the differences among cultures are historical and quantitative.[6] Yet to understand culture in its qualitative and universal sense, he endeavored to adapt and extend Darwin's evolutionary methodology.

Darwin's archetypal savage always remained a Fuegian. They were unforgettable—the most archaic society that he encountered and the one he observed most thoroughly. After leaving the land of the Fuegians, the *Beagle* touched on a number of other ethnographic provinces, and Darwin observed the inhabitants with great curiosity. Although not directly critical of civilization in the manner of some of the Enlightenment philosophers, Darwin nevertheless saw its contact with native peoples, through the colonial situation, bringing about considerable evil. He often gave capsule commentaries on the political situation of the countries he visited and in several instances noted that poverty and human exploitation were not only confined to the natives but also inflicted by the ruling colonizers upon their own ethnics of lower social status.

When the *Beagle* crossed the Pacific and entered the legendary paradise of the South Sea islands, Darwin was captivated. Regarding Tahiti he remarked, "I was pleased with nothing so much as the inhabitants" (*Voyage*, 404). These inhabitants were the complete antithesis of the natives of Tierra del Fuego. To Darwin, they evidenced a mildness of manner that banished the idea of a savage and an "intelligence which shows that they are advancing in civilization" (ibid.). He marveled at their athletic appearance and described the tattoos adorning their bodies as

elegant and noble, not repulsive, as previous observers had referred to them. But Darwin was not carried away by the concept
of the noble savage. He pointed out that the Tahitians are children of the tropics whose reasoning power is not fully developed. Perhaps what impressed him most about the Tahitians—and
it is an aspect of the South Sea peoples that has impressed
travelers from the time of first contact—was their constantly
happy temperaments, a sharp contrast to the dour attitude of
the Fuegians.

When the *Beagle* sailed to New Zealand, Darwin remarked
that the natives of that land were closer to the savage state than
other Polynesian peoples. The final "precivilized" society that
he visited for any length of time was the Australian aborigines.
In his view, they were not as degraded as he had anticipated,
and their admirable skill in the arts of survival induced him to
rank them on a higher level than the Fuegians. In Australia as
elsewhere, Darwin saw the ravages of the white man, greed,
and various diseases leading to the extermination of yet another
human group, and he expressed a sincere and profound lament
over the situation.

DARWIN ON RACE

When Darwin wrote *The Descent of Man*, he addressed himself
to three major questions. The first was whether man, like every
other species, is descended from some preexisting form; the
second, the manner of his development; and third, the value of
the differences among the so-called races of man (*Descent*, 2). A
considerable portion of the work deals with racial variation. The
bulk of this analysis is confined to physical, as opposed to mental, characteristics. The reason for this emphasis is revealed in
the sequel to *The Descent*, *The Expression of the Emotions in Man
and Animals*. In short, Darwin believed that the mental characteristics of the various races evidence greater similarity than the
physical characteristics. A major research tool contributing to
this conclusion was the questionnaire (*Expression*, 15-16) he composed in 1867 and circulated to a number of remote outposts
having intimate contacts with native peoples. The questionnaire

endeavored to gather information on the expressions and gestures found among the various races. The results convinced
Darwin that the mental similarities among the races far overwhelmed the physical differences:

It follows from the information thus acquired that the same state of
mind is expressed throughout the world with remarkable uniformity;
and this fact is in itself interesting as evidence of the close similarity
in . . . mental disposition of all the races of mankind. [Ibid., 17]

In the conclusion to this work, Darwin noted that the theory
of expression, based as it is on so many concrete examples,
"supports the belief of the specific or subspecific unity of the
several races" (ibid., 365). It is unfortunate that subsequent history has paid so little heed to this aspect of his legacy. When
Darwin and race have been discussed in the same context, it has
usually been as a result of the subtitle of *The Origin*—*The Preservation of Favoured Races in the Struggle for Life*. The term *race* in the
subtitle refers not to human physical diversity but simply to
variations in species throughout nature. The term *struggle* signifies a struggle against the environment, not a warlike conflict
between individuals and groups. Social Darwinists tended to
appropriate Darwin's often catchy phrases, applying them su-
perficially and out of context. They also ignored aspects of his
work incompatible with their political philosophy, an example
being his belief in the unity of the races.

The central axis around which Darwin's observations on race
in *The Descent* revolve is the notion that mankind, despite racial
variation, is one species. He noted that in the population of any
race, there is considerable diversity. As an example, he cited the
Australian aborigines, a group held by many to be an example of
racial homogeneity. Darwin demonstrated that even in one tribe,
individuals vary considerably in facial and bodily proportions.
He never fell into the classic ethnocentric trap whereby all people in a given exotic group are said to look alike: "The uniformity
of savages has often been exaggerated and in some cases can
hardly be said to exist" (*Descent*, 27). It is also inaccurate to
assume that there is mental uniformity among individuals of
any racial group in a manner akin to domestic animals because

man's breeding has never been controlled: "No race or body of men has been so completely subjugated by other men, as that certain individuals should be preserved, and thus unconsciously selected, from somehow excelling in utility to their masters" (ibid., 28). This is a direct refutation of the belief that the darker-skinned peoples are ordained, either by God or evolution, for slave status. Darwin added that rather than resembling the homogeneity of domestic animals, the races of man exhibit the variability found in widely ranging species. Groups such as the Polynesians and American Indians have extensive geographical territories, and like widely ranging animal species they exhibit a variability continuous with the variability exhibited by all of mankind. Darwin's approach thus avoids the possibility of misleading racial stereotypes.

For Darwin, the most weighty argument against treating the races of man as distinct species is the fact they grade into one another even when there is no evidence of intercrossing. He remarked that the races can hardly be said to constitute clearly defined units when we note the lack of consistency on the part of writers trying to classify them. In his era the number of races was held to be as few as two and as many as sixty or more. Any conscientious naturalist, according to Darwin, upon perceiving the continuous racial gradation in the human species and the fact that it is doubtful "whether any character can be named which is distinctive of a race and is constant" (ibid., 170), would have to conclude that he was dealing with variations within a single species. These variations are obvious in all of the major racial groups. Darwin used this to buttress a monogenesist argument (the belief in a common rather than a separate origin for the races of mankind).

Although he strongly attacked the notion that human variation is of such magnitude that the different geographical groups constitute separate species, Darwin was not opposed to using the concept of subspecies to describe the phenomenon, although he appears to have been uncomfortable with it. He preferred the term *race*, which he used in a flexible sense to designate a series of traits he believed were in constant flux. It did not signify an unyielding set of fixed morphological categories. Darwin noted that the races of man, unlike animal species, when coexisting in the same geographical locale, freely interbreed and often produce a series of complex crossings. Writing from experience, he recalled a mixture of Indian, Negro, and Portuguese he saw in Brazil and the Indian and Spanish crossing in Chile, noting that the offspring in both cases were vigorous and viable.

For Darwin, the main difference among the races was the obvious one of physical appearance. Races differ in constitution, skin color, bodily proportions, acclimatization, and susceptibility to certain diseases. Because groups inhabiting similar geographical areas in similar latitudes could have different skin coloring, as is the case with South American Indians and Africans, Darwin concluded that a purely environmental explanation for skin color must be inadequate:

With our present knowledge we cannot account for the differences of color in the races of man through any advantage gained, or from the direct action of climate; yet we must not ignore the latter agency, for there is good reason to believe that some inherited effect is thus produced. [Ibid., 191]

To explain the physical differences among races, Darwin leaned heavily in the direction of the preferential mating he termed sexual selection: "Of all the causes which have led to the differences in external appearance between the races of man, and to a certain extent between man and the lower animals, sexual selection has been the most efficient" (ibid., 600). Although the mystery of racial coloration is by no means solved, today we tend to look to natural selection acting either directly or indirectly on the environmental circumstances rather than to sexual selection. Since Darwin adhered heavily to the inheritance of acquired characteristics when dealing with man, it puzzled him when skin color did not change in response to environmental situations over observable generations. We now know that such changes can take place only over a vast expanse of time (when race mixture does not hasten the situation) and that population movements and secondary adaptations make the search for connections between environment and racial traits exceedingly complex.[7]

In the realm of mind, Darwin did not believe that all races were equally endowed. Because of his belief in the inheritance of acquired characteristics, he confused what was learned—cultural content—with its genetic substrate—the capacity for culture. Today with the benefit of modern genetics and the extensive cross-cultural work of anthropologists, we know that the intelligence required to learn any given culture is uniform throughout the species. This uniformity is often referred to as the principle of psychic unity. The fact that Orientals raised in America or blacks in cosmopolitan Europe easily acquire the manners and customs of their cultural contexts does not surprise us because we know it is an instance of learned behavior, not biological transformation. The startling changes that can take place in the repertoire of a group or individual in a generation or two led Darwin to assume that the differences "between the highest men of the highest races and the lowest savages, are connected by the finest gradations.... Therefore it is possible that they might pass over and be developed into each other" (*Descent*, 64). The whole matter of racial intelligence was for Darwin a continual series of gradations in which exposure to a learning situation could produce startling changes in an individual no matter what his race. As far as he was concerned, this process had no limitations. Over 100 years ago, he stood in firm opposition to the position advocated today in a number of quarters that a race can have a particular bent of mind that impairs its capacity to be educated in a certain direction. Nevertheless, his rationale for these assumptions always remained the inheritance of acquired habits and not the belief in a uniform panracial psychic structure.

When evaluating the mental state of the various races, Darwin strongly believed that although differences exist, they are greatly outweighed by the similarities:

The American Aborigines, Negroes, and Europeans are as different from each other in mind as any three races than can be named; yet I was incessantly struck whilst living with the Fuegians on Board the "Beagle", with the many little traits of character showing how similar their minds were to ours; and so it was with a full-blooded negroe with whom I happened once to be intimate. [Ibid., 174]

Shifting away from personal experience, he cited the work of Tylor and Lubbock on the close similarities of the various races in terms of taste, disposition, and habit, manifested in such universal phenomena as music, painting, and language. Darwin followed Tylor's assumption that because various artifacts, like the bow, are found in so many cultures around the world, this must indicate similar operations of the mind in the different races. Darwin's affirmation of the human status of primitive peoples is especially noteworthy considering the shocked sensibility and ethnocentrism that he displayed when describing his encounters with them. These prejudiced descriptions undoubtedly contributed to the racist climate of opinion of the period, and any thorough historical assessment of Darwin must evaluate the impact of these personal asides, as well as his liberal scientific intentions.

MARX, PRIMITIVE SOCIETY, AND THE HUMAN POSSIBILITY

Not having firsthand encounters with primitive peoples did not deter Marx and Engels from making numerous comments about them. In his early writings dealing with the concept of generic man, Marx made reference to the mode of social and productive organization found in savage society. His comments are highly impressionistic, and no source was cited. In later years when he was concerned less with human nature and more interested in history, he found that an understanding of the earliest stages of history (he used the term *prehistory*) became essential. He cited several authors, both social evolutionists and universal historians, in the first volume of *Das Kapital* with reference to their descriptions of non-Western and archaic societies.

After the first volume of *Das Kapital* was published, Marx became increasingly interested in non-Western and archaic societies, probably because of two related facts: a growing belief that history cannot be understood in its entirety until its earliest stages are known in some detail and the great proliferation of studies in anthropology and social evolution that took place in the late nineteenth century. Since Marx was always attuned to the major intellectual developments of his age and their relationship to his own sphere of interest—this is one reason why he immediately grasped Darwin—he was quick to recognize the work of Morgan, Maine, Lubbock, and others on non-Western and primitive peoples. The important but unfinished result of this preoccupation can be found in *The Ethnological Notebooks of Karl Marx*, recently compiled with an introduction by Lawrence Krader.[8] Any comprehensive study of Marx's intellectual development will now have to consider the fascination with anthropology that resulted in these manuscripts.

The Ethnological Notebooks were drafted between 1880 and 1882, shortly before Marx died. He excerpted, compiled for future reference, and critically reviewed the ethnological writings of Morgan, Maine, Phear, Lubbock, and a number of lesser figures. The subjects covered include prehistory, ancient history, and the ethnological study of living peoples. Marx was not uncritical in the assessment of these materials. He was widely enough read in the field to question a number of assumptions. His ethnological knowledge also caused him to be disturbed by the contempt that seeped through John Budd Phear's writings on the peasants of Bengal, the lack of feeling Maine had regarding the Irish, and the obvious ethcentrism in Lubbock, Grote, Gladstone, and Bachofen.[9]

In the introduction to *The Ethnological Notebooks*, Krader remarks that during the latter part of the nineteenth century, the "sciences of man had co-opted the field of ethnology, and anthropology from the philosophical study of the same undertaken by Kant, Hegel, Fichte, Feuerbach, a tradition out of which Marx emerged."[10] The philosophical tradition in anthropology was the source for much of Marx's early writings on generic man and the nature of society. Eventually an empirical tradition, evidencing a concern for the actual study of concrete societies, broke away and established independence, and Marx carefully followed its development. No writer since has so thoroughly spanned the two traditions. As Krader points out, the position in philosophical anthropology Marx developed between 1841 and 1846 has particular relevance to the material brought to light in the later *Ethnological Notebooks*.[11]

Although he dealt with several writers at length in *The Ethnological Notebooks*, Marx thought most highly of the American Lewis Henry Morgan whose *Ancient Society* (1877) has become an anthropological landmark. His desire to present to a German audience the results of Morgan's research in light of his own was fulfilled after his death when Engels wrote *The Origin of the*

Family, Private Property, and the State. Morgan's work is breathtaking in scope and detail, and though it contains a number of errors, compounded by Engels, it is probably the richest source of data and theory on primitive society produced during the nineteenth century. Assessments of Morgan's work abound in anthropology.[12] Of note is Terray's recent argument that Morgan anticipated several major theoretical perspectives developed in twentieth-century anthropology.[13] Engels indicated his enthusiasm for Morgan in a letter to Karl Kautsky, dated April 28, 1884: "Morgan makes it possible for us to look at things from entirely new points of view by supplying us in his prehistory, with a factual foundation that was missing hitherto" (*Moscow*, 776).

In addition to prolific material on comparative social organization, Morgan provided Marx and Engels with an affirmation for the early opinions they had regarding the natural division of labor in primitive society and its unalienated nature. Primitive society, even before its full implications were grasped, gave Marx and Engels an idealized model for the full realization of human potential. They saw civilization, with its artificial as opposed to natural division of labor, as forcing the fullness of human nature into highly specialized social roles. In the hypothetical communist society of the future, new roles would successively be acquired by an individual, and these roles would broaden his humanity rather than reduce it to any one function. The inspiration for this clearly derives from a romantic concept of the primitive:

In communist society, where nobody has one exclusive sphere of activity but each man can become accomplished in any branch he wishes, society regulates the general production and thus makes it possible for me to do one thing today and another tomorrow, to hunt in the morning, fish in the afternoon, rear cattle in the evening, criticize after dinner, just as I have a mind, without ever becoming hunter, fisherman, shepherd or critic. [*German Ideology*, 65]

This eloquent vision was connected to the belief that in primitive society, man's social and natural relations are reduced to their most fundamental and authentic levels. In this primary and irreducibly human social mode, the division of labor results from natural divisions such as age, sex, and seasonality (*Capital*, 1:78). Man transforms nature, and the products of nature's harvest are consumed by the producers themselves. Although Marx regarded the savage state as the childhood of the species, he believed that in no other historical epoch do physical and mental activity align more harmoniously nor does the social take on a more egalitarian frame (*German Ideology*, 81). At the economic level, he emphasized that weaving, making clothing, and herding are direct social functions—products of the families' labor—and not commodities in the capitalist sense. (*Capital*, 1:78). Extending the thrust of Marx's argument by drawing from Morgan's ethnological studies, Engels defined the natural egalitarianism found in primitive society:

They are each master in their own sphere: the man in the forest, the woman in the house. Each is owner of the instruments which he or she makes and uses: the man of the weapons, the hunting and fishing implements; the woman of the household gear. The housekeeping is communal among several and often many families. What is made and used in common is common property—the house, the garden, the long boat. Here therefore, and here alone, there still exists in actual fact that "property created by the owner's labor" which in civilized society is an ideal fiction of the jurists and economists, the last lying legal pretense by which modern capitalist property still bolsters itself up. [*Origin Family*, 218]

RACE AND HISTORY

Because the materialist conception of history gives weight to both economic and biological factors, it leaves open the possibility that a given stage in history can be racially determined, at least be in part. Marx never exercised this option. When his materialism did refer to things biological, it was usually to generic attributes common to all human beings. In *Mein Kampf*, Hitler specifically attacked Marx for recognizing the equal value of all races.[14] This is not to suggest that Marx held a position on race equivalent to the principle of psychic unity established in the twentieth century by Boasian anthropology, a perspective few nineteenth-century thinkers were even close to conceptualizing. Marx's position on race appears to derive from Enlightenment notions of perfectibility. This view holds that the darker-skinned races constitute raw yet nonetheless authentic humanity capable of being improved (*perfected* is the term often used) when placed under favorable circumstances.

One contemporary critic of Marx and Engels, Conway Zirkle, has claimed that the two were racists because they believed in the inheritance of acquired characteristics.[15] Although they did hold such assumptions, to label them racist on this basis is to render an unfair historical judgment. Nearly every major nineteenth-century social thinker held that acquired characteristics are inherited and that there are *psychological* differences among races. Despite holding these views, which never became formally discredited by science until the twentieth century, Marx, Engels, Morgan, Tylor, and Darwin were radicals in their own time on the race issue. They diverged from the accepted standards of their day and expounded positions remarkably consonant with contemporary knowledge. Zirkle tries to strengthen his indictment of Marx by quoting from a letter to Engels in which Marx referred to Lassalle as a "Jewish Nigger," apparently blaming Lassalle's attitudes on his alleged ancestry.[16] But, Zirkle has neglected the other side of the coin. Because of his swarthy appearance, Marx's nickname was "moor," and he was intensely proud of it. He was also proud of the fact that Paul Lafargue, husband of his daughter Laura, was of "colored descent." Also when Theodore Cuno, a close friend of the family, informed Marx that he was going to America, Marx spoke to him of the advantages of marrying across racial lines.[17]

Throughout his theoretical writings, Marx always avoided equating race with a particular historical epoch. When Max Stirner likened the childish state of antiquity to the Negro character and early civilization to the Mongoloid character, Marx was mockingly critical (*German Ideology*, 172-74). Wherever the fetters of slavery were being shed, Marx and Engels showed unbridled enthusiasm. In Jamaica, when former slaves became self-sustaining peasants producing only what they needed for their own consumption, much to the chagrin of local plantation owners, Marx found the situation delightfully rational (*Grundrisse*, 325-26). Like Darwin, he opposed slavery on every front, supported the North in the American Civil War, and was an admirer of Lincoln. Opinions regarding the Negro as a naturally ordained mindless laborer, necessarily dependent on a master, were fiercely attacked

(*Capital*, 2:385-86). Unlike Aristotle, whom he revered as the foremost philosopher of the ancient world, Marx did not regard slavery as an expression of the natural inequalities among human groups. To him, the phenomenon resulted from a particular economic and social situation whereby the owner of the means of production, in conjunction with the owner of labor power, could purchase labor power by buying the laborer himself (*Capital*, 3:385). The Negro slave is not an inherently inferior being; he is placed in such a position by the economic power of society: "a negro... only becomes a slave in certain relations" (*Wage Labour*, 28).

The most telling evidence linking any nineteenth-century thinker to a racist stance is not personal innuendo or provisional scientific hypotheses like the inheritance of acquired characteristics but actual political practice. As Marx stated in his eighth thesis on Feuerbach, "All mysteries which mislead theory find their rational solution in human practice and in the comprehension of this practice" (*Feuerbach*, 84). In the area of political practice, there is little evidence to indicate that Marx's attack on various forms of racist exploitation was anything less than whole-hearted.

Engels and Evolutionary Theory

> From the moment of birth we are immersed in action and can
> only fitfully guide it by taking thought.
> —Alfred North Whitehead

During the waning years of his life, Marx was almost totally preoccupied with the economic analysis contained in *Das Kapital*. This did not prevent him from reading a wide range of scientific and anthropological literature, but it did thwart his efforts to write formally in these areas. Engels was perennially at his side, urging him on in his study of the capitalist system. When Marx died in 1883, with much of his work still incomplete, it was Engels who inherited the task of rendering publishable the second and third volumes of *Das Kapital*. Engels was also aware of the ethnological notebooks Marx had begun compiling in 1880, and the mantle of responsibility for revising and extending these unfinished sketches also fell on his shoulders. The result was *The Origin of the Family, Private Property, and the State*.

While Marx struggled intermittently to complete the second and third volumes of *Das Kapital*, Engels was making numerous and often extensive researches into the natural sciences. On the death of Marx, these studies had to be curtailed in favor of ordering the remainder of Marx's work. How deeply Engels would have probed eventually into scientific theory or how systematic his published results might ultimately have been remain a matter for speculation. It appears highly plausible that his *Dialectics of Nature*, a series of unfinished scientific essays drafted between 1872 and 1880 and published posthumously, could have led to a finished text containing excerpts from Marx's mathematical manuscripts.

The collaboration between Marx and Engels was close and enduring. It is almost amazing then that in the West so much recent literature on Marx has been devoted to revealing a number of divergent points supposed to have existed between them. In these arguments, Darwin often looms as a crucial figure. Fascination with his work and the natural sciences in general is attributed to Engels—not Marx. The effort to separate the scientifically inclined views of Engels from the alleged humanistic vision of Marx stems from the tendency to see the latter in a more critical-philosophical light, particularly one that is Hegelian in tone. This is in part a reaction to the stigma against the association between Marx and science deriving from the Soviet connection, Lenin and Stalin, who tried to transform Marxism into an all-embrasive scientific world view—one that would have been alien to both Marx and Engels.

The new philosophical interpretation of Marx has also been used to criticize a number of earlier, again often Soviet-inspired, interpretations,[1] dividing him into a young, impressionistic humanist and later a more mature and rigorous social scientist. In arguing for a positive assessment of the early Marx and for continuity in his writing, critics like Lichtheim and Avineri have done so at the expense of Engels's and Marx's devout interest in science. For example Engels's explorations into the natural sciences, specifically evolutionary theory, have been described by Lichtheim as private interests diverging from those of Marx and possessing only the remotest connection with his viewpoint,[2] and by Avineri as vulgarizations of Darwinism and biology irreconcilable with Marx's perspective.[3]

Placing a line of discontinuity between Marx and Engels is as erroneous as placing one between the early and the later Marx. It is paradoxical that the argument in favor of a Marx-Engels polarization is used to bolster notions regarding the Hegelian influence in Marx's thought and the importance of the early humanistic writings, concerns for which I have considerable sympathy. They can stand on their own merits and do not require for justification the disavowal of either Marx's scientific proclivities or the role played by Engels in the development of Marx's ideas.

The argument for unity rather than divergence in the writings of Marx and Engels is far from being fashionable in current circles of Marx scholarship in the West. Nevertheless my position is not totally devoid of support. Peter Sedgwick, in a critique directed at Herbert Marcuse's failure to comprehend the significance of the natural sciences in Marxian theory, has justly condemned the widely accepted interpretation of Marx that sees him as the Jesus or Socrates of critical social theory whose teachings have been perverted into an all-embracing doctrine of nature by the Saint Paul-Plato figure of Engels.[4] Sedgwick comments that any discussion of Marx and Engels that fails to communicate their lifelong mental rapport is seriously defective. In response to the current status quo position in the West on the Marx-Engels discontinuity, he wryly remarks, "Against the weight of scholarship, associated with this view, I can only press on regardless."[5] In a similar vein, Bertell Ollman, who has done extensive research on the early Marx, contends that Marx was completely familiar with and fully supportive of Engels's scientific and philosophical writings.[6] This point necessitates further elaboration. Therefore before examining Engels's scientific formulations, in which Darwin is a central figure, I will marshal evidence to indicate that Marx was, or would have been, in accord with most of these views. Unfortunately, any effort to deal with Engels's life and thought must contend with limited biographical materials. Although a great deal exists regarding Marx, albeit of varying quality, a definitive, comprehensive, and up-to-date biography of Engels has yet to be written.[7]

THE MARX-ENGELS RELATIONSHIP

For two thinkers so much of a mind, a contention that has to receive strong support from their extensive collaboration, Marx and Engels had very different temperaments. In their major works, they also illustrate idiosyncratic and contrasting writing styles. Style in communication may be a crucial, if as yet unacknowledged, factor contributing to current opinion regarding the divergence of their thought. It is possible, and highly plausible in the case of Marx and Engels, for two writers to share a common intellectual world view and a political philosophy yet express themselves on the matter in quite different ways. Marx was a profound, unyielding intellect whose convoluted philosophical style, steeped in multiple meanings, probed to the depths of any problem he tackled. When covering similar ground, Engels did so in an easy, engaging manner; his style is lighter, almost journalistic. At times both writers were witty. In Marx, this tendency is expressed in the form of a biting sarcasm. Engels's humor is less searing, frequently mocking in tone, and more often than not overdone.

While Marx's writing drills to the core a limited number of subjects, Engels more casually elaborates the relevant insights of a staggering number of disciplines. Not only did Engels study history, economics, chemistry, physics, astronomy, and languages, he also composed choral music and was an excellent illustrator. He peered into almost every crevice of human understanding. His fascination with military history led to the nickname "General." Had he not served Marx, it has been claimed that he might have been remembered as one of the foremost philosopher-scientists of the nineteenth century.[8] Not only was he one of the most learned men of his day, he was also active in politics, running a business in Manchester, and supporting Marx. If Edmund Wilson's engaging study *To the Finland Station* is accurate, it appears that Marx would not have been able to produce his economic study of the capitalist system without Engels's continual financial, intellectual and personal support.[9]

In his supporting role, Engels wrote a number of articles in Marx's name for the *New York Tribune* during the 1850s. These articles were originally commissioned for Marx who, although needing the money, also needed time to work on his economic theories. Engels wrote the articles at Marx's urging, and Marx received the commission. If nothing else, the episode must surely demonstrate compatibility of thought. (It could also indicate that Marx did not care what appeared under his name, a possibility to which few Marx scholars, no matter what their interpretive persuasion, would subscribe.) When volume 1 of *Das Kapital* was published in 1867, Marx wrote to Engels, "Its completion is due to you and you alone."[10]

Marx and Engels first met in Cologne during the autumn of 1842 while Engels was on his way to Manchester. It was a cool, uneventful encounter. They met again two years later in Paris when Engels returned. By that time they had already carried on a brief correspondence and had read the other's published works. Thus were the seeds of the great collaboration sown. During this time, besides numerous bits of journalism, Engels had written an article, "Outlines of a Critique of Political Economy" (1844), which was later praised by Marx as a "brilliant" study (*Critique*, 22). This article was crucial in launching Marx's interest in economics. Also during this period Engels prepared for publication *The Condition of the Working Class in England*, a study requiring him to be both a fieldworker and a theoretician.[11] From 1845 to 1848, Marx and Engels together produced three major works: *The Holy Family*, a book attacking the previous critical-philosophical school for its failure to comprehend the naturalistic basis for human action and its imperviousness to the important developments taking place in the natural and physical sciences; *The German Ideology*, the first systematic elaboration of the materialistic conception of history; and *The Communist Manifesto*, a practical handbook on the necessity for a revolution and how to prepare for it.

During the period following their joint authorship of the three texts, Engels curtailed his own research and writing in order to be more supportive of Marx. Never one to begrudge Marx his greatness, when Engels had only a few years left to live, he attributed genius to Marx and in the same breath described himself as at best talented. While Engels did claim a certain modest share in laying down the materialist conception of history, he always gave the bulk of credit to Marx for this theory, which "rightly bears his name" (*Feuerbach*, 43). Engels's downplaying of his own importance has never ceased to amaze commentators. The subordination of personal glory to intellectual and personal modesty is a rare historical commodity. The Engels-Marx situation has an interesting, though far from exact parallel, in the Wallace-Darwin relationship.

Darwin and Wallace are generally regarded as the co-discoverers of the theory of evolution by natural selection in light of their joint paper given before the Linnaean Society in 1858 (*Evolution*). However, history has tended to associate the theory with Darwin's name, and this fate is not undeserved. Darwin began crystallizing his ideas under the stimulus of Malthus's *Essay on Population* shortly after he had returned from his voyage on the *Beagle*. In 1842 he wrote a brief sketch of his theory, which he expanded to a longer essay in 1844. The quest for further evidence and his cautious temperament caused him to abstain from publishing; the essay was to be published only in the case of his death.

While Darwin was still marshalling evidence in 1858, he received a letter from Wallace, who was in the Malay archipelago. The letter contained theoretical formulations that converged remarkably with his own: "If Wallace had my manuscript sketch written out in 1842, he could not have made a better short abstract" (*Life*, 2:116). The similarities are close and include the fact that Wallace also had read and derived inspiration from Malthus. Darwin was overwhelmed. Not wanting to act in a "paltry manner" by publishing first, he took Wallace's outline to Lyell and Hooker, who arranged for the joint presentation. History has shown that Wallace never begrudged Darwin's priority; the two became close friends. After Darwin's death, Wallace wrote a book about him, *Darwinism* (1889), reaffirming Darwin's more prominent role in formulating the evolutionary theory bearing the Darwinian label. During the period when both men were alive, Darwin never failed to regard Wallace with courtesy and respect—attitudes Marx was lax in displaying to Engels on a number of occasions.[12]

In writing about the Marx-Engels relationship, Gustav Mayer, a biographer of Engels, has referred to Marx as being motivated by the "harsh good of genius" while Engels was guided by the domination of his rich humanity.[13] It is unfortunate that Marx often failed to give this rich humanity its proper respect, despite his continual dependence on Engels for all manner of support. While Engels was a generous, optimistic, and well-rounded person with endless interests, a Renaissance man in an age in which specialization was rapidly becoming the norm, Marx was somber, intense, and often lacking in human considerations, particularly in interpersonal relations outside of the immediate family. Their personalities could hardly have contrasted more. Yet it was Engels whom Marx regarded as worthy of being his collaborator. He had the utmost regard for Engels's intellect, at times sparing no effort to convince him of even some minor point.[14] Those who emphasize the incompatibility in thought between the two must deal with the fact that Marx had such complete faith in the relationship between his ideas and those of Engels that he left instructions to his family that in the case of his death, Engels could publish the Marx manuscripts in any way he chose.[15]

In retrospect it seems surprising that two such brilliant and independent thinkers could have been in accord on so many points. When disagreement did cause a rift between them, and one such instance is painfully documented in their correspondence, personal and financial rather than theoretical matters were the culprits. If a few of Engels's views differ from Marx's, and a number of writers hold that it may be more than just a few, this does not necessarily place them in opposition. It may serve to pay tribute to Marx by implying that he was not averse to Engels's having some degree of intellectual independence.

COMPARING THE WORK

The current indictment of Engels as a revisionist, or an inaccurate interpreter of Marx, tends to be based on two assumptions: that his preoccupation with the natural sciences, specifically Darwinian theory, was not shared by Marx and that he put forth a vulgar or mechanical materialism that failed to recognize the role of conscious human intervention in history. Two works have borne the brunt of these accusations, *Anti-Dühring* and *Dialectics of Nature*. *Dialectics* was posthumously published from rough notes that Engels had planned to revise. It seems certain that if properly realized, *Dialectics* would have been a joint product containing excerpts from Marx's mathematical manuscripts. Engels first sketched the material in *Dialectics* during the 1870s frequently discussing the project with Marx whom he met with almost every day. In addition, Marx had been aware of Engels's intentions in this direction ever since the initial plan for the study was outlined to him in a letter dated 1858.[16] Marx and Engels were definitely of a mind in their belief in the importance of scientific discovery, and *Dialectics* represents an attempt on the part of Engels to interpret these discoveries in light of the critical theory of history developed by Marx.

Despite the insistence of several contemporary Western interpreters of Marx, *Dialectics* does not represent the manifesto for a Marxist science. There is only one Marxism to which Engels ever paid homage: that of its founder. This is nowhere more clearly expressed than when Engels, near death and with failing eyesight, struggled with Marx's incomplete and often illegible notes to give the world as faithful a rendition as possible of the third volume of *Das Kapital*:

A man like Marx has the right to be heard himself, to pass on his scientific discoveries to posterity in full genuineness of his own presentation. Moreover I had not the desire to infringe...it must seem to me...upon the legacy of so pre-eminent a man; it would have meant to me a breach of faith. [*Capital*, 3:889]

Unlike *Dialectics*, *Anti-Dühring* (1878) is a complete work. Engels's point of departure is a critique leveled at the natural philosophy and socialist theory of Eugene Dühring, a lecturer in philosophy and political science at the University of Berlin. Today Dühring's ideas seem trivial and often absurd. His name survives almost solely because he incurred the wrath of Marx and Engels and became the target for a classic polemic. This polemic is also the most complete statement of the materialist conception of history since their joint collaboration in *The German Ideology*. The technique of explicating one's theoretical biases in the course of attacking a contemporary was not unfamiliar to Engels, since Marx had followed his course in his criticisms of Pierre Proudhon in *The Poverty of Philosophy* (1847) and of Carl Voght in *Herr Voght* (1860).

In *Anti-Dühring* Engels flamboyantly dismantled Dühring's arguments and built in their stead a case for relating socialism and Marx's concept of history to discoveries in the natural and physical sciences. The work is probably the most complete secondary account of Marx's world view; certainly it is one of the most readable. It would have been impossible for Marx, so immersed at the time in economics and politics, to give such a general and accessible overview of his ideas. The logical question then becomes, How accurate a reflection of Marx's perspective is *Anti-Dühring*? It has been argued that the book alters and generalizes

Marxism by looking at it as an interdisciplinary science[17] and also that Marx's views are solely of a historical cast and cannot be reconciled with Engels's scientific formulations.[18] Although generally conceded to be Engels's project,[19] it is worth noting, especially in light of the previous criticisms, that *Anti-Dühring* has also been referred to as being mainly Marx's book, perhaps because in the preface Engels attributed the genesis of and outlook expressed in the book to Marx.[20] He also stated that he read the entire manuscript to Marx and that chapter 10 was written by Marx. There is every reason to assume that the work is a continuation of the collaboration on scientific and philosophical matters that they embarked upon earlier in *The Holy Family* and *The German Ideology*.[21] Whether one accepts Engels's scientific formulations, it seems reasonable to assume that Marx was not only familiar with them, he was also highly supportive.

Engels believed in a naturalistic basis to history and human behavior, a belief hardly alien to Marx. Because Engels was so explicit in expressing these opinions, Avineri has accused him of divorcing history from the mediation of consciousness and as a result producing a mechanical materialism that violates Marx's intent.[22] The priority of consciousness in human action has also been emphasized by Sartre, who in his version of Marxist anthropology refers to freedom as "the irreducibility of the cultural order to the natural order."[23] Yet Marx never made an absolute separation between nature and culture. He believed that freedom and determinism are present in both spheres. Engels, in trying to elaborate the same notions, has been accused of reductionism and expounding a vulgar materialism that omits the individual as creator and innovator.

Yet in his later scientific writings Engels was not averse to explanations involving the individual or free choice. He unequivocally followed Marx in noting that freedom does not refer to a complete and totally random independence from natural laws but in a knowledge of these laws and the possibility that they can be directed to human ends: "[It] consists in the control over ourselves and over external nature which is founded on a knowledge of natural necessity" (*Anti-Dühring*, 125). In other words, man is free to intervene in the events of his environment, but the extent to which he can intervene is constrained by the circumstances of that environment. This is not an alteration of Marx but merely a restatement of one of his fundamental tenets:

Men make their own history, but they do not make it just as they please; they do not make it under circumstances chosen by themselves, but under circumstances directly encountered, given and transmitted from the past. The tradition of all the dead generations weigh like a nightmare on the brain of the living. [*18th Brumaire*, 15]

The materialism of Engels and of Marx always remained consistent with their linked conceptions of the relationship between consciousness and reality.[24] Any criticism of Engels for failing to acknowledge the role of conscious human intervention in natural and historical processes is the result of a shortsighted reading of his work. True, he placed heavy stress on the role of scientific laws, several of dubious validity, but he was also critical of the science of his day for its failure to assess the implications of man's role in changing his external circumstances:

Natural science, like philosophy, has hitherto, entirely neglected the influence of man's activity...it is precisely the *Alteration of Nature by Men*, not solely nature as such, which is the most essential and immediate basis of human thought...[the view that]...nature exclusively reacts on man, and natural conditions everywhere exclusively determined his historical development, is therefore one-sided and forgets that man also reacts on nature, changing it and creating new conditions for himself. [*Dialectics*, 172]

Far from diverging from Marx, Engels's opinions in this context only serve to recall what the senior partner said in his third thesis on Feuerbach:

The materialist doctrine that men are the products of circumstances and that, therefore, *changed* men are the products of other circumstances and upbringing, forgets that circumstances are changed precisely by men. [Quoted in *Feuerbach*, 83]

The two views are equally removed from mechanical materialism and crass positivism.

THE DEFENSE AND INTERPRETATION OF DARWIN

Both *Anti-Dühring* and *Dialectics of Nature* attempt to weigh the effect of the ever-growing mass of discoveries in the natural and physical sciences, the most notable being Darwin's theory of evolution. In the opinion of Marx and Engels, this theory effected a revolution in the intellectual world of the nineteenth century. Engels's assessment of Darwin has been praised by a notable biologist of this century who is one of the founders of the modern synthetic theory of evolution, J.B.S. Haldane. Haldane has evaluated both the strengths and the shortcomings of Engels's analysis. He notes that although Engels took what now appears to be an erroneous position in several scientific arguments, he was usually following the most reputable scientists of his day, and his conclusions as a whole are surprisingly consonant with modern thinking on the various issues.[25] No greater tribute has been paid to Engels's interpretation of science than when Haldane stated that his own researches into evolutionary theory would have been spared a good deal of confusion had he known about Engels's critique of Darwin.[26]

In *Anti-Dühring*, Engels set the stage for his defense and interpretation of Darwin by making frequent reference to the history of science, a field in which Marx also had considerable knowledge and interest. Engels classified scientific models from the previous two centuries as mechanical, largely because they dealt with solid bodies and eternal laws. He acknowledged Newton, begrudgingly, but it is clear that Engels was impatient for a perspective capable of dealing with phenomena moving through and changing with time. The philosophical source was Heraclitus. With respect to Engels's generation, the most recent proponent was held to be Hegel. However, the vision of change in nature did not break through into the realm of science until the nebular hypothesis of Kant was crystallized in the middle of the eighteenth century, an event Engels regarded as one of the great advances in science. For the first time, the notion that nature has no temporal dimension was severely questioned. Engels described the situation prior to Kant as one in which nature was regarded as being in motion, but this motion was a continual repetition of the same processes, processes alleged to have started through a special act of creation (*Anti-Dühring*, 65-66). It was his belief that this perspective served to entrench the idea that species are forever immutable.

In contrast to Newton's world machine cycling endlessly through time with no vestige of a beginning, Kant, much to Engels's relief, gave the origin and development of the universe the status of a scientific hypothesis. This is not to say that cyclical ahistorical hypotheses could not be scientifically legitimate; Engels knew otherwise. But by leaving themselves open to special creation, they were often condoned by Christian orthodoxy, and he found this invariably led to interpretive limitations. For example, the ahistorical scientific world view was used to justify ideologically the status quo by claiming that man's lot, like nature and the heavens, is ordained by the hand of God. Although Engels thought that an evolutionary view of the universe would invariably sever ties with special creationism and Christian orthodoxy, he seems to have overlooked that on a number of occasions Darwin stated that his theory was not a denial of Christianity. He also failed to note that *The Origin of Species* does not deal with the origin of life, an event at that time, and even today, amendable to an invocation of special creation. Despite the fact that a number of nineteenth-century writers, including Engels in his book on Feuerbach, were highly curious regarding the origin of life from nonliving matter, Darwin never showed much interest in this problem.

From his nineteenth-century vantage point, Engels held that Darwin's theory represented a triumph of secular reasoning over religious teleology and man's ability to forge a new destiny over the conditions constraining him since the advent of the state. In his enthusiastic welcome for the evolutionary perspective, he failed to note how it could and did serve as a rationale for conservative thought. By substituting natural destiny for the will of God, the social Darwinists conjured a new legitimation for the old politics.

In his survey of the history of science, Engels examined eighteenth-century precursors of evolutionism. He tried to find developmental concepts dealing with nature similar to those elaborated in the realm of history by Hegel. Hegel saw history as an evolutionary process—an unfolding powered by forces continually in conflict. Marx and Engels accepted this but dispensed with Hegel's notion of the idea or spirit, seeking fulfillment as a final cause. They substituted flesh and blood individuals struggling under conditions inherited from both nature and past generations. Engels believed that Marx's concept of history transformed the Hegelian interpretation by rendering it secular and materially tangible. It also became the logical scientific extension of the Kantian hypothesis of cosmic evolution and Darwin's theory of evolution in organic nature.

Between the cosmic and the organic realms is another highly important theater of evolution in nature, and Engels duly acknowledged it: the geological history of the earth. He singled out Charles Lyell as the figure most responsible for convincingly expounding the idea of a natural history for the earth. For Engels, Lyell was the first person to bring sense to geology in place of the earlier belief, advanced by Cuvier, in a series of cataclysmic creations (*Dialectics*, 10). By demonstrating that the earth has an extended genealogy, Lyell, in spite of not believing in the mutability of species in his early years (although he was a close friend of Darwin), set the stage for the wide acceptance of biological evolutionary theory. Lyell's direct influence on Darwin was considerable, though Engels seems to have been unaware of this. It should be noted that in dealing with the history of biological evolutionary theory, Engels was well aware that Darwin's ideas were not unique. Although Darwin is given credit for the first truly scientific substantiation of evolution, Engels also acknowledged the importance of the earlier contributions of Göethe and Lamarck.

Engels began his systematic examination of evolutionary theory in 1872. At that time, Marx was secure and Engels, having saved and invested, was able to retire from the family business in Manchester. The results of this research were destined to appear in *Anti-Dühring* and *Dialectics*. In defending Darwin against Dühring, Engels brought to light the relevance of many nineteenth-century scientific discoveries in a manner designed to highlight Dühring's inadequate grasp of the same materials. Dühring was an eclectic, a trait that led Engels to remark cynically that his approach dealt with "all things under the sun and then a few more" (*Anti-Dühring*, 10), an accusation that could well have been leveled at Engels himself.

To advance his impressionistic and universal philosophical system, which was also critical of capitalism, Dühring sought to throw Darwin's discoveries into disrepute. In one instance, he accused Darwin of appropriating the defective notions of Malthus. This created an awkward situation for Engels, who agreed that Malthus's notions were defective but also that Darwin's were epoch-making. Engels tried to get around this by pointing out that Darwin would never have attributed the idea of the struggle for existence to Malthus. Engels believed that this struggle is obvious in nature; from here it was applied to human society by Malthus; and from Malthus Darwin received the inspiration to reapply it systematically to the realm of plants and animals. Although Engels appears to be bending the evidence to suit his argument, a similar opinion has independently emerged, nearly one hundred years later. In her extensive biography of Darwin, Gertrude Himmelfarb remarks that Malthus had a keen interest in natural history and natural philosophy and that his speculations about human population, so stimulating to Darwin, were derived from "the more obvious situation" existing among plants and animals.[27] While Engels agreed with Dühring that Darwin may have been a bit uncritical in his assessment of Malthus, he nevertheless forcefully defended the originality of Darwin's researches. He noted that organisms in nature, like human societies, have their own complex laws of population that largely remained uninvestigated except for Darwin's pioneering efforts in this direction (*Anti-Dühring*, 78).

Dühring, as well as a number of other writers, criticized the failure of Darwin's theory to account for the causes of variation in nature. In response to Dühring's contention that Darwin produced individual variations in nature out of nothing, Engels replied that Darwin could not possibly provide all of the answers to the evolutionary problem because he was almost singlehandedly opening up a new area of scientific research and in so doing had to give "too wide a field of action" to master concepts like natural selection (ibid., 79). Despite the fact that neither Darwin nor anyone else could explain the causes of individual variation, Engels insisted they are a concrete reality confronting animal and plant breeders all the time, and the man most responsible for systematically elaborating their consequences "is none other than Darwin" (ibid., 80).

While skillfully parrying Dühring's criticisms of Darwin, it is clear that Engels was not completely satisfied with all of Darwin's formulations. Although Darwin believed in the inheritance of acquired characteristics, in Engels's opinion, he did not use this principle extensively enough. Engels modified evolutionary theory to accommodate further this notion, a direction that has not turned out to be consonant with modern scientific thinking. While the inheritance of acquired traits has been disproven by Mendelian and subsequent genetics, Darwin's most important discovery, natural selection, has grown in importance. It is indeed the master evolutionary principle that Darwin believed it to be in the first edition of *The Origin*, and Engels's comment that Darwin gave it "too wide a field of action" now appears to be a severe underestimation.

Late in life, Darwin began to rely increasingly on the inheritance of acquired characteristics as an agent of evolution. In the first edition of *The Origin*, natural selection was stressed to the point where it appears to be the only agent; however, in subsequent editions, he gradually retreated from this stance. In the sixth and last edition he remarked:

It has been said that I attribute the modification of species exclusively to natural selection, I may be permitted to remark that in the first edition of this work, and subsequently, I placed in a most conspicuous position. . .the following words: "I am convinced that natural selection has been the main but not the exclusive means of modification." [*Origin*, 476]

Two factors might be held responsible for this shift. The first is pressure from his critics, a phenomenon to which he was perhaps unduly sensitive. Darwin was not assertive personally or intellectually, and although he was always convinced of the preeminence of natural selection, it was not wholly convincing to others, so he adhered less forcefully to it over the years. The second factor responsible for the new emphasis had to do with subject matter. In the later work, he was concerned with man, a species capable of extremely rapid change both during a lifetime and over a small number of generations. Natural selection appeared to be too slow to explain these changes, and since Darwin thought that any mechanism of transmutation must be genetic, he leaned in the direction of the inheritance of acquired habits. Haeckel has claimed that near the end of his life, Darwin was just as convinced as Lamarck in the transmission of acquired characteristics.[28] I believe that this is an overstatement. No matter where one looks in Darwin, natural selection remains the master principle, and other modes of explanation, like the inheritance of acquired characteristics, are always secondary. Nevertheless, as far as Engels was concerned, Darwin did not place enough stress on the inheritance of acquired characteristics, and although this opinion does not accord with modern knowledge, it was shared by some of the most reputable scientists of the times. A notable exception was Alfred Russel Wallace who believed that the later Darwin had drifted too far from his earlier and more accurate selectionist position.[29]

Armed with a sound knowledge of the science of his day and a critical imagination, Engels in *Dialectics* set about to recommend several points of modification to Darwin's theory, the most notable being an increased stress on the inheritance of acquired characteristics. To call this Lamarckianism, as a number of critics have, is inaccurate.[30] Engels was totally Darwinian in his approach. He accepted natural selection as well as the struggle for existence and differed from Darwin only by placing more stress on the inheritance of acquired characteristics. Although Lamarck believed in this principle—for good or for ill it bears the label Lamarckianism—it was only one pillar in his evolutionary system. This system did not include struggle, divergent branching, extinction, or anything resembling natural selection—perspectives of importance to both Darwin and Engels.

Since later writers working with the benefit of modern evolutionary theory and genetics have been critical of Engels for his reliance on the inheritance of acquired characteristics, it might be worthwhile to explore his reasons for adhering to the principle. He noted (*Dialectics*, 314) that mathematical axioms obvious to an eight-year-old European child would be difficult to teach to an adult bushman, and this he believed was an inherited capacity. (He was quite aware that the line between the mental capacities of primitive and civilized people is a thin one, and nowhere in the nineteenth century has greater admiration for non-Western society been expressed than in *The Origin of the Family*.) Not being able to separate the content of a group's learned repertoire of behavior, in this case the bushman's, from the innate basis for human behavior as a whole, and recognizing how easily humans can learn so many new things in a generation, caused him to postulate that what is learned in one generation can be biologically passed to the next. How else, he asked, could the experience of the individual extend to the group so rapidly (ibid., 34)? By postulating that individual experience in learning can be replaced to a certain extent by the experiences of a number of ancestors, Engels contributed to the concept of racial memory, a motif that later became prominent in the work of Freud and Jung. However, unlike Engels, Freud and Jung had access to modern genetics, a legacy they chose to ignore.

It has been argued that adherence to the view that acquired characteristics are inherited automatically brands Engels and Marx as racists.[31] While this principle has racist overtones in light of modern scientific understanding, in the nineteenth century its scientific status was of lesser importance with respect to racist implications than was an assessment of the uses to which the principle was put. Like Darwin, Engels used the principle to explain the rapid mutability among the various races—in other words, how quickly the savage, in a generation or two, can learn civilized ways; and therefore how fully human he is in the first place. Whatever label is affixed to Engels for relying on this principle, it is clear that he used it to advance a radical antiracist politics. For Engels or Darwin to have conceived the contemporary position so well articulated by the twentieth-century German-American anthropologist Franz Boas—that the content of a culture, be it bushman or suburban American, is learned on a common, historically unchanging, mental substrate (the psychic unity principle)—before the advent of modern genetics would have required an incredible effort of intellectual foresight. Such conjecture would by necessity have gone against the grain of materialist thinking that proved so fruitful to them in other areas. In the nineteenth century only Alfred Russel Wallace, and perhaps

Edward Tylor, were so imaginative; but in retrospect their views, although compatible with twentieth-century thinking, are less secure in the scientific context of the nineteenth century than the formulations of Darwin and Engels.

Engels grasped Darwinian theory as well as any other intellectual of his era. He accepted the theory of evolution for what it was and still is: the best available scientific explanation for the phenomenon of organic change through time. For Engels, it remained an open-ended hypothesis capable of modification in the light of new evidence. Darwin regarded his theory in the same spirit. Engels lauded Darwin for shattering the rigid metaphysical concept of species and for his scientific rigor in detaching and examining details of the whole from their natural historical context, and refitting them back while providing an explanation for the nature of that context. He believed this demonstrated practical proof for the connection between necessity and chance postulated by Hegel (*Dialectics*, 229). In Engels's opinion, Darwin's theory established continuity between nature, history, and human behavior. Not only did it provide a history of nature, it also yielded the possibility that a prehistory of mind can be traced through successive stages, thus providing a basis for understanding the human brain (*Feuerbach*, 67). Engels was aware of the possibility of unconscious motivation and would have welcomed its investigation.[32] However, when Marxism and psychoanalysis emerged as a topic for consideration during the twentieth century, the direction taken did not correspond to the one that it appears Engels would have followed.

In *Dialectics of Nature*, dialectics constitutes an approach to science dealing with the interconnections and processes that characterize both the natural and historical domains. I have avoided using the term in conjunction with Marx because he did not employ it in the wholesale manner of many of his followers. For Engels, dialectics constitutes a mode of interpretation rather than a methodology, although a number of critics have insisted on seeing it in the latter context. And it is true that in one of his more speculative moments, he did conceive a series of infamous dialectic laws that, as many commentators have rightly pointed out, have no status as scientific laws and are dubious as generalizations. These so-called laws are perhaps best assessed for the way they bring to light the significance of a number of scientific discoveries and experiments that transpired during the nineteenth century.

The overall thrust of *Dialectics* is a cosmological evolution from which man emerged as a free, conscious organism, constrained by natural law. It was Engels's opinion, and one shared with Marx, that an understanding of these laws contributes to the recognition of human necessity and that in the realm of organic nature no one has contributed more to this understanding than has Darwin. To be faithful to its founders, the subsequent Marxian-inspired approaches must reckon both with the legacy of Darwin and the contemporary biological tradition that has followed his lead.

Despite accusations to the contrary, *Dialectics* did not endeavor to make a positivistic science out of Marxism. It is rather an interpretation of the relevance of scientific discovery in the nineteenth century in light of the critical theory of history that Marx developed. In the context of that century, Engels's formulations are surprisingly accurate. This has caused at least one writer, Loren Graham, to comment that a reevaluation of Engels by historians of science is long overdue.[33] Yet Engels did err, most obviously in his stress on the inheritance of acquired characteristics. The crucial question, however, is whether Engels would have modified such notions had he been aware of the rediscovery of Mendel that took place shortly after his death. Would Marx and Engels, both professing fidelity to the canons of pure science, have perceived Mendelian genetics as a scientific breakthrough or as charlantanry? Would the challenge it could have posed to some of their entrenched assumptions have been offset by the new interpretive vistas the Mendelian perspective ultimately opened up?

HUMAN EVOLUTION

On one notable occasion, Engels engaged in some quite specific scientific theorizing. The result is a remarkable, though unfinished, essay, "The Part Played by Laborer in the Transition from Ape to Man," written in 1876. The essay was eventually published, along with a number of other scientific sketches, in the posthumously edited *Dialectics of Nature*. It vividly indicates that Engels absorbed the Darwin of both *The Origin* and *The Descent*. Taking information provided by Darwin, Engels extended it and engaged in some speculative evolutionary reconstruction of his own—similar to what is now being done in the new physical anthropology, an approach that merges the interpretation of fossil and archeological remains with behavioral data from nonhuman primates in order to reveal aspects of human biosocial evolution.

The subject of Engels's essay is the role played by the interdependence of morphological (physical structure) and cultural (particularly tools) factors in the evolution of man from a gregarious prehuman primate to fully developed *Homo sapiens*. He was concerned with how the primate group leading to man interacted with the external natural environment to produce the changing conditions of its own evolution. In anthropology, this is often referred to as the hominid transition and in more philosophical circles as the passage from nature to culture. In his essay, Engels might have been influenced by Rousseau, as well as by Darwin. The spirit of the discussion follows Rousseau's efforts to explain the origin of human society out of a state of nature in his *Discourse on the Origin of Inequality* (1755). While Engels recounted again the saga of man that has captivated the human imagination since Genesis, he managed to reap the harvest of nineteenth-century science en route.

Following Darwin, Engels assumed that man's early ancestors must have been a highly developed race of arboreal anthropoid apes, living in bands. In dealing with human origins, he stressed that it is impossible to find the evolutionary roots of "the most social of all animals, from nongregarious ancestors" (*Dialectics*, 282). On this issue, he made a break with earlier theorists, including Hobbes and Rousseau, who postulated that early man must have lived in an isolated asocial state. These writers held that the dawn of all that is human came with the establishment, through consent, of the social contract, a belief that greatly nurtured bourgeois political economy. Engels echoed Darwin by putting man's social origins well back in natural history. He visualized the arboreal social primates that he believed were the antecedents of man gradually abandoning their habitat in order to begin foraging on the ground. At that point natural selection began operating in the direction of an increasingly erect posture and bipedal locomotion. Engels's description of the behavior of modern anthropoid apes, which he used for comparative purposes, is quite accurate and indicative of a thorough familiarity with the available primate literature. Perhaps like Darwin and the anthropologist E. B. Tylor, Engels made sojourns to the London Zoo to observe anthropoid behavior.

From his knowledge of primate behavior, Engels concluded that the development of the erect posture led to a series of reciprocal actions whereby the hand was freed for tool use. This was accompanied by continual interaction between the manufacture of more efficient tools, increasingly complex social organization, and the emergence of speech:

The mastery over nature, which begins with the development of the hand, with labour, widened man's horizon at every new advance. He was continually discovering new, hitherto unknown, properties of natural objects. On the other hand, the development of labour necessarily helped to bring the members of society closer together by multiplying cases of mutual support, joint activity, and by making clear the advantage of this joint activity to each individual. In short, men in the making arrived at the point where *they had something to say* to one another. The need led to the creation of its organ; the undeveloped larynx of the ape was slowly but surely transformed by means of gradually increased modulation, and the organs of the mouth gradually learned to pronounce one articulate letter after another. [*Dialectics*, 282-83]

In explaining this process he invoked the law of correlation of growth put forth by Darwin during his research on domestic plants and animals:

[*Correlation of growth*]
By this term I mean the whole organization is so connected, that when one part varies, other parts vary; but which of the two correlated variations ought to be looked at as the cause and which as the effect, or whether both result from some cause we can seldom or never tell. [*Variation*, 1:177]

The evolving primate bands Engels described were linked through the development of cooperative social labor. He elaborated the argument by taking and connecting the concept of labor that Marx employed in both his early and later writings to the biosocial evolutionary perspective Darwin outlined in *The Descent*. The result is an imaginative though thoroughly hypothetical reconstruction of the social and behavioral evolution of the primate line leading to *Homo sapiens*. Like Darwin, Engels was aware of the provisional nature of these formulations and the fact that they remain open-ended conjectures faithful to existing facts but modifiable in light of new discoveries. Using his dialectical approach, which stressed the interconnectedness of structure and event and widespread change pervading natural phenomena, he developed a model elaborating a reciprocal feedback between labor and the social necessity. This, in turn, promoted growth of the capacity for abstraction that eventually culminated in language. The nucleus for these activities is the brain, an organ carrying on a dialogue and developing in concert with an ever-changing natural and humanly created environment:

The reaction of labour and speech of the development of the brain and its attendant senses, of the increasing clarity of consciousness, power of abstraction and of judgement, gave an ever-renewed impulse to the further development of both labour and speech. [*Dialectics*, 285]

With benefit of modern evolutionary thinking, we know that Engels's hypothetical constructs can be explained fully through natural selection; nevertheless, he supplemented them with a heavy dependence on that persistent nineteenth-century principle, the inheritance of acquired characteristics. It must have seemed obvious to him that human evolution was relatively rapid in relation to the rest of nature, and since human societies are highly flexible, capable of incredible changes in a few generations, he thought it logical to invoke this principle to explain the situation. However, Engels accepted the principle uncritically, almost enthusiastically. He differed from Darwin, who used it with some degree of reservation, primarily because no viable alternative was apparent.

In the sixth edition of *The Origin*, published in 1872, a year after *The Descent*, Darwin questioned the concept of the inheritance of acquired habits, noting that many behaviors are too complex to be transmitted by habit. He maintained that if a "varying individual did not actually transmit to its offspring the newly acquired character," it might under certain circumstances transmit "a tendency to vary in the same manner" (*Origin*, 101). He further questioned the principle by pointing out that if any habitual action becomes inherited, then it might be reasonable to expect someone like Mozart to play a tune without any practice; however, all we can say about Mozart is that because he could play a tune with very little practice, he might have inherited an instinct for musical behavior (ibid., 244).

His overly enthusiastic dependence on the inheritance of acquired habits notwithstanding, Engels did not neglect natural selection. It is therefore inaccurate to describe his approach as Lamarckian. Nevertheless, Engels did give Lamarck credit for his pioneering efforts in developing an evolutionary perspective, while Darwin was notoriously lax in citing contributions made by his predecessors, despite the fact that his use of the inheritance of acquired habits suggests an unpaid debt to Lamarck. As we have already seen, Lamarck's overview contained basic presuppositions such as a teleology and the denial of extinction, which rendered it incompatible with the overall scientific thrust of both Darwin and Engels.

Engels believed that natural selection was a crucial force operating on our primate ancestors. Those early apelike hordes, he claimed, must have quickly reached the carrying capacity of their environment given that their food intake was chiefly from foraging. This caused him to point to the significance of hunting in human evolution, a fact Marx stressed earlier in *Das Kapital* and a subject that has been the focus of considerable anthropological attention in recent years.[34] By allowing for a more varied diet, the "predatory economy," as Engels called it, gave those individuals and groups who were so engaged a selective advantage over those who were not. Among the factors selected for were intelligence and the kind of sociability characteristic of the human species today: "This predatory economy has powerfully contributed to the gradual evolution of our ancestors into men" (*Dialectics*, 286). Engels went on to note that the meat diet resulting from the hunting way of life greatly shortened the time spent in the quest for food, giving its practitioners advantages over their foraging cousins. In so doing, it helped to bring about such specifically human adaptations as the discovery of fire and the domestication of animals and, eventually, plants. Engels also made reference to the various consequences deriving from the kind of intelligence made possible by the hunting economy. These include the acquisition of agriculture and the invention of metallurgy, factors that enabled the human species to spread throughout the habitable world. At this tantalizing juncture, the incomplete manuscript breaks off.

"The Part Played by Labour in the Transition from Ape to Man" is fascinating on two counts. First, it illustrates the intellectual range and creative scientific imagination of a personality known primarily for his political and economic writings; second, it corresponds in substance, and surprisingly in its conclusions, to contemporary research on human evolution. That is not to say that Engels's argument is without flaw. His quaint description of our early ancestors, his almost total dependence on the inheritance of acquired characteristics to explain the evolution of the hand, and his belief in a direct link between meat eating and the evolution of the brain (the substances in meat feed directly into the brain, causing immediately noticeable changes), have all been discredited by subsequent research. What has survived is his insistence, following and elaborating from Darwin, that no one organ evolves in isolation and his manner of looking at how clusters of traits both morphological and behavioral evolve together in a reciprocating network where one or more can temporarily predominate and exert influence over the adaptive pattern of the entire organism. As an example of this phenomenon, he cited the development of erect posture, which led to the freeing of the hand, tool making, enlargement of the brain, and more elaborate social networks.

Engels also affirmed that evolution is not a teleological unfolding or a mechanical process but an activity whereby the participants actively alter the conditions of their existence:

Animals…change external nature by their activities just as man does, if not to the same extent, and these changes made by them in their environment, in turn react upon and change their originators. For in nature nothing takes place in isolation. Everything affects every other thing and *vice versa*, and it is usually because this *many* sided motion and interaction is forgotten that our natural scientists are prevented from clearly seeing the simplest things. We have seen how goats have prevented the regeneration of forest in Greece; on the island of St. Helena, goats and pigs brought by the first arrivals have succeeded in exterminating almost completely the old vegetation of the island; and so have prepared the soil for the spreading of plants brought by later sailors and colonists. [Ibid., 189-90]

In following this line of thought, Engels insightfully anticipated the ecological approach that has played such a large role in our understanding of natural and cultural relationships during the twentieth century.

_____ **Part IV**

CONCLUSION _____

Assessing the Implications

> If radicalism is to go to the root, as the name implies, it must be prepared to examine the "nature" of man in ways more courageous and less pietistic than those it used in the name of humanism.
>
> —Robert Heilbroner

Colleagues, students, and friends, unaware of the intense debates surrounding Marx interpretation on the one hand and biology and the human sciences on the other, often comment that the analysis I have produced seems rather obvious and straightforward. They usually offer this opinion rather hesitatingly, as if their feeling is that there is nothing remarkably original here. In truth, I regard the study in much the same light. Once the initial connections were perceived, the elaborations that followed have always seemed obvious. They are based on accessible statements in major works.

But although I believe that my line of argument is straightforward, I have always been aware that several contemporary contexts to which it relates have vested interests in seeing otherwise. As French sociologist Raymond Aron has noted, and not without a degree of cynicism, Marx's key ideas would not be so difficult to present if there were not so many self-proclaimed Marxists, and I might add that few of them would subscribe to my interpretation.[1] In a related vein, the relationship of Darwin and biology to the human sciences would not be so difficult a subject were it not for the fact that passionate arguments regarding the inevitable political implications of the enterprise are now commonplace—witness the sociobiology debate. A brief discussion of these areas of controversy, with reference to this study, can shed light on both.

Marx is a figure of enormous political as well as theoretical significance. That I have chosen to emphasize the latter should not be taken as a dismissal of the former. As Sartre once noted, Marx's insights are still relevant today because we have not outgrown the conditions that gave rise to them; Sartre has also pointed out that Marx's legacy is a task to be completed, not a prescribed system. I am sympathetic to both points, though not with Sartre's overall strategy. Marx believed that in order to change the world, we must first understand it, chiefly through science. It is his emphasis on understanding that I have elected to pursue. The unity of theory and practice has to be seen as a variable equation. After all, had Marx died in the streets and not at his desk, the impact of his message would have been greatly diminished.

Perhaps I should reemphasize a division made in the preface between *Marxian* and *Marxist*. It is the Marxian legacy I have selectively elaborated. Marx was very much concerned with human theory in relation to natural scientific understanding. This was a major point of focus in his earlier work, where he dealt with nature, human nature, and society in ways that prefigured Darwin, as well as aspects of twentieth-century anthropology and psychology. Although the emphasis of his work shifted to political economy after 1845 and he no longer elaborated the quest for a unified natural-human science perspective, he clearly worked with reference to this possibility. After 1859 he was fascinated by Darwin and stressed the relationship of his own sphere of interest to that great naturalist's work. I have also argued that this concern for a foundation in nature and natural processes imparts continuity between his early and later work, despite shifts in subject matter and method. Clearly I disagree with the two Marxes concept of Althusser and others.

Although Marx has been utilized by the contemporary social sciences, the appropriation has generally excluded his assumptions on the nature of human nature and society. Recently this aspect of Marx has received consideration from philosophers. Yet both social scientists and philosophers might benefit from examining Marx's assumptions in light of Darwin's work and modern biosocial approaches, such as ethology, comparative psychology, physical anthropology and primatology, sociobiology, and related fields. (I regard sociobiology as one path within a range of possible biosocial strategies, not the all-inclusive discipline its practitioners claim.) Marx's ideas on group process and structure are particularly interesting and worth testing, both with respect to subsequent related thinking in the social sciences, and the biosocial fields. Contemporary social thought can profit from similar cross-fertilization. For example, when the Marx-influenced, but certainly non-Marxist, sociologist Robert Nisbet notes that humankind's quest for community springs from powerful needs of human nature, he is rendering a hypothesis capable of being significantly informed by the kind of natural science understanding the twentieth-century sociology has too frequently avoided.[2]

Another potentially illuminating area, often discussed in the context of Marx and the human sciences in the twentieth century, has been the Marx-Freud synthesis. As a graduate student during the 1960s, I was exposed to formulations in this area by critical theorists such as Herbert Marcuse and numerous seminar discussions of the possibility. At the time I was enthusiastic but felt something was missing. Now I think I see what that absence was, and still is. Discussions of Marx and Freud omitted dealing with the enormous importance the work of Darwin had for both men. Marx was given the social, Freud the individual, and the natural sciences hardly figured in the equation. Marx withstood the appropriation rather well, but Freud posed problems that his followers overlooked. He adhered to an obsolete biology. Although Darwin's work was inspirational to Freud, he failed to agument it with Mendelian genetics and, by extension, the modern synthetic theory of evolution. He died still believing in the inheritance of acquired characteristics, racial memory, and various questionable drives such as the death wish, to which recent biological theory can give no credibility.

Yet Freud has been updated in a number of areas. In particular, links have been drawn between aspects of his human theory and contemporary research in evolutionary anthropology, ethology, and primatology. A notable example is John Bowlby's recent study of mother-infant attachment.[3] It now appears that reworking the Marx-Freud synthesis might be a feasible enterprise, given some of the resources available in the biosocial area. A worthy problem for this endeavor would be the alienation question. Marx and Freud approached it in different but related ways. A contemporary biosocial examination could help augment and complement their analyses. This kind of project, as critical social theory, could also help challenge the widely held assumption that biological informed approaches to the study of human social behavior are invariably conservative apologies for things as they are.

For both Marx and Darwin, as I have tried to demonstrate, humankind is not passive and infinitely malleable, shaped solely through external conditions. However, a good deal of so-called Marxist thinking has proceeded as if this indeed were the case. Soviet science once opted for, and still adheres closely to this model, a situation that was patent during the reign of Lysenko. An interesting problem in the history of the relationship between science and society is that environmentalism was also dominant on the other side of the Iron Curtain. In the United States, under Watson and Skinner, rather than Pavlov, and through psychology rather than biology, environmentalism in the form of behaviorism has meshed rather comfortably with capitalist ideology. Many radical critics of sociobiology and related approaches tend to assume inevitable links between theories that deal with an innate basis for human behavior, and monopoly capitalist-political and economic policy. The opposite may sometimes be the case. For example, in recent years theorists as diverse as Marcuse and Noam Chomsky have worked within a conceptual framework that assumes innate parameters to human nature, yet they have generated searing critiques of the status quo of dominant regimes in both capitalist and socialist worlds.

Unfortunately, the fact that a number of Marxist traditions have emphasized a tabula rasa concept of human nature has caused several theorists in the biosocial field to react negatively to the entire Marx legacy. Ethologist Eibl-Ebesfeldt links Marxism directly to an anti-innate, pro-environmentalist position.[4] Sociobiologist Edward Wilson is even more critical.[5] He refers to Marxism as sociobiology without biology, links it to religion, and claims it is mortally threatened by sociobiology. No doubt much of his hostility derives from the fact that several of the strongest opponents of sociobiology are self-proclaimed Marxists. Both sides seem to have blinders on. Wilson appears unwilling to get past Marxist polemics, to Marx himself, where he might find a scientific materialism close to Darwin's and several observations on human nature and society relateable to sociobiological hypotheses. On the other side, Marxist critics of sociobiology such as Katz-Fishman and Fritz have failed to appraise inclusively the Marx legacy.[6] Not only do they reject sociobiology, they discount the possibility of a biosocial science with a Marxian focus, which might draw from sociobiology but not be governed by it. Marx's concept of materialism was not concerned solely with economic realities, such as relations of production. It also accommodated conditions of life: processes in the natural world and natural processes in the human domain.

Although Marx's concern with the natural sciences has been acknowledged in a number of Marxist traditions, such as Marxist-Leninism, this acknowledgment is linked to a rather dogmatic and inflexible overall assessment of his work. In reaction, an academically successful track of Marx interpretation has arisen in the West. A rather diverse group ranging from critical theorists of the Frankfurt school to several recent philosophers, historians, and sociologists of Marx have emphasized his indebtedness to the German philosophical tradition, especially Hegel. Part of this reappraisal has been the viewing of Marx's work as a continuum. The aim has been to offset both the Soviet distortion of his main ideas and the traditional Western attitude that his work exhibits a rigid determinism. This approach is quite justified and has served to debunk several entrenched misconceptions. However, this new view is not without its own exclusivist tendencies. In particular, it has either downplayed or denied Marx's extensive preoccupation with the natural sciences.

Despite this trend, connections between Marx, Darwin and contemporary biological research have not gone unacknowledged. For example, British historian E. P. Thompson has recently drawn some Marx-Darwin parallels.[7] He notes how important *The Origin of Species* was for Marx, chastises Marx scholars for failing to read Darwin, and debunks social Darwinist misconceptions of Darwin's work. Even more interesting from the point of view of the present study is the Italian Marxian theorist Sebastiano Timpanaro.[8] He criticizes the tendency within recent Western Marxism to dissociate Marx's concept of materialism from biological materialism and defends the legacy of the later Engels. Timpanaro argues against the overwhelming trend to see Marx's formulations in light of an environmentalist bias, and he makes a plea for the inclusion of biological research in a comprehensive Marxian theory of human needs. It is my hope that Timpanaro will help open up a new tradition of Marx interpretation, one in which my own work might find a place.

Owing to its direct social implications and theoretical depth, Marx's work has spawned many interpretations and controversies. Darwin has not been so blessed, or cursed. One has usually accepted, or rejected, his evolutionary theory. Concern with what Darwin really said has not led to scores of books and journal articles, as with Marx. The debates North Americans are most familiar with, such as the Scopes monkey trial in Tennessee during the 1920s, appear as quaint holdovers from the nineteenth century. However, lest I speak too soon, the issue of creationism versus evolutionism appears to be surfacing again, along with the so-called new moral majority and its accompanying conservatism. As of this writing the debate is being assessed in the courts of Arkansas.

Although Darwin's contribution is not debated to any extent in academic circles, numerous assessments of his historical importance have poured out over the last two decades. This Darwin renaissance has been manifest in critical studies, scholarly journals, photographic anthologies, historical novels, and it has even included a movie and television series. The main focus of interest is on the events and circumstances surrounding the voyage of the *Beagle* and the establishment of the theory of evolution by natural selection. The subject of human evolution has received only brief consideration, and Darwin's contribution to the biological basis of behavior has been hardly broached. As a result, I have clearly biased this account toward the latter areas. Considerable emphasis has been placed on Darwin's human theoretical framework—his thinking on human nature and society. Interestingly, although he published formally in this area late in life, he gave the subject some reflection at the outset of his career, as the notebooks unpublished during his lifetime reveal. True, his formulations in this area are more speculative and less rigorous than the theory of evolution, nevertheless they have relevance to the concerns of a number of natural and human science disciplines and can be profitably reassessed. That Darwin's evolutionary formulations, when updated, can be used to challenge some of his speculative human theoretical assumptions attests to the magnitude of his contribution.

What has most hurt Darwin's reception in the human sciences has been the spectre of something not of his doing: social Darwinism. Throughout this study I have noted how social Darwinism misappropriated and misapplied several of Darwin's concepts, such as the struggle for existence and survival of the fittest, rather than utilizing the full range of Darwin's formulations or adhering to the way he actually applied these particular concepts. The phrase *survival of the fittest* actually came from Spencer, who according to several recent interpretations is the true father of social Darwinism. In researching this study, I found and have cited several writers who clearly point out that Darwin's ideas diverge rather markedly from the social Darwinist misinterpretation, so this is not an unacknowledged point of view. Nevertheless Darwin's name still sits uncomfortably in the history of the human sciences, while he is justly revered by the natural sciences.

This is not to suggest that Darwin's work is untainted by certain negative aspects of the nineteenth-century ideology, such as racism. Like Marx he was a child of his times, and to assess him totally in light of present attitudes is somewhat limiting. The context as well as the man must be mutually appraised. In my analysis I have tried to show that although there are racist assumptions in Darwin's work, these assumptions are embedded in what Michel Foucault might call "the true" of nineteenth-century scientific knowledge, a context that also embraced Marx. Even within this frame, Darwin diverged significantly from the dominant ideology of his times. His pronounced liberalism, human compassion, and assessment of the various races in terms of the single-species hypothesis clearly anticipate attitudes familiar to the human science disciplines in this century.

Perhaps the most remarkable, if one of the least-known, aspects of Darwin's contribution is his work on the evolution of the social and moral faculties. Any description of Darwin's human theory in terms of an individualist "might is right" perspective is certainly wanting, although this has been the social Darwinist interpretation. For Darwin, man is and always has been a social animal. His observations on sociability were in fact picked up by socialists such as Ferri, Panneköek, and Kautsky, and the anarchist Kropotkin. During the latter nineteenth century Darwin's name was favorably bandied about in socialist circles; in fact in certain conservative quarters, to be sympathetic to Darwinism was to be a suspected socialist. Although Darwin's work, even when extended using contemporary biosocial resources, cannot provide legitimation for particular political philosophies, it can help us question certain extreme tendencies, such as repressive forms of individualism.

Today several human science disciplines can profitably reassess the history of their dominant concerns in light of Darwin's contribution. This is not to suggest that his influence has not been felt. The various areas of biosocial research owe a significant, if not yet fully acknowledged, debt to the Darwinian revolution. Not surprisingly, these emerging biosocial fields have been the focus of several recent controversies. Attempts to discern the innate, evolutionary basis of human social behavior have been attacked as reactionary, racist, fascist, sexist, and so on. It is not actually a case whereby the practitioners are accused of holding these views; it is more along the lines of, "They know not what they do and what they do will inevitably lead in repressive and discriminatory directions." To summarize and critique these debates would require several volumes.[9] The debates surfaced in response to the work of Edward Wilson and the rise of sociobiology.[10]

As a result of the sociobiology debate, regardless of the merits of the respective sides, *sociobiology* has become a term used to refer to almost any attempt to apply biological understanding to the human realm. I have been a student of this enterprise for fifteen years. When I tell colleagues I am interested in biosocial approaches to the human sciences, they say "Well then, you are a sociobiologist." I try to explain that I think sociobiology is an important and misunderstood area; I draw from it, but my roots are elsewhere. Obviously an assessment of biosocial researches in the human sciences is beyond the scope of the present study. Nevertheless, in passing I should mention the significance I feel characterizes the pioneering efforts of anthropologists Irving Hallowell, Earl Count, and Eliot Chapple.[11] Their research deals with the human evolutionary environment largely unexamined in the work of later sociobiologists. Important biosocial contributions have also been made by Eibl-Ebesfeldt in ethology and Lionel Tiger and Robin Fox in anthropology.[12] Although the work of all three is usually lumped into the sociobiology arena, they have independent genealogies and more radical implications than either their critics, or they themselves, suspect. More recently Pierre van den Berghe has used sociobiology to produce a revealing biosocial framework for sociology; his biosocial roots also predate sociobiology.[13]

Neither sociobiology nor other biosocial areas of study represent social Darwinism resurrected. The belief that human nature has innate parameters does not invariably lead to a justification of the status quo. In fact sociobiology has even had a radical fringe of sorts. The anarchist Kropotkin was probably the most authentically Darwinian political philosopher who ever wrote. On the other hand a predominantly environmentalist position can be used to justify repressive political attitudes, as the recent history of monopoly capitalism attests. I find no contradiction in the fact, for example, that one of the most preeminent theorists in the human sciences, and one of the most radical, Chomsky, believes that specific innate parameters underlie the acquisition of human language. However, a number of his sympathetic political allies seem rather perplexed by his human science orientation.

To advocate a biosocial approach to the human sciences is not to advocate a rigid determinism. The social cannot be explained in whole by reference to the biological. Wilson's somewhat overzealous attempt to reduce traditional areas of study in the social sciences and humanities to sociobiological theory suffers the flaws of other reductionistic attempts at human understanding.[14] It creates a hierarchy, whereby the new approach (sociobiology) attempts to subsume the old (traditional social science and humanities inquiry); this is not unlike the attitude taken by several social sciences at the turn of this century, when they argued for disciplinary legitimacy and a mandate for studying human social behavior by denying the natural sciences any significant role in the enterprise. At times human sociobiology exhibits a direct overreaction to this unfortunate exclusion. It has sought to be the final arbiter on many areas within the human disciplines, when at best it can be an informative adjunct, paralleling and enlightening traditional approaches.

If the nature of our species is as sociobiologists like Wilson suggest, and I think he is right on a number of key issues, then the claims made for sociobiology can never gain the acceptance its practitioners hope for. True, we are a species capable of extensive elaborations in the logical arena of science, but we are also guided by other modes of apprehending the world, which cannot be subsumed to the canons of scientific inquiry. Recently one of the more astute critical theorists, William Leiss, seems inclined in this direction when he notes that science does not have, or should it aspire to, a monopoly on our understanding of either nature or human nature; such a monopoly can only lead to an unhealthy "conceptual imperialism."[15] In light of this I find it ironic that Wilson criticizes Marx and the Marxist tradition for failure to be scientific enough, when the real source for many of the quandaries in orthodox Marxism resides in its overly enthusiastic acceptance of what is signified by the label *scientific*, a bias rooted in the progressivist ideology of the nineteenth century.

These observations may appear to be a retreat from the major thrust of this book: that natural science understanding can and should inform the human disciplines. However to be informed by is not the same as being governed by. This distinction parallels that between a biosocial approach and sociobiology. What goes on in the human sphere cannot be reduced in whole to the biological. Yet there are regularities. Certain needs, even institutions, recur in a diversity of social and historical contexts. That these recurrences can be partly explained with reference to a scientifically inspired understanding of human nature and its evolution is a possibility the human disciplines have too long avoided. The legacy of Marx and Darwin might be one place to redress this oversight.

Finally, when it comes to informing human practice, what role can a biosocial perspective building on the tradition of Marx and Darwin play? Philosopher Vernon Venable provides a key when he refers to the negative science of man as conceived by Marx and Engels—in other words that a knowledge of human limitations is part of a positive emancipation it it frees us from misdirected activity.[16] I believe a biosocial approach can be relevant, not if it advises us regarding what to do, but if it charts limits by suggesting or warning us of things we should refrain from doing. In this area we cannot derive "ought" from "is"—to recycle David Hume's famous terminology—but we may be able to discern "ought not."

Notes

CHAPTER 1

1. Kernig 1972, p. 306.
2. Lefebvre 1969, p. 22
3. Harris 1970 tries to establish Herbert Spencer's priority in this area; his position has been severely challenged by Freeman 1974.
4. I am indebted to Caroline Ridout-Stewart for this observation.
5. Popper 1965; Popper 1969.
6. Barzun 1958.
7. Mayr 1964, pp. xi-xii.
8. Ghiselin 1972, pp. 4, 102.
9. Gruber and Barrett 1974.
10. Mayr 1967, p. vii.
11. Barzun 1958, p. 1.
12. Hook 1931, p. 290.
13. Bottomore and Rubel 1964, p. v.
14. Popper 1969, p. 3.
15. While the twentieth-century social science tradition has shown little interest in Marx and the human nature question, philosophers like Venable 1945 and Meszaros 1972 have emphasized its importance.
16. Popper 1969, p. 108.
17. Ibid., p. 107.
18. Ghiselin 1972, p. 67.
19. Cornforth 1968, p. 28.
20. Quoted in Fromm 1971, p. 256.
21. For example Avineri 1967; Avineri 1971; and McLellan 1973 have echoed this view.
22. Seigel 1974, p. 39.
23. Uranovsky 1973, p. 139.

24. Fromm 1971 and Sartre 1963 argue for this interpretation.
25. See Tylor 1898.
26. Avineri 1971.
27. Struik 1948.
28. Liebknecht n.d., p. 106.
29. Gruber and Barrett 1974, p. 71.
30. Cited by Gruber 1961, p. 583.
31. Cited by Timiryazeff 1927, p. 174
32. Cited by Colp 1974, p. 335.
33. Colp 1972; Feuer 1975; Colp 1976; Feuer 1976; Carroll 1976; Colp 1977, Fay 1978; Carroll 1978; Feuer 1978.
34. In Carroll 1976.
35. Feuer 1975.
36. Aveling 1897.
37. Colp 1976.
38. A personal opinion expressed by Lionel Tiger.
39. Hofstadter 1967, p. 92.
40. "I am no Marxist." Quoted in Becker and Barnes 1961, 2:701.
41. Rogers 1972, p. 272.
42. Colp 1974 and Avineri 1971 discuss Marx's attitude to the work of Friedrich Lange and Ludwig Buchner.
43. Aveling 1897.
44. Quoted in Ferri n.d., p. 13.
45. Pannekoëk 1912, p. 28.
46. Komarov in Bukharin 1973, p. 224.
47. Ferri n.d.
48. Hofstadter 1967, p. 152.
49. Pannekoëk 1912.
50. Kautsky 1918.
51. Lenin n.d.
52. Medved 1969; Joravsky 1970.
53. Medved 1969; p. 17.
54. Ibid., p. 25.
55. Zirkle 1959.
56. Graham 1971, p. 6.
57. Ibid., p. 195.
58. Ibid., p. 22.
59. Ibid., p. 8.
60. Lichtheim 1971, p. vii.
61. Sedgwick 1966, p. 183.
62. Sartre 1963.
63. Marcuse 1962; Marcuse 1968; Marcuse 1969.

64. Schmidt 1971.

65. Graham 1971, pp. 27, 30.

66. Marx's reputed uncritical attitude toward science is discussed in Habermas 1971.

CHAPTER 2

1. Althusser 1970, p. 14.

2. Himmelfarb 1968; Gruber and Barrett 1974.

3. See, for example, the appropriate discussion in chapters 1 and 9.

4. Himmelfarb 1968, p. 423.

5. Ghiselin 1972, p. 38.

6. Ibid., p. 46.

7. Lovejoy 1960.

8. These changes, as they occur in the ideational sphere, are eloquently described in ibid.

9. Himmelfarb 1968, pp. 27-28.

10. Ibid., p. 42.

11. These notebooks have recently been published in Gruber and Barrett 1974.

12. Eiseley 1961, p. 98.

13. Ghiselin 1972, p. 31.

14. This conversion is well documented in Himmelfarb 1968.

15. Eiseley 1961, p. 67.

16. Quoted in ibid., p. 73.

17. Harris 1970, pp. 122-23.

18. Freeman 1974.

19. Eiseley 1961, p. 179.

20. Vorzimmer 1970, p. 4.

21. Quoted in Himmelfarb 1968, pp. 160-61.

22. Ibid., p. 167. Although Himmelfarb, like a number of other writers, believes Marx thought he was standing Hegel on his head, the actual reference, in the introduction to *Das Kapital*, is to standing Hegel on his feet after finding him on his head, the obvious way a materialist such as Marx would be expected to operate.

23. In the foreword to *Origin*, p. 3.

24. I am indebted to biologist Tim Perper for these observations.

25. Ibid.

26. Ghiselin 1972, p. 46.

27. Ibid., p. 47.

28. As, for example, Harris 1970 does with Spencer.

29. Reprinted in *Evolution*.

30. The several works of David McLellan, from whom I have liberally drawn, are probably the best overall studies of Marx's life.

31. Darwin's illness has been the subject of some psychohistorical speculation. In his foreword to *The Voyage of the Beagle*, Leonard Engel cites Chaga's disease, a prolonged debilitating ailment caused by a South American parasite, as a distinct possibility. Colp 1977a has provided an exhaustive study of Darwin's affliction(s).

32. For example, Avineri 1971.

33. A good discussion of this period can be found in McLellan 1969b; McLellan 1970.

34. See especially the Martin Nicolaus edition cited in the chronological bibliography.

35. McLellan 1973 rightly emphasizes this.

36. Quoted in Singer 1974, p. 27.

37. Fromm 1971, p. 13.

38. Burrow 1970, p. 10.

39. Nisbet 1966, p. 208.

40. Godelier 1970, pp. 341-42.

41. Wilden 1972.

42. Graham 1971, p. 30.

43. Earlier, in a letter to Bloch dated September 21, 1890, Engles had tried to extricate himself and Marx from the accusation that their approach to history is predicated on a single factor. Note that in the following citation he used the term *materialist* conception of history, not *historical materialism* or *dialectical materialism*:

According to the materialist conception of history the determining element in history is *ultimately* the production and reproduction in real life. More than this neither Marx nor I have ever asserted. If therefore somebody twists this into the statement that the economic element is the only determining one, he transforms it into a meaningless abstract and absurd phrase. The economic situation is the basis, but the various elements of the superstructure—political forms of the class struggle and its consequences, constitutions established by the victorious class after a successful battle, etc.—also exercise their influence upon the course of historical struggles and in many cases preponderate in determining their form....We make our own history, but in the first case under very definite presuppositions and conditions.... Marx and I are ourselves partly to blame for the fact that younger writers sometimes lay more stress on the economic side than is due to it. We had to emphasize this main principal in opposition to our adversaries, who denied it. [*Torr*: 475-77]

44. This was written two years prior to the publication of *The Origin of Species*.

45. "Nature makes no leaps."

CHAPTER 3

1. One of the few commentators to downplay Hegel's influence on Marx is Althusser 1970.
2. Hyppolite 1969; Marcuse 1968.
3. Lowith 1967; Berlin 1963.
4. Ritchie 1893.
5. Hyppolite 1969, p. 129.
6. Petry 1970, p. 26.
7. Hegel 1970, p. 213.
8. Ibid.
9. Ibid., p. 218.
10. Ibid., 2: 216.
11. Hegel 1861, p. 58.
12. Ibid., p. 57.
13. This argument is elaborated in Ritchie 1893, p. 83.
14. Quoted in Lowith 1967, p. 226.
15. Quoted in Diderot 1963, p. 58.
16. This list of favorites is reprinted in Fromm 1971, p. 257.

CHAPTER 4

1. This view is elaborated in Eibl-Ebesfeldt 1972.
2. The history of science (including psychology) and philosophy in the Soviet Union is definitively surveyed by Graham 1971.
3. Marcuse 1961 extensively employs the rubric *Soviet Marxism* in the book of the same name.
4. Fromm 1971, p. 24.
5. Ollman 1973, p. 75.
6. The Scottish moral philosophers include Adam Smith, David Hume, Adam Ferguson, Thomas Ried, Francis Hutcheson, Dugald Stewart, Lord Kames, Lord Monboddo, and several lesser-known figures. An excellent anthology of their major statements can be found in Schneider 1967, and a useful interpretive survey has been written by Bryson 1945. Marx indicates that he was well versed in the writings of most of the Scots.
7. Marx himself was guilty of failing to integrate human nature with historical charge in his writings prior to 1845.
8. Feuerbach 1972, p. 243.
9. Ibid., p. 172.
10. Althusser 1970.
11. Meszaros 1972; Pappenheim 1968; Fromm 1971; Ollman 1973.

12. A stance central to Schmidt 1971; Avineri 1967; Avineri 1971.

13. Feuerbach 1972, p. 21.

14. Quoted in the introduction to ibid., p. 21.

15. Lenin n.d.

16. The foremost proponent of structuralism is French anthropologist Claude Lévi-Strauss.

17. This literature is assessed in chapter 9.

18. Lévi-Strauss 1969.

19. A point well substantiated in Bauman 1972. For an assessment of this work, see Heyer 1975.

20. For the contemporary anthropological view of tool use and manufacture, see Oakley 1967 and Washburn 1962.

21. Feuerbach 1972, p. 293.

CHAPTER 5

1. For a discussion of pangenesis, see Ghiselin 1972.

2. The Huxley-Wilberforce debate is recounted in Himmelfarb 1968; and Eiseley 1961.

3. Darwin's early notebooks are discussed in Gruber and Barrett 1974.

4. Darwin's ideas on sexual selection are explicated in Ghiselin 1972.

5. LeGros Clark 1959, p. 173.

6. Wallace 1889.

7. Fox 1975, p. 338.

8. For an elaboration of the paradigm concept in the history of science, see Kuhn 1970.

9. Quoted in Mepham 1973, p. 111.

10. Especially Chomsky 1972 and Lyons 1970.

11. Syntactic behavior is analyzed by Hallowell in Montagu 1968.

12. Tylor 1958, p. 2.

13. In Gestalt psychology see Kohler 1972; and for the ethological perspective, Eibl-Ebesfeldt 1970.

14. Quoted in Stern 1967, p. 103.

15. Among the more notable works in this rapidly increasing body of literature are Goodall 1972 and Schaller 1963.

16. This situation, as it is manifested in anthropology, is discussed in Fox 1975.

CHAPTER 6

1. As, for example, in Mannheim 1936.

2. The primary concern of Berger and Luckmann 1967.

3. I am indebted to Anthony Wilden for aiding my understanding of the importance of levels of constraint in human activity.

4. It was Wilden who showed me the implications of the periscope effect. He has expanded on it in the forthcoming second edition of *System and Structure*.

5. It is obvious, however, that Engles read Darwin's *Descent of Man* quite scrupulously. Reference to this aspect of Darwin appears in *Dialectics of Nature*, in particular the remarkable essay, "On the Part Played by Labour in the Transition from Ape to Man." Since Marx and Engels were in almost daily contact during this period (the 1870s), it seems unlikely that Marx would not have read the work as well, or at least received a summary of it from Engels.

6. At this stage (early 1840s) Marx had not yet acknowledged his own materialist bent. His approach can perhaps be described as a naturalistic humanism.

7. Feuerbach 1972, p. 156.

8. Ibid., pp. 244-245.

9. This hypothesis is discussed in the essay on the role of labor in human evolution, which will be assessed in chapter 9.

10. For a thorough recent examination of Rousseau, see Masters 1976.

11. A notion that anticipates the twentieth-century tradition of social psychology, particularly the work of G. H. Mead.

12. The term *social organism* was used extensively by Durkheim. The *superorganic* was originally coined by Spencer to denote the social aggregate. However, the contemporary use of *superorganic* derives from the formulations of anthropologists Alfred Kroeber and Leslie White. Both the social organism and the superorganic refer to the social as a phenomenon sui generis, a process separate from the qualities of the individuals comprising it and one that is inexplicable by any reference to psychology and biology.

13. These traditions include ethology, the new physical anthropology (new referring to a concern with behaviorial evolution as opposed to the old physical anthropology, which focused more on fossil interpretation), and sociobiology.

14. A view overlooked by almost every contemporary Marxist tradition.

15. That humankind is prefigured or predisposed for the social is a recurring theme in Bergson n.d., who is discussed in chapter 7.

16. These studies are documented in Krader 1972 and are discussed in chapter 8.

17. The so-called hunting hypothesis has been elaborated in popular form by Ardrey 1976; more academic accounts of it can be found in Lee and DeVore 1968; Coon 1971; and Service 1967.

18. The idea that in primitive or nonstate societies social and natural

relations are more fully congruent has been recently elaborated by the renowned anthropologist Claude Lévi-Strauss 1969a and 1969b.

19. In this sense he can be seen as an anticipator of the links between language and culture implied by the Sapir-Whorf hypothesis. It is interesting to note that Edward Sapir extensively read Herder and held him in high esteem.

20. Quoted in Berlin 1965, p. 51.

21. Kaufman 1966a, p. 103.

22. For example in Salter 1971; Salter 1978; and in Salter's forthcoming *The Agency of the State*.

CHAPTER 7

1. Looking comparatively at the similarities and differences between species.

2. The attack was waged in *BioScience* 26, no. 3, and *New York Review of Books*, November 13, 1975.

3. This process is most fully described in Spencer 1912.

4. For the notion of social and cultural evolution as a viable twentieth-century perspective, see Steward 1955; White 1959; and Sahlins and Service 1960.

5. Wilson 1975, pp. 3-4.

6. Ibid., p. 118.

7. Alland 1967 makes a strong case for this position.

8. Bradley 1967, p. 170.

9. Ibid., p. 174.

10. Tönnies 1963. In another earlier edition, the title of the work was translated as *Community and Association*.

11. Ibid., p. 208.

12. Ibid., p. 105.

13. Ibid., p. 107.

14. This point is well argued by Pappenheim 1968.

15. *The Search for Society: Darwin and the Legacy of Durkheim.*

16. Durkheim 1966, p. 13.

17. Durkheim 1964, p. 197.

18. Bergson n.d., p. 15.

19. Ibid., p. 14.

20. Ibid., pp. 55-56.

21. Ibid., p. 100.

22. A notable attempt to inject Bergsonian notions into a contemporary social science perspective can be found in the structuralist analysis of totemism undertaken in Lévi-Strauss 1969b.

CHAPTER 8

1. I use the term *primitive* in its highly respectful anthropological sense to indicate the existence of humanity prior to the advent of the state or civilization. For a full elaboration of this concept, see Diamond 1975 and Montagu 1968a.

2. Rousseau 1964, p. 93.

3. Eiseley 1961, p. 9; Himmelfarb 1968, p. 377.

4. Quoted in Eiseley 1961, p. 303.

5. Ibid., p. 312.

6. A historical assessment of Tylor can be found in Stocking 1968. He uses the phrase *cultural Darwinism* to describe Tylor's perspective.

7. The classification and explanation of racial variation is a controversy far from being resolved. An interesting but by no means orthodox attempt can be found in Brace and Montagu 1965.

8. Krader 1972.

9. Ibid., p. 58.

10. Ibid., p. 44.

11. Ibid., p. 12.

12. A thorough survey of the literature can be found in Harris 1970.

13. Terray 1972.

14. Deborin 1973, p. 112.

15. Zirkle 1959.

16. Ibid, p. 33.

17. Cuno n.d., p. 212. The advantages are not stated.

CHAPTER 9·

1. Althusser 1970 is an example of a more recent Marx interpreter taking this stance.

2. Lichtheim 1971, p. 66.

3. Avineri 1971, pp. 69-70.

4. Sedgwick 1966, p. 183.

5. Ibid., p. 191.

6. Ollman 1973, p. 52.

7. Mayer 1936 remains the standard interpretation.

8. Bernal 1935, p. 506.

9. Wilson 1953.

10. Quoted in Henderson 1967, p. 11.

11. Marcus 1974 provides an informative account of the events and circumstances surrounding this period in Engles's life.

12. The inconsiderateness of Marx is particularly evident in the correspondences asking Engles for money.

13. Mayer 1936, p. 67.
14. Lafargue 1971, p. 238.
15. Mayer 1936, p. 238.
16. Ollman 1973, p. 53.
17. Hodges 1965, p. 298.
18. Avineri 1971, p. 69.
19. Nova 1967, p. 84.
20. Bober 1965, p. 286.
21. Sedgwick 1966, p. 190.
22. Avineri 1971, pp. 65-66.
23. Sartre 1963, p. vii.
24. Korcsh 1970, p. 92.
25. Haldane 1969, p. xii.
26. Ibid., p. xiv.
27. Himmelfarb 1968, pp. 160-61, 245.
28. Haeckel 1909, p. 140.
29. Wallace 1889.
30. Zirkle 1959 takes this track.
31. Ibid.
32. Haldane 1969, p. 156.
33. Graham 1971, p. 35.
34. As noted in chapter 4.

CHAPTER 10

1. Aron 1968, p. 145.
2. Nisbet 1966.
3. Bowlby 1972. The Freud-Darwin link has also been insightfully explored in Sulloway 1979.
4. Eibl-Ebesfeldt 1972.
5. Wilson 1979.
6. Katz-Fishman and Fritz 1980.
7. Thompson 1978.
8. Timpanaro 1978.
9. Caplan 1978 has compiled a useful preliminary compendium.
10. Wilson 1975, 1979.
11. Hallowell 1971; Count 1968; Chapple 1970.
12. Eibl-Ebesfeldt 1970; Tiger and Fox 1974.
13. van den Berghe 1978; van den Berghe 1979.
14. Wilson 1979.
15. Leiss 1979, p. 396.
16. Venable 1945.

References ⸻

WORKS BY MARX, ENGELS, AND DARWIN CITED IN THE TEXT

Karl Marx (1818-1883)

Early Texts	*Early Texts*. Translated and edited by David McLellan. New York: Barnes and Noble, 1971. Contains various excerpts written before 1845.
Critique Hegel	*Critique of Hegel's Philosophy of Right*. Edited, with an Introduction and Notes by Joseph O'Malley. London: Cambridge University Press, 1970. Originally written 1841-1843.
Paris Manuscripts	*The Economic and Philosophical Manuscripts of 1844*. Edited with an Introduction by Dirk V. Struik and translated by Martin Milligan. New York: International Publishers, 1972. Unpublished during Marx's lifetime and probably not intended for publication.
Holy Family	and Frederick Engels. *The Holy Family*. Translated by R. Dixon. Moscow: Foreign Languages Publishing House, 1956. First published 1845.
German Ideology	and Frederick Engels. *The German Ideology*. Moscow: Progress Publishers, 1964. Originally written 1845-1847 and unpublished in their lifetime, though attempts were made.
Poverty Philosophy	*The Poverty of Philosophy*. New York: International Publishers, 1973. First published 1847.
Wage Labour	*Wage Labour and Capital*. Moscow: Progress Publishers, 1974. Given as a series of lectures in 1847, which later became articles in 1849.

Manifesto and Frederick Engels. *The Communist Manifesto.* New York: International Publishers, 1969. First published 1848.

18th Brumaire *The Eighteenth Brumaire of Louis Bonaparte.* New York: International Publishers, 1969. First published 1852.

Grundrisse *Grundrisse: Foundations of the Critique of Political Economy (Rough Draft).* Translated with a Foreword by Martin Nicolaus. Middlesex, England: Penguin Books Ltd., 1973. Unpublished notebooks drafted 1857-1858.

Critique *A Contribution to the Critique of Political Economy.* Translated by S. W. Ryazanskaya and edited with an Introduction by Maurice Dobb. New York: International Publishers, 1970. First published 1859.

Theories *Theories of Surplus Value.* Translated by G. A. Bonner and Emile Burns. New York: International Publishers, 1952. Originally written 1861-1863 and published after Marx's death as volume 4 of *Capital,* edited by Karl Kautsky.

Capital 1, 2, 3 *Capital: A Critique of Political Economy.* Translated by Samuel Moore and Edward Aveling and edited by Frederick Engels. New York: International Publishers, 1967. First edition of vol. 1 published 1867, vol. 2 1887, vol. 3 1894.

Critique Gotha *Critique of the Gotha Program.* New York: International Publishers, 1970. Originally written in 1875 and first published by Engels in 1891.

Moscow and Frederick Engels. *Selected Correspondence.* Moscow: Foreign Languages Publishing House, 1953.

Torr and Frederick Engels. *Correspondence, 1846-1895.* Translated by Dona Torr. New York: International Publishers, 1936.

Americans and Frederick Engels. *Letters to Americans, 1848-1895.* New York: International Publishers, 1957.

Kuglemann *Letters to Dr. Kuglemann.* New York: International Publishers.

Frederick Engels (1820-1895)

Outlines	*Outlines of a Critique of Political Economy.* Reprinted in *Paris Manuscripts.* First published 1844.
Working Class	*The Condition of the Working Class in England.* Translated and edited by W. O. Henderson and W. H. Chalmers. Oxford: Blackwell, 1971. First published 1845.
Anti-Dühring	*Anti-Dühring.* Translated by Emile Burns. New York: International Publishers, 1970. First published 1878.
Dialectics	*Dialectics of Nature.* Translated and edited by Clemens Dutt, with a Preface and notes by J. B. S. Haldane (1939). New York: International Publishers, 1963. Unpublished during Engels's lifetime, probably written between 1872 and 1880.
Origin Family	*The Origin of the Family, Private Property, and the State.* With an Introduction and notes by Eleanor Leacock. New York: International Publishers, 1972. First published 1884.
Feuerbach	*Ludwig Feuerbach and the Outcome of Classical German Philosophy.* New York: International Publishers, 1970. First published 1888.
Socialism	*Socialism Utopian and Scientific.* New York: International Publishers, 1969. First published 1892.
Selected	*Engels: Selected Writings.* Edited with an Introduction by W. O. Henderson. Baltimore, Md.: Penguin Books, 1967.
Lafargue, 1, 2, 3	*Engels, Frederick, Paul and Laura Lafargue: Correspondence.* 3 vols. Moscow: Foreign Languages Publishing House, 1959, 1960.

Charles Darwin (1809-1882)

Evolution	and Alfred Russel Wallace. *Evolution by Natural Selection.* London: Cambridge University Press, 1958. Contains Darwin's sketch of 1842, his essay of 1844, and the joint paper of 1858 with Wallace.

Voyage   *The Voyage of the Beagle*. Annotated with an
                            Introduction by Leonard Engel. New York: Dou-
                            bleday, 1962. First published in popular form
                            in 1845, although an earlier version appeared
                            in 1839.

Origin 1st   *On the Origin of Species by Charles Darwin: A
                            Facsimile of the First Edition*. Introduction by
                            Ernst Mayr. 2 vols. Cambridge: Harvard Uni-
                            versity Press, 1964. First published 1859.

Variation 1, 2   *The Variation of Animals and Plants under Do-
                            mestication*. 2 vols. New York: Appleton, 1898.
                            First published 1868.

Descent   *The Descent of Man and Selection in Relation to
                            Sex*. New York: Rand McNally & Company,
                            n.d. First published 1871.

Expression   *The Expression of the Emotions in Man and Ani-
                            mals*. Preface by Konrad Lorenz. Chicago: Uni-
                            versity of Chicago Press, 1970. First published
                            1872.

Origin   *The Origin of Species*. Foreword by G. G. Simp-
                            son. New York: Collier, 1969. The sixth and
                            last edition was published in 1872.

Life 1, 2, 3   *The Life and Letters of Charles Darwin*. Edited by
                            Francis Darwin. 3 vols. London: Murray, 1887.

More Letters 1, 2   *More Letters of Charles Darwin*. Edited by Fran-
                            cis Darwin and A. C. Seward. 2 vols. New
                            York: Appleton, 1903.

OTHER SOURCES CONSULTED

Adams, H. P.
        1972   *Karl Marx in His Earlier Writings*. New York: Antheneum.
Alland, Alexander, Jr.
        1967   *Evolution and Human Behavior*. Garden City, N.Y.: Natu-
                ral History Press.
Alpert, Harry
        1939   *Emile Durkheim*. New York: Columbia University Press.
Althusser, Louis
        1970   *For Marx*. New York: Random House, Vintage Books.
Appleman, Philip, ed.
        1970   *Darwin*. New York: W. W. Norton.

Ardrey, Robert
    1976   *The Hunting Hypothesis*. New York: Bantam.
Aron, Raymond
    1962   *Introduction to the Philosophy of History*. Boston: Beacon Press.
    1968   *Main Currents in Sociological Thought*. Garden City, N.Y.: Doubleday.
Aveling, Edward B.
    1889   *Darwin Made Easy*. London: Progressive Publishing Co.
    1897   Charles Darwin and Karl Marx. *New Century Review* (June).
Avineri, Shlomo
    1967   From Hoax to Dogma: A Footnote on Marx and Darwin. *Encounter* (March).
    1971   *The Social and Political Thought of Karl Marx*. Cambridge: Cambridge University Press.
Barash, David
    1979   *The Whisperings Within: Evolution and the Origin of Human Nature*. New York: Penguin Books.
Barnett, S. A., ed.
    1959   *A Century of Darwin*. Cambridge: Harvard University Press.
Barzun, Jacques
    1958   *Darwin, Marx, Wagner*. Garden City, N.Y.: Doubleday.
Bauman, Zygmunt
    1972   *Culture as Praxis*. London: Routledge & Kegan Paul.
Becker, E.
    1968   *The Structure of Evil*. New York: George Braziller.
    1971   *The Lost Science of Man*. New York: George Braziller.
Becker, Howard, and Harry Elmer Barnes
    1961   *Social Thought from Lore to Science*. 3 vols. New York: Dover.
Berger, Peter, ed.
    1969   *Marxism and Sociology: Views from Eastern Europe*. New York: Irvington.
Berger, Peter, and Thomas Luckmann
    1967   *The Social Construction of Reality*. Garden City, N.Y.: Doubleday.
Bergson, Henri
    n.d.   *The Two Sources of Morality and Religion*. Garden City, N.Y.: Doubleday.
Berlin, Isaiah
    1963   *Karl Marx*. New York: Oxford University Press.

1965   Herder and the Enlightenment. In *Aspects of the Eigh-
            teenth Century*. ed. E. R. Wasserman. Baltimore, Md.:
            Johns Hopkins Press.

Bernal, J. D.
1935   Engels and Science. *Labour Monthly* 17, no. 8.

Bernstein, E.
1967   *Evolutionary Socialism*. New York: Schocken.

Boas, Franz
1968   *The Mind of Primitive Man*. New York: Macmillan. First
            published 1911.

Bober, M. M.
1965   *Karl Marx's Interpretation of History*. New York: W. W.
            Norton.

Bock, Kenneth E.
1955   Darwin and Social Theory. *Philosophy of Science* 22, no.
            2.

Bottomore, T. B., and Maximilien Rubel, eds.
1964   *Karl Marx: Selected Writings in Sociology and Social Philoso-
            phy*. New York: McGraw-Hill.

Bowlby, John
1972   *On Attachment*. Middlesex: Penguin Books.

Brace, Loring, and Ashley Montagu
1965   *Man's Evolution*. New York: Macmillan.

Bradley, F. H.
1967   *Ethical Studies*. Oxford: Oxford at the Clarendon Press.

Bryson, Gladys
1945   *Man and Society: The Scottish Inquiry of the Eighteenth Cen-
            tury*. Princeton, N.J.: Princeton University Press.

Bukharin, Nikolai
1969   *Historical Materialism*. Ann Arbor: University of Michi-
            gan Press.

Bukharin, Nikolai, et al., eds.
1973   *Marxism and Modern Thought*. Westport, Conn.: Hyperion
            Press.

Burrow, J. W.
1970   *Evolution and Society*. Cambridge: Cambridge University
            Press.

Butler, Samuel
1924   *Life and Habit*. London: Jonathan Cape.

Caplan, Arthur, ed.
1978   *The Sociobiology Debate*. New York: Harper and Row.

Carneiro, Robert L.
1970   A Theory of the Origin of the State. *Science*, 169.

Carroll, Thomas
    1976   On the Darwin-Marx Correspondence. *Annals of Science* 33.
    1978   Correction to Margaret A. Fay's Article. *Journal of the History of Ideas.* 34, no. 4 (October-December).

Carter, C.S.
    1960   *A Hundred Years of Evolution.* London: Sidgwick and Jackson.

Chambers, Robert
    1969   *Vestiges of the Natural History of Creation.* New York: Humanities Press.

Chapple, Eliot
    1970   *Culture and Biological Man.* New York: Holt, Rhinehart and Winston.

Charbonnier, Georges
    1969   *Conversations with Claude Levi-Strauss.* London: Jonathan Cape.

Chomsky, Noam
    1972   *Problems of Knowledge and Freedom.* New York: Random House.

Cohen, Ronald, and Elman Service
    1978   *Origins of the State.* Philadelphia: Institute for the Study of Human Issues.

Colp, Ralph, Jr.
    1974   The Contacts between Karl Marx and Charles Darwin. *Journal of the History of Ideas,* 35, no. 2.
    1976   On the Darwin-Marx Correspondence. *Annals of Science,* 33.
    1977   Darwin's Complaint. *New York Review of Books,* October 27.
    1977a   *To Be an Invalid.* Chicago: University of Chicago Press.

Coon, Carleton
    1971   *The Hunting Peoples.* Boston: Little, Brown.

Cornforth, Maurice
    1968   *The Open Philosophy and the Open Society.* New York: International Publishers.

Count, Earl
    1968   The Biological Basis of Human Sociality. In *Culture: Man's Adaptive Dimension,* ed. Ashley Montagu. New York: Oxford University Press.

Cuno, Theodore
    n.d.   Reminiscences of Marx and Engels. In *Reminiscences of Marx and Engels,* ed. Foreign Languages Publishing House. Moscow: Foreign Languages Publishing House.

Darwin, Francis, ed.
    1958   *The Autobiography of Charles Darwin and Selected Letters.*
            New York: Dover.
Deborin, A. M.
    1973   Karl Marx and the Present. In *Marxism and Modern Thought,*
            ed. N. Bukharin et al. Westport, Conn.: Hyperion Press.
Desan, Wilfred
    1966   *The Marxism of Jean-Paul Sartre.* Garden City, N.Y.:
            Doubleday.
Diamond, Stanley
    1975   *The Search for the Primitive.* New Brunswick, N.J.: Trans-
            action Press.
Diderot, Denis
    1963   *Diderot: Interpreter of Nature,* ed. Jonathan Kemp. New
            York: International Publishers.
Durkheim, Emile
    1964   *The Division of Labor in Society.* New York: Free Press.
    1966   *The Rules of the Sociological Method.* New York: Free Press.
Eibl-Ebesfeldt, Irenaus
    1970   *Ethology: The Biology of Behavior.* New York: Holt, Rine-
            hart, and Winston.
    1972   *Love and Hate.* New York: Holt, Rinehart, and Winston.
Eiseley, Loren
    1961   *Darwin's Century.* Garden City, N.Y.: Doubleday.
Fay, Margaret A.
    1978   Did Marx Offer to Dedicate *Capital* to Darwin? *Journal of
            the History of Ideas.* 39, no. 1 (January-March).
Ferri, Enrico
    n.d.   *Socialism and Modern Science.* Chicago: Charles H. Kerr &
            Company.
Fetscher, Iring
    1971   *Marx and Marxism.* New York: Herder and Herder.
Feuer, Lewis
    1975   Is the Darwin-Marx Correspondence Authentic? *Annals
            of Science* 32.
    1976   On the Darwin-Marx Correspondence. *Annals of Science*
            33.
    1978   The Case of the 'Darwin-Marx' Letter. A Study in Socio-
            Literary Detection: *Encounter* (October).
Feuerbach, Ludwig
    1957   *The Essence of Christianity.* New York: Harper & Brothers.
    1972   *The Fiery Brook,* trans. Zawar Hanfi. New York: Doubleday.

Findlay, J. N.
    1970   *Hegel: A Re-examination*. London: Allen and Unwin.
Firth, Raymond
    1972   *The Sceptical Anthropologist? Social Anthropology and Marxist Views on Society*. London: Oxford University Press.
Foreign Languages Publishing House
    n.d.   *Reminiscences of Marx and Engels*. Moscow: Foreign Languages Publishing House.
Foucault, Michel
    1973   *The Order of Things*. New York: Random House.
Fox, Robin
    1975   *Encounter with Anthropology*. New York: Dell.
            The Search for Society: Darwin and the Legacy of Durkheim. In preparation.
Freeman, Derek
    1974   The Evolutionary Theories of Charles Darwin and Herbert Spencer. *Current Anthropology* 15 no. 3 (September).
Fromm, Erich
    1966   *Socialist Humanism*. New York: Anchor Books.
    1971   *Marx's Concept of Man*. New York: Ungar.
Ghiselin, Michael T.
    1972   *The Triumph of the Darwinian Method*. Berkeley: University of California Press.
    1973   Darwin and Evolutionary Psychology. *Science* 179 (March).
Glass, Bentley, et al., eds.
    1968   *Forerunners of Darwin, 1745-1859*. Baltimore, Md.: Johns Hopkins Press.
Godelier, Maurice
    1970   System and Structure in *Das Kapital*. In *Introduction to Structuralism*, ed. Michael Lane. New York: Basic Books.
Goodall, Jane
    1972   *In the Shadow of Man*. New York: Dell.
Gould, Stephan Jay
    1979   *Ever Since Darwin: Reflections in Natural History*. New York: W.W. Norton and Company.
Graham, Loren
    1971   *Science and Philosophy in the Soviet Union*. New York: Knopf.
Greene, John C.
    1959   *The Death of Adam*. Ames: Iowa State University Press.
    1961   *Darwin and the Modern World View*. Baton Rouge: Louisiana State University Press.

Gregor, A. James
   1965   *A Survey of Marxism*. New York: Random House.
Gruber, Howard E.
   1961   Darwin and Das Kapital. *Isis* 52, no. 170 (December).
Gruber, Howard E., and Paul H. Barrett
   1974   *Darwin on Man*. New York: E. P. Dutton.
Habermas, Jurgen
   1971   *Knowledge and Human Interests*, trans. Jeremy J. Shapiro. Boston: Beacon Press.
Haeckel, Ernst
   1909   *Last Words on Evolution*. London: Watts.
Haldane, J.B.S.
   1963   Preface to *Dialectics of Nature*, by Frederick Engels. New York: International Publishers.
   1969   *The Marxist Philosophy and the Sciences*. Freeport, N.Y.: Books for Libraries Press.
Hallowell, Irving
   '1968   Self,Society and Culture in Phylogenetic Perspective. In *Culture: Man's Adaptive Dimension*, ed. Ashley Montagu. New York: Oxford University Press.
   1971   *Culture and Experience*. New York: Schoken Books.
Harnad, Stevan, et. al., eds.
   1976   *Origins and Evolution of Language and Speech*. New York: New York Academy of Sciences.
Harris, Marvin
   1970   *The Rise of Anthropological Theory*. New York: Crowell.
Hegel, G.W.F.
   1861   *Lectures on the Philosophy of History*. London: Bohn.
   1961   *The Phenomenology of Mind*. London: Allen and Unwin.
   1969   *Hegel's Science of Logic*. London: Allen and Unwin.
   1970   *Hegel's Philosophy of Nature*, ed. N. J. Petry. London: Allen and Unwin.
Heilbroner, Robert L.
   1970   *Between Capitalism and Socialism*. New York: Random House.
   1972   *The Wordly Philosophers*. New York: Simon and Schuster.
   1974   The Human Prospect. *New York Review of Books*, 22, nos. 21-22, January 24.
Henderson, W. D., ed.
   1967   *Engels: Selected Writings*. Baltimore, Md.: Penquin Books.

Hewes, Gordon
    1973   Primate Communication and the Gestural Origin of Language. *Current Anthropology* 14, nos. 1-2.

Heyer, Paul
    1975   Review of *Culture as Praxis* by Zygmunt Bauman. *Leonardo* (Winter).

Himmelfarb, Gertrude
    1968   *Darwin and the Darwinian Revolution.* New York: W. W. Norton.

Hobsbawm, E. J., ed.
    1971   *Pre-Capitalist Economic Formations by Karl Marx.* New York: International Publishers.

Hockett, Charles F., and Robert Ascher
    1964   The Human Revolution. *Current Anthropology* 5, no. 3.

Hodges, Donald Clark
    1965   Engels' Contribution to Marxism. *Socialist Register* (annual).

Hofstadter, Richard
    1967   *Social Darwinism in American Thought.* Boston: Beacon Press.

Hook, Sidney
    1931   Marx and Darwinism. *New Republic*, July 29.
    1968   *From Hegel to Marx.* Ann Arbor: University of Michigan Press.

Hume, David
    1969   *A Treatise of Human Nature.* Baltimore, Md.: Penguin Books.

Huxley, Thomas H.
    1959   *Man's Place in Nature.* Ann Arbor: University of Michigan Press. First published 1863.

Hyppolite, Jean
    1969   *Studies on Marx and Hegel.* New York: Basic Books.

Innis, Harold
    1964   *The Bias of Communication.* Toronto: University of Toronto Press.

Irvine, William
    1956   *Apes, Angels, and Victorians.* London: Reader Union.

Jackson, T. A.
    1936   *Dialectics.* Toronto: Frances White.

Joravsky, David
    1970   *The Lysenko Affair.* Cambridge: Harvard University Press.

Kamenka, Eugene
    1970   *The Philosophy of Ludwig Feuerbach.* New York: Praeger.
    1972   *The Ethical Foundations of Marxism.* London: Routledge &
             Kegan Paul.
Katz-Fishman, Walda and Jon F. Fritz
    1980   The Politics of Sociobiology. *The Insurgent Sociologist* 10,
             no. 1 (Summer).
Kaufman, Walter
    1966a   *Hegel: A Reinterpretation.* New York: Doubleday.
    1966b   *Nietzsche.* New York: Meridian Books.
Kautsky, Karl
    1918   *Ethics and the Materialist Conception of History.* Chicago:
             Charles H. Kerr.
Kernig, C. D.
    1972   *Marxism, Communism, and Western Society: A Comparative
             Encyclopedia.* New York: Herder and Herder.
Kohler, Wolfgang
    1972   *The Task of Gestalt Psychology.* Princeton, N.J.: Princeton
             University Press.
Korsch, Karl
    1970   *Marxism and Philosophy.* New York: Monthly Review Press.
Krader, Lawrence
    1972   *The Ethnological Notebooks of Karl Marx.* The Netherlands:
             Assen.
Kuhn, Thomas
    1970   *The Structure of Scientific Revolutions.* Chicago: The Uni-
             versity of Chicago Press.
Lafargue, Paul
    n.d.   *The Evolution of Property.* Chicago: Charles H. Kerr &
             Company.
    1971   Reminiscences of Marx. In Erich Fromm, *Marx's Concept
             of Man.* New York: Ungar.
Lamarck, J. B.
    1914   *Zoological Philosophy.* London: Macmillan. First published
             1809.
Landmann, Michael
    1974   *Philosophical Anthropology.* Philadelphia: Westminster Press.
Laughlin, Charles
    1974   *Biogenetic Structuralism.* New York: Columbia University
             Press.
Leacock, Eleanor
    1972   Introduction to *The Origin of the Family, Private Property*

and the State, by Frederick Engels. New York: International Publishers.

Lee, Richard, and Irven DeVore
1968   *Man the Hunter*. Chicago: Aldine.

Lefebvre, Henri
1969   *The Sociology of Marx*. New York: Random House.

LeGros Clark, W. E.
1959   The Study of Man's Descent. In *A Century of Darwin*, ed. S. A. Barnett. Cambridge: Harvard University Press.

Leiss, William
1974   *The Domination of Nature*. Boston: Beacon Press.
1979   "Scientific Culture in the Contemporary World" in *SCIENTIA-International Review of Scientific Synthesis* edited by U. Mathieu and P. Rossi. Milan.

Lenin, V. I.
n.d.   *Materialism and Empirio-Criticism*. Moscow: Foreign Languages Publishing House.

Lévi-Strauss, Claude
1963   Rousseau, Father of Anthropology. *Unesco Courrier* (March).
1969   *The Raw and the Cooked*. New York: Harper Torchbooks.
1969a   *The Scope of Anthropology*. London: Jonathan Cape.
1969b   *Totemism*. Boston: Beacon Press.

Lichtheim, George
1964   *Marxism*. New York: Praeger.
1969   *The Origins of Socialism*. New York: Praeger.
1971   *From Marx to Hegel*. New York: Herder and Herder.

Liebknecht, Wilhelm
n.d.   Reminiscences of Marx and Engels. In *Reminiscences of Marx and Engels*, ed. Foreign Languages Publishing House. Moscow: Foreign Languages Publishing House.

Linden, Eugene
1976   *Apes, Men, and Language*. New York: Penguin.

Lindsay, Jack
1949   *Marxism and Contemporary Science*. London: Denis Dobson Ltd.

Loewenberg, J.
1965   *Hegel's Phenomenology*. La Salle, Ill.: Open Court.

Lorenz, Konrad
1971   *Evolution and Modification of Behavior*. Chicago: University of Chicago Press.

Lovejoy, Arthur O.
1960   *The Great Chain of Being*. New York: Harper & Row.

Lowith, Karl
    1967   *From Nietzche to Hegel*. New York: Anchor Books.
Lucretius
    1968   *On the Nature of the Universe*. Baltimore, Md.: Penguin
              Books.
Lyons, John
    1970   *Chomsky*. London: Fontana.
Macbeth, Norman
    1973   *Darwin Retried*. New York: Dell.
McLellan, David
    1969a   Marx's View of the Unalienated Society, *Review of Poli-
              tics* 31, no. 4 (October).
    1969b   *The Young Hegelians and Karl Marx*. New York: Praeger.
    1970   *Marx before Marxism*. New York: Harper and Row.
    1973   Karl Marx: *His Life and Thought*. New York: Harper & Row.
McLellan, David, ed.
    1972   *The Grundrisse by Karl Marx*. New York: Harper Torchbooks.
Mandelbaum, Maurice
    1971   *History, Man & Reason*. Baltimore, Md.: Johns Hopkins
              Press.
Mannheim, Karl
    1936   *Ideology and Utopia*. New York: Harcourt, Brace and World.
Marcus, Steven
    1974   *Engels, Manchester and the Working Class*. New York: Ran-
              dom House.
Marcuse, Herbert
    1961   *Soviet Marxism: A Critical Analysis*. New York: Vintage
              Books.
    1962   *Eros and Civilization*. New York: Random House.
    1968   *Reason and Revolution*. Boston: Beacon Press.
    1969   *One-Dimensional Man*. Boston: Beacon Press.
Masters, Roger
    1976   *The Political Philosophy of Rousseau*. Princeton: Princeton
              University Press.
Mauss, Marcel
    1970   *The Gift*: London: Routledge & Kegan Paul.
Mayer, Gustave
    1936   *Frederick Engels*. New York: Alfred A. Knopf.
Mayr, Ernst
    1964   Introduction to *On the Origin of Species by Charles Darwin:
              A Facsimile of the First Edition*. Cambridge: Harvard Uni-
              versity Press.

Mead, G. H.
 1970 *Mind, Self, and Society*. Chicago: University of Chicago Press.

Medved, Z. A.
 1969 *The Rise and Fall of T. D. Lysenko*. New York: Columbia University Press.

Mehring, Franz
 1969 *Karl Marx*. Ann Arbor: University of Michigan Press.

Mepham, John
 1973 The Structuralist Sciences and Philosophy. In *Structuralism: An Introduction*, ed. David Robey. London: Oxford University Press.

Merz, John Theodore
 1965 *A History of European Thought in the Nineteenth Century*. 7 vols. New York: Dover.

Meszaros, Istvan
 1972 *Marx's Theory of Alienation*. New York: Harper Torchbooks.

Meyer, Alfred G.
 1970 *Marxism: The Unity of Theory and Practice*. Cambridge: Harvard University Press.

Montagu, Ashley
 1962 *Culture and the Evolution of Man*. New York: Oxford University Press.

Montagu, Ashley, ed.
 1968 *Culture: Man's Adaptive Dimension*. New York: Oxford University Press.

 1968a *The Concept of the Primitive*. New York: Macmillan.

 1980 *Sociobiology Examined*. New York: Oxford University Press.

Moore, Stanley
 1967 Marx and the State of Nature. *Journal of the History of Philosophy* 5, no. 2 (April).

Morgan, Lewis H.
 1868 *The American Beaver and His Works*. Philadelphia: Lippincott.

 1969 *Ancient Society*. Cleveland, Ohio: Meridian Books. First published n.d.

Murphy, Robert
 1971 *The Dialectics of Social Life*. New York: Basic Books.

Nasmyth, George
 1916 *Social Progress and the Darwinian Method*. New York: Putnam's.

Nisbet, Robert A.
 1966 *The Sociological Tradition*. New York: Basic Books.

1969   *Social Change and History*. New York: Oxford University Press.

Nova, Fritz
1967   *Frederick Engels: His Contributions to Political Theory*. New York: Philosophical Library.

Oakley, Kenneth
1967   *Man the Tool Maker*. Chicago: University of Chicago Press.

Odajnyk, Walter
1965   *Marxism and Existentialism*. Garden City, N.Y.: Doubleday.

Ollman, Bertell
1973   *Alienation: Marx's Conception of Man in Capitalist Society*. New York: Cambridge University Press.

Owens, Rochelle
1974   *The Karl Marx Play*. New York: E.P. Dutton and Company.

Panneköek, Anton
1912   *Marxism and Darwinism*. Chicago: Charles H. Kerr & Company.

Pappenheim, Fritz
1968   *The Alienation of Modern Man*. New York: Monthly Review Press.

Parsons, Talcott
1967   *The Structure of Social Action*. New York: Free Press.

Peckham, Morse, ed.
1959   *The Origin of Species by Charles Darwin: A Variorum Text*. Philadelphia: University of Pennsylvania Press.

Penniman, T. K.
1965   *A Hundred Years of Anthropology*. London: Gerald Duckworth & Co. Ltd.

Petry, N. J.
1970   *Introduction to Hegel's Philosophy of Nature*. London: Allen and Unwin.

Petryszak, Nick
1978   The Sociology of Human Nature. Ph.D. dissertation, Simon Fraser University.

Plaine, Henry., ed.
1962   *Darwin, Marx, and Wagner: A Symposium*. Ohio: Ohio State University.

Plekhanov, G. V.
1934   *Essays in the History of Materialism*. London: John Lane.

Popper, Karl R.
1965   *The Open Society and Its Enemies*. 2 vols. Princeton, N.J.: Princeton University Press.

1969   *The Poverty of Historicism*. New York: Harper & Row.

Ritchie, David G.
1893   *Darwin and Hegel*. New York: Macmillan.

Robey, David, ed.
1973   *Structuralism: An Introduction*. London: Oxford University Press.

Robinson, Paul
1969   *The Freudian Left*. New York: Harper & Row.

Rogers, James Allen
1972   Darwinism and Social Darwinism. *Journal of the History of Ideas* 33, no. 2 (April-June).

Rosenberg, Alexander
1980   *Sociobiology and the Preemption of Social Science*. Baltimore, Md.: Johns Hopkins Press.

Rousseau, Jean Jacques
1964   *The First and Second Discourses*, ed. Roger D. Masters. New York: St. Martins Press.

Ruse, Michael
1980   *Sociobiology: Sense or Nonsense*. Dordrecht Holland: D. Riedel Publishing Company.

Ryazanoff, D., ed.
1927   *Karl Marx: Man, Thinker and Revolutionist*. New York: International Publishers.

Sahlins, Marshall, and Elman Service
1960   *Evolution and Culture*. Ann Arbor: University of Michigan Press.

Salter, Liora
1971   Regulatory Agencies and the Nature of the State. *Proceedings of the Canadian Political Science Association* (May).
1978   State, Agencies in Corporate Control. *Proceedings of the Canadian Sociology and Anthropology Association* (May).

Sartre, Jean-Paul
1963   *Search for a Method*. New York: Random House.

Schaff, Adam
1963   *A Philosophy of Man*. New York: Dell.

Schaller, George
1963   *The Mountain Gorilla*. Chicago: University of Chicago Press.

Schmidt, Alfred
1971   *The Concept of Nature in Marx*. London: New Left Books.

Schneider, David, ed.
1967   *The Scottish Moralists*. Chicago: Phoenix Books.

Sedgwick, Peter
    1966   Natural Science and Human Theory. *Socialist Register* (annual).
Seigel, J. E.
    1974   Review of *Karl Marx: His Life and Thought*, by David McLellan. *New York Review of Books* 21, no. 17 (October 31).
Service, Elman
    1967   *Primitive Social Organization: An Evolutionary Perspective.* New York: Random House.
Seward, A. C.
    1909   *Darwin and Modern Science.* Cambridge: Cambridge University Press.
Singer, Peter
    1974   Discovering Karl Popper. *New York Review of Books* 21, no. 7 (May 2).
Smith, T. V., and Marjorie Grene
    1967   *Berkeley, Hume, and Kant.* Chicago: University of Chicago Press, Phoenix Books.
Solloway, Frank J.
    1979   *Freud, Biologist of the Mind.* New York: Basic Books.
Somit, A.
    1976   *Biology and Politics.* The Hague: Mouton.
Spencer, Herbert
    1852   A Theory of Population Deduced from the General Law of Animal Fertility. *Westminster Review* (April).
    1912   *First Principles.* New York: Appleton.
Stern, Bernard J.
    1967   *Lewis Henry Morgan: Social Evolutionist.* New York: Russell & Russell.
Steward, Julian
    1955   *Theory of Culture Change.* Urbana: University of Illinois Press.
Stocking, George Jr.
    1968   *Race, Language and Culture: Essays in the History of Anthropology.* New York: The Free Press.
Stone, Irving
    1980   *The Origin: A Biographical Novel of Charles Darwin.* Garden City, N.Y.: Doubleday.
Struik, Dirk V.
    1948   Marx and Mathematics. *Science and Society* 12, no. 1 (Winter).

Terray, Immanuel
  1972   *Marxism and Primitive Society*. New York: Monthly Review Press.
Tiger, Lionel
  1970   *Men in Groups*. New York: Random House.
Tiger, Lionel, and Robin Fox
  1974   *The Imperial Animal*. New York: Dell.
Thompson, E. P.
  1978   *The Poverty of Theory and Other Essays*. New York: Monthly Review Press.
Timiryazeff, K.
  1927   Darwin and Marx. In *Karl Marx: Man, Thinker and Revolutionist*, ed. D. Ryazanoff. New York: International Publishers.
Timpanaro, Sebastiano
  1975   *On Materialism*. London: New Left Books.
Tönnies, Ferdinand
  1963   *Community and Society*. New York: Harper & Row.
Trigger, Bruce
  1967   Engels on the Part Played by Labour in the Transition from Ape to Man: An Anticipation of Contemporary Anthropological Theory. *Canadian Review of Sociology and Anthropology* 4, no. 3 (August).
Tucker, Robert C.
  1964   *Philosophy and Myth in Karl Marx*. New York: Cambridge University Press.
  1968   *The Marxian Revolutionary Idea*. New York; W. W. Norton.
Tylor, Edward B.
  1898   *Anthropology*. New York: Appleton.
  1958   *Primitive Culture*. New York: Harper Torchbooks. First published 1871.
Uranovsky, Y. M.
  1973   Marxism and Natural Science. In *Marxism and Modern Thought*, ed. N. Bukharin et al. Westport, Conn.: Hyperion Press.
van den Berghe, Pierre L.
  1978   *Man in Society: A Biosocial View*. New York: Elsevier.
  1979   *Human Family Systems: An Evolutionary View*. New York: Elsevier.
Venable, Vernon
  1945   *Human Nature: The Marxian View*. New York: Alfred A. Knopf.

Vico, Giambattista
  1968   *The New Science of Giambattista Vico.* Ithaca, N.Y.: Cornell University Press.
Vorzimmer, Peter J.
  1969   Darwin, Malthus, and the Theory of Natural Selection. *Journal of the History of Ideas* 30, no. 4 (October-December).
  1970   *Charles Darwin: The Years of Controversy.* Philadelphia: Temple University Press.
Wallace, Alfred Russel
  1889   *Darwinism.* New York: Humboldt.
Washburn, Sherwood
  1962   Tools and Human Evolution. In *Culture and the Evolution of Man,* ed. Ashley Montagu. New York: Oxford University Press.
Wasserman, Earl R., ed.
  1965   *Aspects of the Eighteenth Century.* Baltimore, Md.: Johns Hopkins Press.
White, Leslie
  1959   *The Evolution of Culture.* New York: McGraw-Hill.
Whitehead, Alfred North
  1964   *Science and the Modern World.* New York: Mentor.
Wilden, Anthony
  1972   *System and Structure.* London: Tavistock.
Wilson, Edmund
  1953   *To the Finland Station.* New York: Doubleday.
Wilson, Edward O.
  1975   *Sociobiology: The New Synthesis.* Cambridge: Harvard University Press.
  1979   *On Human Nature.* New York: Bantam Books.
Zirkle, Conway
  1959   *Evolution, Marxian Biology, and the Social Scene.* Philadelphia: University of Pennsylvania Press.

Index ─────────────────

About the Author

PAUL HEYER is Assistant Professor of Communications at Simon Fraser University, Burnaby, British Columbia. His earlier works include *Culture, Communication, and Dependency: The Tradition of H. A. Innis* (with W. Melody and L. Salter).